THE AUTOBIOGRAPHY OF
A LIVERPOOL IRISH SLUMMY

Most people who read this book will find it difficult to believe. But anyone who actually saw the squalor of the Scotland Road district of Liverpool in the early years of this century, will realise that this book recreates, vividly and dramatically yet with complete accuracy, the appalling physical and mental filth in which people lived. Mr. O'Mara not only survived the conditions, but despite abject poverty and a violent and drunkard father, also managed to become an omniverous reader and to teach himself to write.

He escaped from Liverpool to the comparative ease and comfort of life at sea on board tramp steamers, and it was here that his ability to write began to flourish. He writes extremely well; sometimes his style may seem a little raw, but it has the innate rawness of the life he describes, and his autobiography is both a compelling book and a shattering insight into the way people lived a mere fifty years ago.

A 8029 01 332185

Author

Title

BOOK-STORE

Books or discs must be returned on or before the last date stamped on label or on card in book pocket. Books or discs can be renewed by telephone, letter or personal call unless required by another reader. After library hours use the Ansafone Service (01 - 698 7347). For hours of opening and charges see notices at the above branch, but note that all lending departments close ~~all~~ on Wednesday and all libraries are closed on Sundays, Good Friday, Christmas Day, Bank Holidays and Saturdays prior to Bank Holidays.

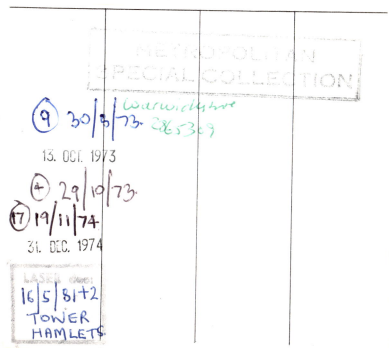

THE AUTOBIOGRAPHY OF

A Liverpool Irish Slummy

PAT O'MARA

CEDRIC CHIVERS LTD.
PORTWAY
BATH

First published 1934
by
Vanguard Press Inc.
This edition published in 1968
by
Cedric Chivers Ltd
by arrangement with the copyright holder
at the request of
The London & Home Counties Branch
of
The Library Association
Reprinted 1972

SBN 85594 629 6

Reproduced and Printed by
Redwood Press Limited, Trowbridge & London
Bound by Cedric Chivers Ltd, Bath

TO

ALL SLUMMIES

CHAPTER ONE

LIVERPOOL, ENGLAND, where I was born and raised, is, or was when I left it some fourteen years ago, the greatest seaport in the world. There are seven miles of docks, stretching from the Herculanean, at the most southerly tip, to the Hornsby, at the most northerly. Skirting these docks, and taking in practically all of the slums, is the overhead railway, and it is from this vantage point, if you will accept me as your guide of some twenty-five years ago, that you may glimpse the more significant phases of the city of that time.

But before we look at Liverpool, which is on our left, let us glance swiftly across the Mersey to Birkenhead, biggest city in lovely Cheshire, which is on our right. Over there, you can see black, smoking Cammell Laird's internationally known shipyard; but over there also lies Port Sunlight, that benign innovation of the soap-manufacturing Lever Brothers. And all around it is beautiful rural-seaside Cheshire. Strange people over here, very quiet and very English—as the few of us sensitive Irish slummy children knew whenever our periodic "Bank Holiday" excursions to such delightful places as Egremont, Seacombe, and New Brighton would be made. This was the land of the "One-eyed" people—a sarcastic nickname given them by less shrewd Liverpudlians. The Mersey separated us. It was an effective separation.

Now if we look to the left, as our overhead train drones peacefully along, we see an entirely different picture. It, also, is England, but how different from that across in Cheshire! That low-lying structure in the immediate foreground is the Sailors' Home. Here, sailormen of every color and race commingle, sign on, get paid off. When getting paid off, sailormen can leave their wages safely in the bank provided for that purpose in the Home, drawing out as they see fit. Usually, however, they take their entire pay-off and march across the way to the FLAG OF ALL NATIONS, that big alehouse in the immediate foreground, so named because of the diverse flags bedecking its interior. Here they meet the pimps and, after the pimps, the whores from Brassey Street in the South-End and Scotland Road in the North-End, or the semi-whores and semi-pimps (out o' workers), or the numerous begging children, the progeny of the last-named. Then begins a brief and torrid festival, ending sometimes fatally and nearly always tragically.

Over there, meandering northward from Whitechapel, just behind the Walker Art Gallery, lies that acme of all British slums, the internationally famous Scotland Road. Midway in this thoroughfare stands Paddy's Market, also internationally known, where the refuse of the Empire is bought and sold. Old clothes, old boots, bits of oilcloth, turbans, frayed domestic and foreign underthings—to sell

4

such stuff brazen female hawkers seated on the flag-floor lure Coolies, Chinamen, African Negroes and other Empire Builders with the consumptive cackle: "Now, John, ninepence for that coat! Come 'ere! Come 'ere!"

Just across from Paddy's Market stands Richmond Row, where, in its squalid shacks—sleeping sometimes ten in a single room for threepence a night—live most of these transient women hawkers. The majority of these young women, after peddling their wares in or outside the Market, sally forth at night toward Lime Street, there to barter anew—this time with their bodies, up alleys, for a mere pittance and to anyone, regardless of color or race. After such nocturnal forays they meander homeward, get drunk on methylated spirits, engage in internecine warfare, and usually end the night in that stumpy little structure up the road, the Rose Hill lock-up.

A little farther up than Paddy's Market stands Sebastopol, a vicious narrow artery named very appropriately, housing, for the most part, pimps (Hi-Rip lads), whose specialty is waylaying foreign sailormen lured there by the women decoys—or waylaying anyone else, for that matter, suspected of having a few shillings. The bobbies walk up here in pairs. Every old-time sailorman knows Sebastopol.

Now if we gaze due north, we will see the Working Boys' Home, where pauper and destitute children from Liverpool and other manufacturing towns can get, free, a mug of tea, bread, a pair of strong Blucher boots and a bed, to sustain them while they scour the city for work. All derelicts are registered, and, of an evening, when tired feet double into unfilled bellies, agents from landowners in various parts of the Empire dazzle them with exaggerated stories of the immense dinners and splendid opportunities that await them on the Canadian Prairies, in the Australian Bush, in the African Veldt or the Gold mines. Most colonists come from here.

Immediately in the foreground squats the George's Hall, where all the major criminal cases are tried and political speeches and free-for-all fights are held. Just beyond it stands the lovely Royal Court Theatre, where old British actors are to be seen in old British plays. Higher up a bit, looms the Dale Street lock-up, frequented for the most part by rowdy sailormen, usually picked up wounded and penniless in dank alleys.

That large group of low-lying gray buildings away inland, sprouting from its hill to the sky, is the Brownlow Hill Workhouse, named after the elevated section of the city on which it sits. If one's eyes could stretch that far, one would see the brightly attired pauper men, women, and children wheeling loaded handcarts across the cobblestoned pathways and carrying baskets on heads. The men are dressed in black tam o' shanters, navy pilot coats, heavy Blucher boots, gray shirts and white moleskins; the women in gray stripe print dresses, heavy boots and white starched caps; the children, not on the breast, in little red uniforms (how well I remember mine!); suckling children are swaddled in gray calico dresses. Thus it would be hard to abscond with and pawn the institution's clothes. They are confiscated the day of the inmate's release, when his or her bundle of rags, now soundly fumigated, are returned. There is no pay but plenty of hard work in Brownlow Hill. It is occupied mostly by wretches tired of battling for existence on the outside, who have come here to stop worrying, to work and to die. It is a lost city.

Inmates get into the Workhouse usually on the recommendation of the Board of Guardians. It, having gotten them off the streets, promptly forgets all about them. The food consists of bread, tea, porridge without milk or sugar for breakfast; a lump of hard-boiled meat, two jacketed potatoes and a piece of bread for lunch; a piece of cheese, bread and a pint mug of tea for supper. The answer to the entering challenge: "Is there anyone to claim you in case of death?" is usually "No." When the older inmates start to lean too heavily on the institution's hospital, they die very rapidly. The sexes are segregated and everyone, even mothers with suckling babies, works, usually at the task at which one is most adept. Despair is in the air; humor non-existent. Occasionally one might hear a sardonic joke from a husband chancing by his wife or child, for this would be the only opportunity to talk, since knock-off time means separation. Then at nightfall perchance a surreptitious pennyworth of gin or methylated spirits smuggled in, and finally sleep—to awaken early the following morning, as hopeless and as helpless as the night before. And in most cases on and on until chronic incapacity develops—then swift, mysterious death.

Just beyond this necropolis, you may see its subsidiary, Olive Mount Training School, where the pauper children are sent as soon as the family shows evidence of a lengthy stay in the Workhouse. Once inside here, children rarely see their parents again—though few of them ever regret it—and from Olive Mount they usually graduate to those

7

two decrepit square-riggers you see anchored out near the mouth of the Mersey—the *Ackbar* and the *Clarence*.

The *Ackbar* reforms Catholic delinquents and the *Clarence* reforms Protestant delinquents. They are, one might truthfully say, the alma mater of the internationally known Liverpool Prig. The process of reformation is very simple. Slummy boys, after batting aimlessly from alley to alley, are subjected five years to strict discipline; then, they are adjudged sailormen and given assistance in procuring berths on merchant ships. Only one ray of sympathy penetrates the harsh routine that is theirs, (welcomed usually with a lively distaste by the boys); the weekly visit of the pastor or the priest with accompanying threats of hell-fire and damnation.

All this, of course, does not apply to that Nelsonesque square-rigger, the *Indefatigable,* that you see in a little toward the quay. It is a training and not a reform ship and is restricted to orphan boys of proved respectable people, functioning under the auspices of the Seaman's Orphanage. Here, as in the case of H. M. S. *Eagle,* that relic of Trafalgar tied up in the Salthouse dock to the left, an interest is taken in the boy himself, since he is destined to become a mercantile marine officer—a pinnacle rarely attained by a graduate of the *Ackbar* or the *Clarence*.

Let us leave the river for a moment and switch our gaze over Lime Street. Every sailorman knows Lime Street: and certainly every foreigner knows Italian "Jew" Grossi's Trocadero, the English counterpart of the Continental boozer-bordello, in the basement of the Hotel St. George. The big Sailors' Outfitters' Store over to the left in Paradise Street is also owned by Mr. Grossi. Here sailormen took their advance notes and had them exchanged, seventy-five per cent merchandise, twenty-five per cent cash—this last usually finding its way back to Grossi via his Trocadero. The courtesans frequenting this place are semi-professional—usually young slummy girls not making much money at their regular factory tasks, who are essaying the payless role of barmaid-enchantress as preparation for bigger game. The hygienic ignorance of most of these "economic" prostitutes has given many foreign sailormen reason to remember the old Troc!

Such is Lime Street, a wind-swept thoroughfare of whores and amusement places. Out beyond all this—in line with the equestrian stone effigies of Queen Victoria, consort Albert, and grim Disraeli—on wide Belmont Road, you can see the spot where, up to a short time ago, stood the old *Test House*, a governmental amenity to destitute, roving men and women. Here tramps could enter, have their clothes fumigated, take a bath, and obtain a night's lodging. In the morning, after doing their prescribed domestic chores, a mug of tea and a piece of bread would be served, whence they could push off, refreshed, to the next town's Test House. Whole families availed themselves of this charity, arriving sometimes with furniture and bedding strapped to their backs. Shelter from the impending rain, a doss, tea and a butty in the morning—it was nothing to be sneezed at! Alas, the Test House is no more: I mentioned it simply to show the changed atmosphere of the town.

To the left, that dumpy little structure is Mission "Cob" Hall, where all the young ungodly waifs, not as yet aboard the *Ackbar* or the *Clarence,* are coaxed from

9

windy street corners by Mr. "Gypsy" Smith and other evangelical men by the promise of a big fresh bread cob—*after* service.

Perhaps, haphazardly, the better class of people around whom most English literature centers, have heard of the Workhouse, the Test House, "Cob" Hall, and the other landmarks of Liverpool. But they have no actual contact with them. These institutions are part and parcel of the sinewy arteries that branch off from these seven miles of docks and comprise the slums—a bit of Ireland united, save in religion. This rends them. The Catholic elements have their stronghold in Scotland Road along with a goodly segment of the southern end of the Dock Road. In the South, the Protestants have Clive Street and Jerry Hill, and in the North, Netherfield Road and Lodge Lane —scattered bits grouped under the name of the Orange River. The religious issue is sharply defined and anyone foolhardy enough not to heed it gets scant sympathy from the English bobbies when trouble ensues. Connaught is Connaught and Ulster is Ulster and never the twain shall mix—save in desperate battle on St. Patrick's birthday and on that eventful day when Prince William of Orange crossed the river Boyne.

CHAPTER TWO

SUCH is a brief outline of the significant places in Liverpool that I knew best; my immediate environment, however, should give them more vividness. I was born thirty-two years ago in "Auld" Harris's tenement house in Bridgewater Street, facing the Queen's Dock, but we moved from there (as usual, evicted) shortly afterward. Most of my early life was spent on Brick Street, a street of abominably overcrowded shacks near by. Negroes, Chinese, Mulattoes. Filipinos, almost every nationality under the sun, most of them boasting white wives and large half-caste families, were our neighbors, each color laying claim to a certain street.

The Negroes, many of whom were firemen and trimmers on the Elder-Dempster "Monkey" boats, had their headquarters on Gore Street and Stanhope Street, at the foot of which, into the Coburg Dock, the Monkey boats used to come from sea. Not only were these ugly tribal-scarred fellows from the West Coast of Africa accepted by white women as equals; many times they were considered the white man's superior. The main reason, of course, was

11

economic—they made far better *pater familiae*. Some families, like my mother's, abhorred the practice of inter-marriage, but it was so prevalent that they had to keep their beliefs to themselves. There were others who had great pride in our colored neighbors, and when Jack Johnson won the heavyweight boxing championship, many of them tried desperately to prove him a Britisher.

The fact that most of the black fellows followed the sea had much to do with the local white girls marrying them—much better, reasoned the girls, to put up with a Negro three months in the year (while drawing his steady salary) than to marry a young dock walloper and be continually starved and beaten. The most amusing thing about this intermarrying business was the Negro's pen-chant for blondes, a large number of whom came from overcrowded cities like Cardiff, London and Manchester. For the most part they were half-starved illiterates, des-perately anxious to secure economic independence, espe-cially when it came in the manner of a husband away at sea nine months of the year.

Sometimes wifely plans went awry, as in the case of "Galley" Johnson, a repulsive-looking old Negro I knew. Galley married Mollie McGuire and gave her seven half-caste children before she died. He had put in twenty years stoking on the Elder-Dempster boats when she died. A few months later he married Maggie McCoy, an Irish girl younger than Galley's own eldest half-caste daughter. A week afterward he opened a Negro boarding house and installed himself as janitor. There was to be no more roving, he told Maggie, whose looks had some-thing to do with his retirement from the sea. Maggie left.

A more humorous case was that of Bridgett Hylands. A week after Paddy, her father, brought her over from Connaught, Bridgett heard Joe "Black" Diamond strumming *The Yaller Rose of Texas* on his banjo and immediately fell in love with him. A few days later she brought the shy Joe home to her father and told of the marriage. When Paddy recovered his breath, he threw Joe out and on bended knee begged his daughter to go down to the dock and throw herself in—"The good Lord will forgive you, daughter!" he pleaded. Bridgett followed Joe out, swearing that she'd "Plaze herself!" and later she confided to my mother that Father Ryan, who married them, had said, "If Joe's face is black, his heart is white!" Shortly afterward they moved to Cardiff and opened a Negro boarding house.

The same thing occurred among the Chinamen in Pitt Street (Chinatown), so far as the women were concerned. I think the Chinamen chose their white wives with a little more discrimination, for, esthetically and intellectually, they were on a much higher plane than the Negroes. With the exception of a few honest laundrymen and grocerymen, their main business was opium. A rookie bobby arrested one of these opium dealers once and told the court that the Chinaman had tried to bribe him.

"What did he say?" asked the Court.

"I givee you one hundred pounds if you lettee me go," replied the bobby.

"Sir," said the accused, "I don't speak in that idiom: I was educated in Hong-Kong." The case was dismissed, and the bobby censured.

Humorous, too, were the deportation proceedings. A

13

group of convicted dope dealers, after serving their six-months' sentence, would suddenly reappear in their old haunts despite the ruling that all convicted dope-dealers be deported. The *racket*, apparently, was in Cardiff, for they all came back through that port. I liked the Chinese better than the others. There was mystery and glamor in Chinatown, never to be found among the Negroes or the Flukes. I used to love to wander about the base of Chinatown near the Sailor's Home, mostly for the sight of the peculiar buildings (landlords never had to fix any Chinese dwellings: the Chinese arranged all the mysterious alleyways and passages themselves) and the strong tang of opium in the air.

Then at the end of Frederick Street (Flukey Alley) the brownish element had their quarters. "Flukes" we used to call them on account of their flat faces. Hawaiians mostly, these fellows were in greater demand by the girls than either the Chinese or the Negroes; and this made them so conceited that there resulted few marriages and many bastards. Few of the Flukey Alley boys with whom I played knew their fathers. I think the Flukes' progeny, more than any other factor, were responsible for the Board of Guardians. It always seemed to me that the local authorities were much too liberal with these fellows, but the women liked them, for they played the ukuleles to perfection and made excellent pimps. Perhaps the keenest insult one could offer would be to call one of them a Negro.

Brick Street, however, though in the midst of all this, was different from its neighbors: it was peopled for the most part by West-of-Ireland folk or their descendants. There was the same poverty, but no Negroes or Chinese or Flukes. The men were dock laborers or carters and their wives and children chip-choppers and oakum pickers but when washed, all white. Splendid stock, too, occasionally, as in the case of my mother's people, or the jetsam of elegant bourgeoisie, as in the case of my father's.

Of my father's family, I know little, save that it had money and position and was well known in Cheshire. My father's father came from an old Tipperary family that dated far back into Irish history. A big dark-complexioned, generous fellow, he left Ireland, as most ambitious young Irishmen do, and came to England, where he met and married my grandmother, a very snobbish English domestic. Much prosperity and seven children were the issue, my father, I think, being the fifth to arrive.

An inherent rogue from his earliest boyhood, my father would never conform to the elegant life prescribed for him by his mother, nor respect his proper sisters and brothers—nor the comfortable estate. After causing much family strife, at sixteen he ran off to sea on an Elder-Dempster boat, returning to the estate nine months later with no money, only a sea bag. And the same thing later on. And again. At twenty-five we find him loafing around the estate, tolerated only by his sentimental father. One day the hired man was sick, and my grandmother asked my father to take the cartload of vegetables into the Birkenhead Market to sell to her regular commission man. James took it to another commission man and sold not only the cargo, but donkey and cart and harness as well—and off to sea again. Years later he returned, broke as usual, and was forgiven by his father, who, seeing much of his own idiosyncrasies in his son, loved him in-

tensely. The following day, as a sort of gesture of grati-
tude, my father eloped with his father's Sunday suit and
pawned it for thirty shillings—and off again. Years after
his father had died, my father showed up at his brother's
death-bed. His brother gasped out that should Jimmy
(my father) stay sober three days, he could have the gold
watch now in keeping of my grandmother. My father
faithfully promised his dying brother he would keep the
pledge; but on the third day after his brother's death he
came for his prize hopelessly drunk. No watch. Chagrined,
he ran off and this time joined the Horse Artillery of the
British Army.

Here he got in with a scapegoat like himself. Shortly
after enlistment, both these patriots deserted up in Here-
fordshire and got jobs as hop-pickers. Then, because of
my father's gentlemanly training, some obscure English
squire hired him as coachman and he left his fellow deserter
flat; the latter returned later to his regiment for dinner
and returned the favor. My father was hauled back,
courtmartialed and sentenced to twenty-eight days. The
sentence served, he struck a Gandhi pose and again was
brought before the tribunal. This time he refused to answer questions until his old Colonel would testify as to
his general character. "But the Colonel is in India!"
argued the Court. "Then bring 'im back!" said my father.
"For if I was in India and the Colonel asked for me, you'd
bring me. Now fair play's bonny play; so get him here."
It was a good point, but the Court couldn't see it. My
father's case was considered *incamera,* and on Queen Victoria's Golden Jubilee, when all erring British warriors

were given special indulgence, he was drummed out of the Army.

After this, he heaved up in Liverpool as a horse-hack driver for Mr. McGuire at Low Hill, near the present Adelphi Hotel. The first day he appears to have behaved himself; after that, along with horse and hack, he was missing two days and nights. Midnight of the third day, he faced the irate Mr. McGuire, who cooled down considerably when, in the darkness of the stable, my father handed him a half-sovereign. But later, after my father had gone Mr. McGuire discovered that the half-sovereign was a sixpence, he boiled up again and scratched my father off the payroll.

Later, my father turned up in Fleetwood as a tramp, frequenting the Test House and knocking on door bells. The next record in this *Odyssey* shows him on an Isle-of-Man boat without any ticket, the passengers subscribing the necessary expense. Shortly after this he is hanging around the Liverpool Docks, the mecca of all British jetsam. He was thirty-seven then, and, it was about this time and in such circumstances that he met my mother. She was his complete antithesis in everything, but, like all the girls of her class, looking for an "economic," though in her case white, marriage.

CHAPTER
THREE

MY MOTHER'S people, it always seemed to me, were, despite their poverty, of far better stock and much more interesting than my father's. Like my father's father, both their histories go back into Ireland. My mother's father was the Shaw type of Irishman: witty, sympathetic, liberal, a terrible foe. He was a soldier as his father before him and his father before that; and when he left the Army, he took up tailoring and began the intensive reading that was to make of him an agnostic, plant dynamite within the family. My mother, when a young girl, once betrayed him to Father Flynn. That champion converter came up on the run from the parish house. "Get down on your knees, John!" he commanded my grandfather, "and say a Hail Mary!" My grandfather obeyed meekly and promised to make amends, but the moment the priest was gone he called my mother in and, shaking his finger in her face, said: "If I ever get ye interferin' again with my affairs, Polly, oi'll make yer bottom look like a piece of beef steak!" But he wouldn't of course; he just wanted to impress, upon a particularly zealous member of his family, the importance of his being left to himself and to his books.

My grandmother was a fine, big woman, akin to my grandfather in everything save religion. Anything pertaining to the church was true to her. A sample tale: Mike O'Dunne, an old shoe wax (a cobbler) living in Dublin, heard his two recently born twins cursing each other like adult drunkards. Whereupon, convinced they were Banshees, he put both of them into a bag and threw them in the river. And when he got back, lo! there was his wife holding on her knee the same two children, this time conversing like little angels! The point in the story was that I should never grow up and be a bad man like my father, from whom, at the moment, mother had fled.

My grandmother, too, was a tailor; and it was in this capacity that she met and married my grandfather in St. Andrew's Church in Dublin, shortly after his discharge from the Army. Then later, after the arrival of four children, stark poverty, that driving urge of all Irish people, brought them in search of work to Liverpool—perhaps the most Irish city in the world outside of Ireland.

Their first home was in the upper part of Stanhope Street, just above the Negro white-wife element. Later, disgusted, they moved into a big barracks of a house in St. James Street, hard by St. Vincent's Catholic Church, then presided over by the internationally known Father Flynn, with whom my bookish grandfather was soon to be in constant conflict.

The "barracks" itself was an awful hovel to contemplate. Tenants rented as many rooms as were needed. First my grandparents took one room, then two and later on three. To get an extra room would sometimes necessitate a stretching of ethics, as they would have to find a scheme to get rid of the other occupant. Of the nine children all except four were born in Dublin: my mother (she points this out very proudly) was included in the Irish births. The others, all born in this neighborhood, used the barracks as their mutual base for the rest of their lives.

Of the nine children, seven lived to maturity, five girls and two boys: Leisha, the eldest; Johnny; Mary (my mother); Janie; Katie; Jimmie; and Lizzie, in the order named. All of them were big, healthy children. My mother was the dreamer, keenly sensitive and highly imaginative. None could tell tales so well as she.

There was no schooling or shoes or regular meals for any of them as children. All reading was limited to the Weekly *Post*. Most of the children started to work at fourteen as store helpers in the Fish Market or such places, and from then on the children were left pretty much to themselves. There would be bits of timely advice for them from either of their parents, but never any browbeating. They brought home to my grandmother whatever wages they earned, out of which they would be given their "pocket money." But all other problems, major or minor, were settled in their own youthful minds.

All the girls eventually married, but not the two boys. Johnny, the elder son, was my especial favorite, because he had so much in common with my mother. He had only one arm, having lost his right one when nine years old while stealing some sugar from a wagon passing into the Queen's Dock. This incapacitation, combined with his sullen sensitiveness over it, drove him to excessive drinking and a premature death. He knew almost nothing and read little; but he felt life very deeply—perhaps more deeply ·than his gravely bookish father, whom he used to sit and watch for hours, as the other worked his needle or read. In childhood, my mother and he, being of like natures, had been inseparable companions. They loved music and dancing. One of my mother's fondest memories was how, when the hurdy-gurdy sounded below their window after they had been put to bed, Johnny had tied a rope around her waist, lowered her to the street, and joined her in the dance a moment later. When I was quite young, I recall his saying to me: " 'Tis better, Timmy, were you never born at all, than into *this*. . . ."

Jimmy, his younger brother, was more of a sport, early showing up as the hack-driver-bachelor type. His pronounced "ladies' man" traits made him very distasteful to his sisters, who liked to think of their men as brawny, unsentimental dockers. "Sibby the bitch!" was what his intimate knowledge of feminine foibles got him. "It's skirts ye ought to have on!" my grandmother used to say when seeing him primp in front of the looking-glass. My grandfather liked him. "That lad'll marry into money some day!" he used to say. "You're all jealous of him—that's what."

Of the five girls, two married "satisfactorily" and settled into the usual dull life. Lizzie and my mother married tragically, Janie married humorously. I think the only genuine love affair was between Leisha and her husband, Johnny Roche. Johnny Roche was that rare being: a Liverpool docker who was a hard-working, sober, homeloving man. They were well-mated and kept no secrets from each other—my grandmother once getting a sharp rebuke from Johnny over an attempt to tell him something not for Leisha's ears. While other dockers were drinking on Saturday night, Johnny Roche would be home mending boots for his twelve children. Up at four in the morning, he would walk the seven miles to the Langdon Dock to save overhead railway fare and be on the stand at six—on the slim chance of getting work.

The other marriages all had their inception in economics, with Janie's case being about the worst. A big, lumbering woman, always either in extreme ecstasy or complete despair, there was something about her that invariably fetched a smile. "Plate-face" was the sobriquet my grandmother had given her in token of that baffling expression that might presage almost anything After having a love-child by a Spanish sailorman, whom none of us ever saw, she turned around and accepted a proposal of matrimony from Joe Lonnigan, an argumentative elderly clerk, who kept bachelor's quarters in one of the top rooms. My grandmother detested Lonnigan for four reasons: coming uninvited into the Molloy circle, covering the fire at all times with his bottom, his penchant for argument, and later his pro-German talk. Born in Manchester, of English-born parents, and never in his life outside of England, he declared himself an Irishman and denounced England at any and every opportunity.

The bans of Janie's marriage to him were published from St. Vincent's pulpit and the neighbors all prepared for the eventual spree. But in the meantime Janie had met up with a more malleable man and when the sacred hour arrived, she was nowhere near the church. Joe became the laughing-stock of the neighborhood, but some six weeks later, when his erring sweetheart returned, he beat her publicly in front of the barracks, thus vindicating himself among his cronies. A little while later Janie married the other man, Johnny Murray, a consumptive widower with two half-caste children, Anne and Maria, still very young and needing a mother's care. Reversing the usual procedure, this Irishman had married a colored woman, only to have her "die on him" shortly after the birth of the second child. The stage was set. Mr. Murray was brought into the family amid veiled imprecations from the other members, but it was not long before the two half-castes were shipped away to a colored relative and forgotten both by old father and new mother. Nor were they sorry, for during their brief sojourn in the barracks, every remark of their foster mother to them was prefaced with "You black so-and-so!"

From then on, the new Mrs. Murray started training her husband. She made his clothes for him, apportioned him his pocket money, and even forbade him the traditional practice of drinking at the bar with his fellow workmen. He had been in a warehouse, but on account of the bigger wages to be made at the docks, Janie decided to teach him dock laboring. A dummy ship's hatch was rigged up in their room with a coil of rope and, to his bewilderment, they practiced how to work a winch and later how to roar orders down a ship's hatch. After this, she hammered home the importance of determination and speed, so much so that pretty soon, because of his agility in springing from one dock to another, he earned for himself the sobriquet "Raffles." When work at the docks was light, she·criticized him unfairly. One morning after he had just returned from a futile quest for work, his wife, leaning out the window and espying a certain much-married lady, called him over and sighed: "Maggy Gorman there, Johnny—she's just buried her fourth husband! Some people have all the luck!" Then the worm turned. "What you want me to do—drown meself?" Sarcastic: "No, Johnny, you'll take good care you won't do anythin' like that . . . !" Then she opened wide all the windows because she knew he wanted them shut.

Lizzie. Poor, beautiful Aunt Lizzie! She confused *comfort* with love and paid dearly for her mistake. She was eighteen when she met Chris Hazeman, young-man-about-town of very comfortable German parents. He was Lutheran and she was Catholic—but the Hazemans lived in such a splendid house! Six months after the initial meeting, she walked into the barracks and announced to my grandmother that she had married this young man in the Protestant church. She walked out about an hour later, leaving a house full of broken hearts (with the exception of my grandmother) and continued on happily to the elegant little house provided for them by Chris's mother. But ten years later, as a boy holding onto my own tragic mother in the gloomy barracks, I heard this once beautiful girl (now a handful of gaunt bones) yell at her husband in drunken bitterness: "You! You gave it to me at nineteen! The syph! At nineteen!" Her first born, Jimmy, was big and healthy, and lived; the second, Charles, died of violent convulsions within two months. A week prior to this, Lizzie, very sickly and ashamed, came to the barracks and asked my grandmother to accompany her to

24

the dispensary. "Charlie's cryin' all the time," she said. "I want you to take him in—I don't feel like it."

My grandmother, with perplexed simplicity, agreed. The doctor, after examining the screaming child, asked my grandmother in a mildly contemptuous tone: "Are *you* the mother of this child?"

"No," she said.

"Then where is the mother?"

"She's outside."

"Tell her to come in."

In a moment Lizzie, ashamed and abashed, stood before him.

"Do you feel sick?" he asked.

"No," she lied.

"Well, see that this child is kept clean, particularly his groin."

"But I do keep him clean. . . ."

"I don't mean that," cut in the doctor contemptuously. "I mean keep it clean with this ointment."

A week later, the baby died. As the infant lay dead, the father, in convivial spirit and not aware of what had happened, came in the parlor playing his accordion as usual. There had been much bad feeling on the part of the father, due to the child's perpetual crying. Lizzie, incensed, seized the accordion and ripped it in two. "Now!" she screamed, "he'll cry no more!"

Four years later, Sydney was born and was hurried off secretly by my grandmother to be baptized. This was the only time I ever knew my grandmother to stir vigorously from out her armchair. She was gone all that day and, though very tired when she returned to sink back into it, there was an intensely happy gleam in her eyes. Sydney, as I remember him, was a very sickly child and his mother spent many hours in the Children's Infirmary waiting to have his recurring sore eyes treated. One time, returning late from the Infirmary, to her elegant little dwelling in Crump Street (she still was very proud of it) and being scolded by her mother-in-law for not having Chris's supper ready, she flew into a rage and threw cups and other utensils at the bewildered old German woman. A letter for Chris, written in German, came the following day from the mother, and Lizzie got a sound scolding from him. From then on beautiful Lizzie died gradually— no other words fit quite so accurately, for I watched the process and I know.

About eight years after the German letter, she staggered into the gloomy barracks, a horrible-looking, boneless hulk and threw herself down at my grandmother's feet. "I want to lie down, mother!" she groaned. There was a rosary in her hand. "I've been to Mass—look!" My grandmother put her to bed. She recovered sufficiently to go home that night, but the next day she came back and threw herself down again. That night she staggered home, this time followed dubiously by my Aunt Janie, who had been dispatched after her by my grandmother. Janie saw her go upstairs and tear her clothes off. Lizzie recognized Janie and pointed to the elegant furniture and some money scattered on the table, screaming: "Dross! Look at it! Take it away from me—dirty, bloody dross!" She died the following day in the most horrible agony. She was thirty-seven. Her husband, Chris, was prostrated, and carried on desperately at the funeral. Ten months later in that very room, with Jimmy his son standing for him as sickly Sydney looked on, he married big Bridgett Kelly. Two years later, Bridgett died of internal hemorrhages. Ten years later, at the behest of the authorities, Chris was forcibly taken from a public house and put in segregation. His face was nearly eaten away. A few months later, he died in an institution.

Katie. My Aunt Katie was the beloved snob of the family and it was no more than natural that she marry a very snooty (and improvident) Englishman. He was an insurance collector or something like that when he first met her while she was working in John's Fish Market— with a sister who had just started out working and seeing things. They were married shortly after that. Katie discarded her shawl, left the old barracks and Liverpool and the next thing we knew, the newlyweds were living in a magnificent place in New Brighton. Tales of servants and other such stuff seeped through to us. A few years later on a visit there, my sister and I fascinated, stared at the elegant children clad in Eton collars and expensive dresses, talking with broad "A's" and allegedly our cousins! Mr. Patterson we did not see, for it was always "Papa's up in his study." I think it was Katie who did the studying. She was a genius at getting credit and extending it. "Jack" was the foil, and never ungrateful. "Give mamma a coat instead of that horrible shawl," he'd tell the children, "and she'll get you the empire."

Katie could be humble, too. About four years after the New Brighton bubble burst, she showed up at the barracks with two handcarts full of salvaged furnishings, back home and broke. A couple of rooms were apportioned the refugees (eight, including Mr. Patterson) and everybody did his bit toward the Patterson rehabilitation. They lived here for about five years, the children bearing the come-down stoically. Presently, Katie's ambition stirred anew. A little fruit shop was started in the basement of the barracks, causing great consternation among the neighbors, who peeped into it wonderingly, no doubt thinking one of the Molloys had gone mad. But the fruit store prospered and once again the exodus took place. Elegant Nile Street came next and such splendid schools as Skerry's College and the Technical School for the children. And on and up and up until a certain day was to find the entire family in a Riverside Drive (New York) apartment with one of the daughters confiding to another (out of hearing of the mother, thank God) that "We owe our intelligence and push to our father, and our health to our mother. . . ."

My mother. With the possible exception of Lizzie's, my mother's story was the most tragic. Surely, hers is the classical example of what cumulative economic fear will do to a nature inherently opposed to all material acquisition! Like her sister Katie, to wrench herself free from poverty and dirt was a passion with her. She could neither read nor write, but she was not content, like the brother Johnny whom she loved, to lie down and die under it. I recall a Molloy reunion, with everyone present save Auntie Katie and my father (not allowed inside the place). All of us were crowded around a typically "Irish" table (littered with foodstuffs and spilled water), the men in white corduroys (the dockers' Sunday outfit), the women in white-and-black aprons and we children shoeless and in rags. Everyone was talking except my grand-father and grandmother—to this day I can see that fine, grave face of his as he contemplated the crowd, and then excused himself to go to his books.

Then my mother did a peculiar thing, as she often did when under the influence of drink. Feeling my sweaty hands, she looked down at me, disclosing the tears in her eyes, and yelled aloud: "Oh, Jesus, sufferin' Christ, won't you *ever* take me out of this!" Better than anything else did this ejaculation reveal her deep desire to rise above the squalor and poverty into which she had been born.

CHAPTER
FOUR

IT WAS just such desperation of spirit that made my mother throw in her lot with my father, now a dock laborer, whom she met in Penny's pub in Rathbone Street. At the time, she was working in Peter Williams's Clothing Factory in Paradise Street, making about twelve shillings a week piece-work—a hard job, holding out little economic hope. Now she listened avidly to my father's talk about his family's estate and how much it would mean to him if he would only settle down and get married. Surreptitiously, my mother inquired about the O'Maras of Rock Ferry, forgetting, however, to find out how my father stood with them. Learning that his story was true, she fell an easy victim.

How she must have listened to his deprecation of her slummy surroundings and how much more pleasant it would be on the ancestral grounds in Cheshire! Unlike her other sisters, she had held out until she was thirty; now here indeed was a reward for her patience! After the marriage ceremony, she brought my father up to the barracks and, although he was white and Catholic (this last the main consideration), it is a strange fact that the entire Molloy clan went on record as hating him intensely. My grandfather, with his uncanny insight, said my father was deceitful and frankly warned my mother to be on her guard. My grandmother's and my Uncle Johnny's initial reaction was to throw the new member out. Nor was there any love lost, my father, with his peculiar pride, experiencing a similar reaction. He never made a second visit to the barracks; the Molloys never asked him again.

When the newlyweds left the barracks, their total resources were nine shillings and sixpence, held discreetly by my mother. They wandered the streets for a while in the rain, my mother's new "marriage" shoes hurting her painfully, until they finally found a furnished room in Heath Street just off London Road, five shillings a week, parlor, bedroom, bathroom, toilet, kitchen all in one. Here my father behaved himself for a time, doing an occasional day down at the docks, while my mother worked steadily in the clothing factory; then, gradually, he reverted to type, more speedily as my mother's interest in the ancestral estate began to show. One day, after work, my mother had gone to help the sick wife of one of my father's docker friends, assuming no doubt that this gesture would be appreciated by my father. Instead, his late dinner angered him beyond all reason, and he let loose a vocabulary so terrible that my mother, thinking him gone mad, left the place and ran to the barracks.

Eventually his penitence, his religion and the mirage of the eventual Rock Ferry inheritance brought her back.

Soon he started in again, Saturday (pay day) being the regular day for the weekly "fight." Three months after taking this honeymoon room, the landlady, who previously had thought nothing was too bad for her house, was forced to eject the newlyweds. Their few belongings were bundled into a handcart and wheeled over to Hampton Street to a similar room, in which my mother got her first beating. Upon my mother's recovery, they were ejected from here, showing up in another shack close by. Two weeks later they were ejected again, moving to Negro-white-wife Stanhope Street in Court No. 14. And here a little explanation is in order.

The term, of course, is ironic; what the "Court" represented was a narrow alley receding off the street to a larger areaway, like an unseen tooth cavity, and ending in a conglomeration of filthy shacks. About twenty-five large families—dock laborers, hawkers, sooty artisans and their children—lived in the average court. Two revoltingly dirty toilets stood in the areaway and were always in demand; a queue usually waited in line, newspapers in hand. The shacks were so closely packed together and their walled partitions so thin that one had no choice but to listen to what went on on either side. Screams often rent the air at night—one courter waylaying another in the darkness. The cheaper elderly whores favored the Courts, and could always be found attending to their furtive business in the darker corners. Huge cats continually stalked the place, their eyes an eerie phosphorescence in the darkness. The great pastime was hiding on rent day from the Corporation landlord, who usually lacked humor and any other human traits. The Courts ran in numbers, like the cells in a penitentiary.

The customary domestic procedure of the courters

was to drink and fight, sometimes within the family and sometimes shack against shack. The men considered it a traditional duty to beat their wives and the wives considered it a traditional penance to accept the continual beatings. Even in these surroundings my father was looked upon as undesirable. The others occasionally did let up on their wives, but not my father—he was always drunk and at his task. The mirage of the Rock Ferry ancestral estate had gone completely from my mother's mind now, and the only reason she put up with the torture was because of her pregnancy and the rigid laws of the Catholic Church in the matter of marriage. When my mother was delivered of her first child, May, my father was lying drunk on the floor upstairs, having exhausted himself beating her prior to the arrival of the bewildered midwife. This beautiful child was a nervous wreck until she died six years later.

Shortly after the birth of May, my parents were forcibly put out of Court No. 14 as objectionable to the other courters and moved to Court No. 3, farther down the street. Here, the same story again and this time another birth, a big boy, Jimmy, named for my father. Jimmy died in violent convulsions nine months later. After two years here and the birth of two more children, both born dead, there followed another forcible ejection.

After this, they turned up in what was perhaps the most abandoned of the Courts, Stanhope Court, unlike the others named and not numbered. Here the same ritual and the birth of Katie, to die some three years later. Next came Alice, my sister who lived. Just before Alice was born, my mother received what she alleges was

33

her worst beating—a bashing in of the eyes and head—and she fled in desperation with Alice to her sister Leisha, then the very happy though poverty-stricken Mrs. Johnny Roche.

Here three important factors brought my mother back to my father—sensitiveness at being kept by her sister, whose economic problems with her growing family were very acute; her religion, which demanded she make sacrifices for her child; and the repentant outpourings of my father, whose belly was beginning to miss his meals and his legs to miss the comfortable feel of clean white moleskin trousers. Back she went, and this time they heaved up in "Auld" Harris's tenement house in Bridgewater Street close to the Queen's Dock. At the time, this house I was to know so well later on was occupied on the first floor by "Auld" Harris, barber, teacher of the fiddle, his dipsomaniac wife and perennially crying baby, Emma. On the second floor were three families: Mrs. Wylie and her two grown docker sons; colored bachelor "Charlie the Carpenter"; and Mrs. Harris's sister, widowed Mrs. Craft. On the third floor were a middle-aged couple of vagrants named Simpson who, total strangers, had recently met and married each other when both were emerging from Walton Gaol; the man now worked around the docks. They had the front room. We took the back. It was in this windowless room that I was born.

CHAPTER
FIVE

My mother always thinks of my birth in Harris's as the most horrible experience of her miserable married life. She should have been delivered late Saturday night, but the terror engendered by my father's drunken capers (he was in a fearful mood that night), and her own forgetfulness in not taking the necessary oils delayed my birth until eight o'clock Sunday morning. All through the night my mother lay in bed terrified and suffering fearfully. My father was beside her, jabbering incoherently, hopelessly drunk. At three o'clock in the morning, he kicked her off the bed, in which cramped position she lay groaning until seven o'clock, when a scream from her brought the tipsy Mrs. Harris upstairs. A nurse was gotten from Princess Road Nurses' Home. When she came, my father crept out of the room under her astounded stare. I was delivered. I have no record of what happened to my sister Alice during this period. She, two-and-a-half years old then and a very nervous child, was the lone survivor of the "Court" life. Now I was here to keep her company.

Gradually, by that mysteriously baffling recovery so

typical of her, my mother got well again and settled into the torture for which she seemed to be fated. All hopes, dreams of legacies, were gone now. That she was living with a madman—and would have to keep on living with him in order to live at all—was quite obvious to her by now. Moreover, being very religious, this had another, deeper, aspect for her. The children must somehow be raised as good Catholics—that must come first. If she left my father, this would be impossible, for little economic help was furnished to husband-deserters. My mother's application for a separation would have been listened to unsympathetically, as well she knew, and there would never have been much effort made to make my father support us. The government at that time (this was before the days of Mrs. Pankhurst) didn't take the Single Standard seriously. So my mother's choice lay between suicide and torture, and as the former was impossible (since she was a Catholic), she had no recourse but to submit grimly to the latter.

My father by now was a regular dock laborer, living the usual life of a dock laborer of that period, seeking work when and where he liked and chucking it when he liked. He hated my mother intensely, because by now he realized that she had married him for the alleged legacy and stayed with him only for the sake of the two children. Added to this was the Molloy clan's contempt for him. During this hectic period my grandmother used to scan the evening papers with trepidation, fearful and expectant of reading, as she used to say, of "some awful tragedy nearby. If it was me—I'd *do* for him!"

To even things, my father waxed very contemptuous

about my mother's people. He had a stock criticism for my mother: "You're all bloody slummies and were raised in S——houses!" He never looked for more than a couple of days' work. This would ensure the rent and enough to get the barest necessities of living. Two days' work would net him ten shillings, out of which, on Saturday, my mother, after much wrangling, would be lucky to get six, the other four being kept by him as entrée to the public houses where he could ply his baiting of sailors or other available "catch-ons."

This baiting business was his favorite pastime; we never knew who was coming into our rooms next. At three years of age, I myself, with my mother's vivid imagination and my father's unconscious tuition, was an inveterate and expert cadger and always knew how best to maneuver a new guest—even a foreigner with scant knowledge of English—into giving me a penny or a halfpenny. The baiting trick worked something like this. My father had an old fireman's book—stolen from someone —which gave him entrée to maritime habitats usually not open to landlubbers. Accordingly, either around frigid Cannon Place or at the bar of the Flag of All Nations, he would ferret and ferret until something resembling an easy mark turned up, usually in the guise of some young Scandinavian sailorman, just paid off and in a very convivial mood. These impromptu guests were a constant source of worry to my mother, who could see through the whole rotten game and who more often than not, after they had departed, received a beating from my irate father for allowing her sympathies to assist them out of a predicament. Sometimes, when these fellows would sober up, they would wonder what my mother could be doing with such a man and very often openly expressed their views. My father would say nothing, but, after they had gone, he would first accuse my mother of infidelity, then beat her. These sailormen would come to the house with the obvious intent of seducing my mother (having been through similar situations before), but the moment the actual circumstances dawned upon them, the thought would vanish from their minds.

Most of these "catch-ons" were reckless Scandinavians, generous to a fault. When they would be corralled in our rooms, all my father's mates and their wives and their children would come trooping in to try to secure pawnable material from the guest of honor. First, all the children would have to have new boots, the women, new aprons and boots and so on until the guest was cleaned out. Then he would be thrown out or, more bitter still, left alone and ignored in another shack, the owner of which usually would make the accusation of burglary. Nearly all the houses around our neighborhood went in for this.

The *Elba*, a four-masted Scandinavian barge, docked in the Queens one day, and among those getting paid off were two young fellows I recall as Otto and August. The *Elba* had been out from Scandinavia eighteen months. Mr. Gollen, a gentleman of the same stripe as my father, got hold of Otto and brought him up to his sister-in-law's, Mollie Doran, a four-time widow and "white liver" suspect [i.e., a woman continually burying husbands] who ran a huckster shop nearby. August went with a whore, promising to meet his pal when the *Elba* signed on again. Presently Otto had furnished Mollie and all her relatives with select "Scotch fitting" boots and new reversible shawls. There were hacks and theater parties and endless drinking bouts for almost two weeks. At the end of the first week, it was arranged to "engage" Otto (who was still very drunk) to Mollie's anæmic sister, Kate, the marriage to take place at the termination of Otto's next eighteen-month trip.

A ring, costing thirty-two shillings, was purchased with Otto's fast-dwindling roll, and put upon the bewildered Kate's hand as proof of his seriousness. At the end of the second week, Otto's funds ran out. A family council deemed it advisable—since he was going to become a member of the family—that he go down and sign on the *Elba* (which peculiarly enough was signing on about the time Otto was spent out) and fetch back his advance note, which Mollie would willingly cash for him and his new fiancée. Otto obeyed with the fatalism of a man who feels he has erred so badly that a little more erring can't hurt, and brought back his advance note, out of the cashing of which I managed to get my first pair of boots. The whole Gollen outfit, with the assistance of the O'Maias and others who came to offer their felicitations to the coming bride and bridegroom, had a grand time. After the money was spent and the runner from Maggie Smerden's boarding house had warned Mr. Gollen that the *Elba* was ready for sea, young Otto was filled to the gills with whisky and escorted by Mr. Gollen (carrying Otto's bag, filled with three old mats) down to the Queen's Dock.

All was intense happiness at the huckster's. Most of the four-pound-ten cash which Mollie had given Otto for his advance note had been spent in the store and on pawn-able clothes for the family. Three days later, too, she would get her money back when Otto was safely on the high seas. But crossing the inside bridge of the Queens, in sight of the *Elba*, Otto lurched, slipped and fell, striking his head against the hard cobblestones. A half-hour later, after much wrangling in the darkness between Mr. Gollen and the bobby on watch at the gate, the ambulance came and took Otto to the Southern Hospital, and from the Southern Hospital to the morgue. And there, lying on the next slab, was August, his pal, who a few hours previously had been picked up in an alley. The cause of August's death was never quite unraveled. There was much talk about this for months after—not about the tragedy of the boys, but how sagacious Mollie Doran had been hooked out of her advance note.

My mother never quite forgot this tragedy, but not my father. He got the proceeds of pawning the boots Otto had bought me. These shoes and blonde, reckless young Otto are fixtures in my mind; so, too, is the recurring vision of two old Scandinavian mothers wondering how their sons met their deaths.

In addition to sailor-baiting, another trick at which my father was adept was mulcting compensation bureaus. This was a practice not only with him but with all his pals—yet I think he was easily the best trickster. When he was fixing himself up in our room at night, preparatory to a visit the following morning to a compensation doctor, everybody would have to be on the *qui vive*. I recall, after one of these alleged accidents, a last-minute council with a gang of his docker cronies over a subtle point to be discussed the following morning. My father had met with one of his supposed injuries, though mother and I and my sister (and, of course, everyone else present) were convinced there was nothing at all the matter with him. One croaking adviser counciled, "If they ask you to stoop over, Plunger [my father's nickname], don't you do it—they bluffed me that way once." Another ventured sententiously: "Tell 'em you shake all night in yer sleep—that's a bloody good one I invented meself." After they had gone, my mother, Alice and I took turns in scalding his back with hot poultices, the idea being to give his back the appearance of having been recently bruised.

My father, of course, won his skirmish with the compensation people, to the extreme delight of his docker advisers. Another time a clerk, indignant at my father's efforts to get paid in a hurry, had patted my father's hands with a ruler. Leaving his day's wages there, my father hurried off to a lawyer and entered suit for physical injury. It was a palpable fraud, but my father's cunning won him the day. His claim was that the injury incapacitated him from pursuing his occupation—he couldn't use his dock hook.

As the testimony proceeded he forgot which hand it was that had been injured. "You see," said the defense to the Court, "he doesn't know which hand was injured, yet he comes up here and says he was incapacitated. Gentlemen, you can see the man is a fraud." But my father replied quickly, "No, sonny! Both hands of a docker are his chief hands. When you're working in the left-hand side of the ship's hold, why, you use your left hand; and when in the right-hand side, you use your right hand.

And if you had four hands you could work four ship's holds. And if you had eight hands. . . ." He won the case and was awarded nine pounds.

The following night he almost murdered me—not deliberately. The three of us were fleeing his drunken rage when a huge cast-iron frying pan flashed down from the top room window, a few inches past my head, and smashed at my feet. The pan had been aimed at my mother, to whose apron I was clinging. We went through hell until the nine pounds were spent.

CHAPTER SIX

THESE incidents I have described occurred a few years later, in the interval between our first and second stay with the Harrises. Shortly after I was born, the old fiddler-barber, convinced like all the other people who knew him, that my father was mad, had us put out. Next we went to live in Court No. 6, and from here, a few years afterward, mother, Alice and I went into Brownlow Hill Workhouse. Desperate for ale money, my father had been caught stealing some lead piping from the New Branch then being added to the Queen's Dock. This time the Court won and he was given a month in Walton jail. Unable to work because of my recent birth, my mother appealed to the Parish and was given four shillings a week to support the three of us.

At the end of the month my father returned with ten shillings earned in jail, all of which was spent in Cain's public house at the top of the street. Then, he repaired to our shack and gave my mother another fearful beating. Though I was very young, the picture of her, covered with blood, lying on a stretcher and being carried to the ambulance, is still very vivid in my mind.

For this my father was given two months in Walton. As soon as my mother recovered sufficiently we were again dispossessed. We had by this time acquired quite a neighborhood reputation and no one wanted to take us in. But somehow we got a little room in Kent Square and, though very hungry, we lived happily in the new peace and quiet we found, on the four shillings a week contributed by the Parish. After his two months were up, my father asserted his legal rights and again rejoined us, stayed normal for about a week, then broke loose once more. He attempted to throw my mother bodily down the stairway and failed in this only because of the combined efforts of all three of us. It was a strange thing that he would listen to us children, particularly to me, whom he liked very much. But although he was thwarted at the stairway episode, he beat my mother so badly that she was again carried to the Southern Hospital for a week's stay, while he was taken to Walton jail, this time for four months.

When my mother returned with bandaged head the landlady, gripped with fear, asked us to leave. It was the last straw. Broken in spirit, my mother trudged, with us wonderingly at her side, up to the Workhouse and surrendered. This was indeed gall for her to take, since, despite her seeming lack of spirit, she was an inherently proud woman and would work off her finger tips, as proved in later years, if only she could get something to do and if she could reconcile the desertion from my father with her very Catholic conscience.

A LIVERPOOL IRISH SLUMMY

If there had been any decent government institution into which to put us children without fear of losing that vital faith she cherished, my mother would have done so immediately and put my father out of her life. But there seemed no such haven. The governmental tendency, as I have said, was to frown upon any slummy woman with two children, seeking matrimonial separation—particularly when opposed to her plea, denying everything alleged against him, was a man as tricky as my father.

Alice was five and I was three when we entered the big iron gate so dreaded by the slummies; and though our stay was only to be brief—three weeks, enough time for my mother's head and crushed spirit to heal—for a while it looked as though we were to go the way of all permanent inmates. But upon recovery, frightened at this frigid necropolis, my mother applied for release. What visible means had she of support with her husband in jail? asked the Board. Then my mother told of her sister's (my Auntie Janie) working as a charwoman in Heilbron's Emigrant House, a Cunard Line passenger agency in Great George's Square, inferring that Janie would obtain work for her.

It was a plausible story and the Board was sympathetic. Off came our little red frocks and my mother's gray striped dress and on went our old rags reeking with fumigation gas. Outside in the street my mother proudly brought forth two shillings which she had concealed in her hair (for fear that it might be taken from her in the workhouse). She treated us all to meat pies and tea in such a nice peaceful shop that I still remember it and her contented look.

When we left here, my mother, pocketing her shame, repaired first to St. Vincent's Church, where she said a few tense prayers in the darkened quietness as we knelt beside her wonderingly. Then we went straight into the barracks. Here she found my grandmother, confined to her rocking chair by a cancer which the family called indigestion, rocking in silence and staring; my grandfather showing indubitable signs of decay (he was ninety-odd then), sewing away; Johnny, my one-armed uncle, dying on his feet, and at the moment repairing his rags for entry into the hospital of the very institution we had just left. Janie was down at the Emigrant House dodging as much work as possible (of course, this was long before her marriage to the malleable Mr. Murray); the rest of the girls were now married and away with their husbands and children and worries—this last applying particularly to my ambitious Auntie Katie, then in the midst of her New Brighton venture. My Uncle Jimmy was temporarily away from home due to a fracas in which he had beaten up a bobby. Joe Lonnigan, of course, was there with his Anglophobiac philosophy and his bottom in front of the fire, but, sensing a sad story in my mother (he liked to look on the bright side of things), he mooched off upstairs, to my grandmother's extreme satisfaction.

My mother received the usual calm, motherly counsel: "Get away from that madman, Polly; he'll kill you if you don't. Let Janie get you a job and you can lave the childer here."

That part about Janie's getting her a job sounded all right to my mother, but leaving us in the barracks she knew to be impossible. She looked to my grandfather, then to the one-armed brother she loved so well; but they, sensing the hopelessness of everything, nodded their heads in silence.

We stayed there all afternoon, my mother awaiting the arrival of Janie from work, commiserating with my silent uncle about his visit to the hospital and with reckless abandon spending her few coppers on ale. But after the third quart was sent for, my grandfather looked up gravely from his needle and, with shaking head, admonished my mother:

"You've spent enough, Polly—kape the rest of that bit you've got for childers' bellies!" Then he whispered something to my Uncle Johnny, but the latter, in the manner of a man preparing his coffin, kept on packing his bundle. There was a silence for a moment; then my grandmother flared out:

"Trouble! Trouble! There's Johnny goin' to the Workhouse and Jimmy with the bobbies after him. . . . Trouble!"

My once beautiful Aunt Lizzie came in about seven o'clock, carrying her sick boy Sydney and voicing her usual bitter complaint about her husband, Chris.

"The fly turn [ladies' man] had his tea and took his accordion out with him! Sometimes I wish he'd never come back! Or I'd never met him!" Then she turned to Johnny and, after being told that he was going to the hospital, tried to kiss him. But Johnny warded her off. He detested sentimental demonstrations—even from my mother, his pal —and anyway I think he had a premonition of death. Lizzie immediately sent for more ale as a sort of thankful gesture for what my grandmother had done in getting

Sydney christened in St. Peter's the preceding afternoon —in spite of Lizzie's fear of what would happen if her husband's people ever found it out.

Later, Aunt Leisha and her husband, Johnny Roche, and their little boy, Bernard, came in—to the extreme satisfaction of my grandfather and my uncle Johnny, both of whom admired Roche very much, and he, being a sensible man, admired them. After my mother insisted upon spending her remaining few coppers (Johnny Roche, though amiable, was very careful with money and never sent for ale), our problem was taken up again. Not for long, however; mention of my father's name instantly cast a gloom over everything—and silence. Presently heavy footsteps lumbered along the hall and my grandmother smiled and sighed:

"Here she comes—Plate-Face. Now you'll hear all about it!"

Auntie Janie had her apron full of variegated foodstuffs—the remnants of meals served in the Emigrant House—and we all went at it eagerly, particularly Berny and I. As the ale went into this vast woman, Aunt Janie reverted to her usual humorous loquaciousness. Certainly, she'd try to get my mother a charing job at the Emigrant House—but let it stop at that.

"Don't talk in this house about that baste you married, Polly!" So once again, talk about my father was shelved and only Molloy business allowed to be spoken of. On they talked and on they guzzled and on they moaned and the hum of the tramcars came to us from outside and the screeching of the children playing in and around the house and the mellow accordion music floated in through the long hall every so often as gangs of merry-makers went their way; and all the while Alice is standing there very pale-faced hanging on to my mother's apron strings and my mother is trying to be merry and I am trying to be merry but I know in all three minds recurs the parenthetical thought: after we leave here, what then?

But inevitably humor comes from "Plate-Face." She is telling of something preposterous that happened to her after last Saturday's "do" [party]. At about four the following morning she had gone up the "Mount" (the elevated section about St. James's cemetery at the top of St. James Road) to "blow the bloody cobwebs off her brain." And here in this quietude, the hand of the world-famed evangelist, Gypsy Smith, on the hunt for derelict souls, touched her arm, as he softly said: "Now, my dear woman, don't you think it time that you gave up this mode of living in sin (inferring, of course, she was a derelict prostitute) and turn to the Lord? . . ." And Janie, indignantly: "Go away, you dirty rotten auld swiper or oi'll batter your bloody face in for you!" Whereupon, according to Janie, Gypsy, much abashed, "snaked away".

After the roar of laughter had subsided I found myself playing with my cousin Bernard—soldiers and sailors, with knives and forks. We were thrusting at each other, he the sailor, I the soldier. "Here's the way we attack," he would explain and run out along the long dark lobby chasing an imaginary enemy, and I would follow him until the exhaustion I felt so quickly, overcame me. Darkness came on gradually, the sisters one by one departed, my grandmother and grandfather retired into the back room and we were left in the parlor alone, Alice and I on my

49

mother's knee. Presently, however, as the oil lamp burned low and darkness enveloped us, the front door reopened, letting in the hum of the passing tramcars. I went out to shut it and looked up the street. Darkness and gloom and rain. Then, as I closed the door and turned, I faced my Uncle Johnny, just come back from the pub, very pale and drunk. He kissed me and bade me good-bye.

"I'm going to the slaughter house in the morning, Timmy. Take care of your mammy—you've got a good mammy. . . . We always were playmates, me and your mammy. . . . So long. . . ."

He died shortly after that, as he predicted, in the hospital. And there was much drinking and carrying on in the barracks when he was negligently buried against his wish—he had been Catholic enough to ask to be put in the consecrated Ford Cemetery—in non-consecrated Anfield.

CHAPTER SEVEN

SHORTLY after this Janie obtained a charing job for my mother down at Heilbron's Emigrant House, and she took a little room for the three of us in Kent Square, where for a brief period we tasted real happiness and real food. Roast meats, green peas, puddings, stewed fruits, cakes— all mingled in a paper mass carried home in her apron, and were pounced upon eagerly by Alice and me, when mother would come home exhausted but happy. I was so elated with this new-found nourishment that I used to take my dish and sit at the open window in a swankish spirit, showing passersby what the dish contained.

The only family conflicts I recall here were in the arguments Alice and I used to have as to who had protected my mother most from my father. In this protecting business we had very definite stations, mine being at my father's side, holding him back, and Alice's at my mother's, shielding her. Obviously, mine was the more difficult assignment and I insisted upon getting full credit for it, say, in the form of receiving an extra dish of Heilbron's rice pudding. Those memories are the most pleasant to recall, my mother sitting here with Alice, silent and absorbed, on one knee, and me, excited and jabbering incessantly, on the other. Three whole months without a single fight, without once racing barefoot through the night for the bobby—it seemed impossible that such happiness should come our way.

But our bliss was not to continue. Once out of jail, my father returned, begging and beseeching that my mother take him back. He was like a saint, and very sober, with presents of oranges for Alice and me. The oranges won us, particularly Alice, who, all through her life, despite the unworthiness of our father, has shown a devotion to him that is inexplicable. He kissed us and sat us on his knee. Mrs. Sweinson, the landlady, came up; like good slummies we were all more or less sentimental. My father sent for some ale with the money he had earned in Walton and we all drank. Resolutions were in order—there was to be no more of the old life. That night he took my place, next to my mother in bed.

It required only a month for my father to return to his old habits. This time it was worse for my mother, because not only did she absorb the beatings but she also was the breadwinner. My father's efforts at the dock, now that he saw the barest necessities being provided by her, were negligible and confined mostly to stealing stuff and selling it to some fence for a pittance, this to be absorbed in drink. Here once again his caginess stood him in good stead. The beatings were never so bad as to incapacitate my mother from her charing job at the Emigrant House. But they were of such frequency, with the consequent appearance of the bobbies, that eventually Mrs. Sweinson had us put out.

The next place we turned up in was the cellar of a tenement house in Pitt Street above Chinatown, near Great George's Street. We rented the cellar and two attic rooms from the owner, "Nobby" Perkins, a Manchester man who had come to Liverpool at the time of the making of the new docks and who lived close by. Two other families lived in the house, navvies from Macclesfield in to complete the new docks. Mr. and Mrs. Will Hasty and their two small boys; and elderly relatives of old "Nobby's," a Mr. Tibbett and his wife. A peaceful old couple these last; after navvying all week, Mr. Tibbett, of a Saturday night, would get some ale and the two would sing hymns in their room together. The Hastys were very quiet too, and whenever my father would be "in" Mrs. Hasty would tell her husband in suppressed and fearful voice, "Will, he's in downstairs." Whereupon Mr. Hasty would sit in sullen silence, knowing of the terrible row that was to follow in our cellar. I liked Mr. Hasty very well, for he was a kindly man. I always got pennies from him—a big thing with any slummy boy.

Here, the same old things began to happen again with the same grim regularity. How many times my mother went to the dispensary I don't know; how many times during the week my father was due for an eruption, we could never foretell. But the Saturday-night affair was a fixture, and my mother and Alice and I always prepared for it. All week long my father would occupy his time between surreptitious visits to the docks, sailor-baiting, mending the family boots, thinking up schemes to defraud the compensation people—always, if sober, in malignant silence.

He was very generous to both Alice and me. If he worked a day at the dock, we knew he would almost always steal something from the ship's hold and bring it home to us. If he was sober our happiness would be transcendental; but the slightest hint of drink (presaged usually by a wearing of his flat hat) would make us uneasy. It might have seemed humorous to watch the two of us bringing our reason to bear upon my father and mother as Alice shielded her and I restrained him. If my mother, incensed at a vicious, undeserved blow, swore back at my father, little Alice in bared feet and long tresses, would shriek: "Mammy, please don't talk back to him—you know he isn't worth it! There, now—*shut up*!" (Her hand would be over my mother's mouth.)

I, on the other hand, would be counseling my roaring father: "Daddy, she's no bloody good! She's a slummy—you know that! Not like your nice people over in Rock Ferry! Don't pay any attention to her. Come on up to bed!"

Sometimes we would succeed in our endeavors and avoid bloodshed, and we would feel the glow of accomplishment as we watched our mother pray and heard our father snore upstairs. But more often we were swept aside and treated to the sight of our mother being kicked around the floor. One dreaded Saturday night my father caught us all hiding where we kept the coal in the cellar. Alice and I were cast aside and buckets of water were thrown on my mother and then shovelfuls of coal in an effort, it appeared, to bury her.

A LIVERPOOL IRISH SLUMMY

One night, shortly after getting settled in this new place, my sister awoke to find my father setting fire to my mother's hair as she lay in bed. She screamed and awakened my mother. Again, in the middle of the night the place was wrecked, pictures, ramshackle furniture, everything—which was followed by another hurried visit in the night to the dispensary. But nothing was done by the bobbies, who, seemingly unappreciative of my mother's dilemma, had contempt for her. A few days later, only a miracle saved my mother from being thrust out the third-story window. With Alice and me screaming and tearing at his hands, my father carried my mother bodily to the window, despite her frantic kicks, and tried his best to push her through to certain death. The window was too small, however, and Mr. Hasty came up to our assistance and reasoned with him—as men always could.

In "Nobby" Perkins's house, with comparatively little danger of being put out (since "Nobby" didn't live on the premises), my father had decidedly more freedom. Whatever little restraint he had shown in the other houses, due to a fear of being evicted, did not operate here. We hung on at this place almost two years when, after numerous requests from "Nobby" to move had been disregarded, Nobby came down with his two brawny nephews and dumped our bits of furniture out on the sidewalk. My father fled to the public house and from there to the fourpenny lodging house; my mother, Alice and I put the furniture in a handcart and wheeled it to the yard in back of the barracks.

The three of us stayed there a week, but the illness of our grandparents made it necessary for us to move. Everyone had his or her hands full, and it was a matter of "each for himself and God for us all". My mother still had her job at the Emigrant House and Alice and I were, according to custom, ready to make our bow at school. We needed a home—a home of any sort—and again my mother, at the behest of religion, made the big sacrifice.

CHAPTER EIGHT

THE next place we took was the shack in Brick Street mentioned earlier in the book. Dirtier even than the Courts out of which we had been driven, this dilapidated shack at the head of the long entry was rented to us for three shillings and sixpence a week. It had one bedroom upstairs with one little window, and as this opened up on the wall of the shack next to us, the sun never entered our room. All excretions went into the two buckets provided for that purpose, along with a dirty piece of newspaper covering them. One of my favorite games was clipping wings of the huge blue-bottle flies that buzzed over the buckets and around the room. We slept on the floor on mattresses. I used to lie on the mattress and, following the example of my father, spit on the wall or the floor. Later, when my lungs weakened, the spitting became intensified.

To the right of the shack the entry widened into a sort of imitation court having three other shacks like ours. One of these was tenanted by a large family, the head of which was the only human counterpart I have ever seen of my father—a tall, lean, Leinster Irishman named Francis O'Rourke; about fifty years of age, his specialty was to parade on the roof naked, calling foul epithets to anyone chancing by. Every dock laborer had one nickname, but Francis had two, the "The Black Prince" and "The Hombre," both given because of his extremely dark complexion.

Francis, as well as thundering curses at strangers, occasionally used to tear the bricks from the roof and start heaving them at passing bobbies, who usually had a very difficult time subduing him. He used to brandish a huge carving knife and yell: "I'm the hombre who can use the knife!" One time my father and the hombre hooked up, throwing bricks at each other from the roofs, but only once. After viewing Francis' long knife, I think my father rather respected Francis' prowess and steered clear of him, drunk or sober. Francis' wife, Anne Jane, was a poor misguided idiot, almost as terror-stricken as my mother. There was one son, Jimmy, and two girls, Mary Anne and Sissy. One night Anne Jane, the mother, threw herself out of the third-story window to escape the hombre's knife; she is lame to this day. Jimmy, the son, was addicted to violent fits all his life; but later, as a man, though suffering very badly, was (along with the dole) his father's sole support. The girls married rather young and fled into other sections of the slums.

To the left of us was another shack, occupied by long-suffering Harry Gavney and his wife, "Gentle Annie," a chip-chopper with twelve children, most of whom garnered the wood chopped and sold the finished product. Gentle Annie's shack was perhaps dirtier and more sparsely furnished than either the Hombre's or ours. Parents and children slept on the floor, whereas we had mattresses. Every Monday morning the landlord, Mr. Gillen, would come around to collect the rents of the occupied houses—not the Gavney residence, however, since he had put them out sometime before. Just before he put in an appearance, the Gavney children would carry out behind the house all the Gavney accoutrements, and the "House to Let" sign, that had been taken out of the window temporarily, would be put back into its place. After Mr. Gillen, satisfied the house was still unoccupied, departed, the process would be reversed.

The remaining shack farther to the left of the court was occupied by Mr. and Mrs. George Gollen (already mentioned in the *Elba* case) and their four children, Jimmy, Johnny, Sam and Lizzie. Mrs. Gollen took a great pride in her maiden name and was known everywhere as Polly Tucker. Very improvident, she was the only slummy Catholic woman I knew who did not belong to a burial club. Father Ryan once admonished her on this improvidence and she replied testily: "If they won't bury me for love, father, they will for stink!"

Later on, jealous of the Gavney's racket, Polly perfected a technique to beat Mr. Gillen out of his rent. The good Mr. Gillen (thanks to the slummy *esprit de corps*) hadn't discovered as yet the trick perpetrated upon him. She told Mr. Gillen she was leaving—and she did, but only during the day. One Monday, Mr. Gillen caught Polly (still drunk from the night before) unawares. Ostensibly, her shack was, like the Gavneys, "To Let." This particular morning, after gimpsing the wary Gavneys's "To Let" sign in their window, Mr. Gillen was surprised to see no "To Let" sign in Polly's window. He opened the door to see if all was well (perhaps the sign had fallen down, he mused) and was surprised to see all of the same old Gollen furnishings—an orange box, bucket, two corn-beef cans, two more boxes and several rags.

Suspicions aroused, he went upstairs and peered into the top room (Polly, giggling, was behind the door as he opened it, but kept hidden); and he returned downstairs in great fury, breaking up the "furniture," throwing it all out into the yardway and departing. A few minutes later, Polly recovered what was recoverable of her chattels (the corn-beef cans which were the cooking utensils, etc.) after which, she came in to see my mother, giggling with laughter, saying: "Mrs. O'Mara, holy sufferin' Jesus Christ, Mr. Gillen's just been in and kicked me things out in the yard. . . . And I was behind the door all the time! Good job the children or George didn't come in. . . !" From then on the Gavneys renewed their vigilance.

Of Polly's children, Jimmy, a lanky lad, later went to fight in France, came back and married a war widow, only to step out, rather pleased, when the husband returned; and Johnny, mentally deficient, stayed at home, as did Sam, as a munitions worker. Lizzie, a good quiet girl something like my sister Alice, married and was swallowed up in another section of the slums. As children, the horde of us (save Alice and me when the usual battle started) would romp and play in rags and bare feet up and down the entry, much to the chagrin of Mr. Tommy Brody, who lived in an elegant little house near Park

Lane and who used our entry to make unlicensed race-horse books.

My father was a constant source of irritation to Mr. Brody, for when the bobbies would come to arrest my father, it would almost always mean the suspension of Brody's business. A sixpence flung to the Hombre would keep him quiet. It would have required a bank to silence my father. Mr. Brody made a lot of money from this bookmaking and later went into politics and was elected first to the Select Vestry of the Board of Guardians and later to the City Council when, on the advice of his sons attending college, he changed his name to Thomas D. Brody, II. Shortly after this he almost beat Sir Something or other for Parliament. I don't think Mr. Brody could write his name, but most of his councilman's work was done for him by his educated sons. He was very popular with us slummies, however, because his position on the Select Vestry gave him the power to help us get food and clothes during distress, which he did very willingly. All day long, the line of men making bets with him at our entry was a familiar sight, as also was the furtive stand of his touts on each corner of Park Lane farther up the street—a position I eagerly looked forward to filling some day. In the event of a raid, the touts would all duck up the entry and into any shack they cared to, then out the back way. For this privilege the children were thrown an occasional penny; every one of mine, I remember, I used to keep for my mother and offer it to her with a grand show-off—then beg it back from her a little while later, when the joy of giving had waned.

CHAPTER
NINE

THE three-cornered warfare between Mr. Gavney, his vast brood, and the School Board, then starting an intensive campaign for the education of slummy children, took place about this time. Mr. Gavney never recalled the names or whereabouts of his children, except when he was carted off to jail to atone for their truancy. The way this new governmental solicitude used to function was very humorous. Coming out of Walton jail, after doing twenty-eight days for Bridgett's aberration, Harry was turned over to another bureau, this time doing six weeks for child Paddy's absence. (In the same ratio that the child missed school the father put in time in jail.)

I always knew when Mr. Gavney was returning from jail, for he almost always cursed and kicked out of his way any of the brats he passed playing in our entry. Or the evidence of his wrath came from his house. Like the rest of the women of this neighborhood, Gentle Annie did all her baking (when there was flour, of course,) in a big pan mug which Harry (if just out of jail) would empty over her head. Then she would come running out into the yard crying happily, face covered with flour. "Oh Mrs. O'Mara, look what 'Arry's done to me!" The Black Prince and my father were fortunate in that their children were only too eager to get into the better atmosphere of the school. But not poor Harry; his brood were inveterate truants.

Gavney and the Black Prince got along together fairly well—except once. The Black Prince had signed on as fireman on one of the Cunard boats. While he was down in The Curio Vaults squandering his advance note, he threw Anne Jane out and ordered her home to pack his sea bag. Anne Jane, furious at this treatment, borrowed the Gavney floor-mat and packed her husband's bag pretty much the way George Gollen had packed the ill-fated Otto's of the *Elba*. Out on the high seas, the Black Prince, recognizing the mat, put two and two together and when he returned home accused Harry of philandering. There was almost murder that night; I think all concerned went to the hospital before going to jail.

To the left of our alley, just above bookmaker Brody's elegant little house, was Harris's pawnshop, no relation, however, to the Harrises who had ejected us from Bridgewater Street. This pawnshop was an integral part of this neighborhood's social and economic life. Sunday was the only day for us to wear civilized clothing. Hence the obvious question: Why keep good clothes and boots loafing in the house all week when they could be pawned? Every Monday morning a *queue* would line up outside Harris's pawnship, pledging the elegant little things worn (with the creases still in them) so proudly of a Sunday. What a badge of shame for a boy or girl to appear at mass on Sunday morning in the same old week-day rags! It did not hurt Alice and me much because we were hardened to this. My father's moleskin trousers, his docker's hook and belt and his union button—it seemed to be my task to pledge these every Monday, to be redeemed the following Saturday if my father had earned the redemption price at the dock during the week.

This pawning-redeeming routine kept up until the pawnable material had deteriorated to a point viewed with skepticism by the very cynical Mr. Harris. I recall one furtive fellow placing his sweater on the counter and saying, "Gimme eighteen pence on that, Mr. Harris."

"There's enough on that right now," replied the veteran pawnbroker, inferring, of course, vermin, as he rejected the pledge.

Mrs. Haggerty, who lived below our entry, for years pawned her false teeth every Monday morning, and when she died, Mr. Harris hopefully put them up for sale in his front window, taking them out eventually and putting them in the storeroom. It was always a source of worry as to when Mr. Harris would term a pledge no longer pledgeable. Prior to pawning, frayed cuffs and edges of suits were always discreetly smoothed out and sewed up by prudent pledgers. We all got very nervous when Mr. Harris reached for his spectacles, for this meant minute scrutiny and minute scrutiny almost always meant condemnation. Sometimes this condemnation was very poignant. Once, the only hope we had for a loaf of bread was in pawning my Sunday boots—an item that had always fetched two shillings and that had been redeemed with much misgiving on my father's part on the preceding

Saturday night for me to wear with the other boys at Sunday Mass. Of course, we looked forward with almost certainty to getting back the two shillings on Monday; in fact, we had so arranged our budget—my father was to get the price of a pint, the most important item, and the rest was to go for bread and tea. When Mr. Harris adjusted his spectacles and said to me, "I'm sorry, sonny, but these boots are no use here any more" I felt very weak.

"But my mammy just got them out on Saturday!"

"I'm sorry, but these boots are no use here any more, sonny."

"But, Mr. Harris, we've got nothing to eat! And my daddy, if he doesn't get his pint, will beat my mammy again."

Again he looked at them, shook his head and pointed to a small gap between the sole and the upper that I, better than anyone else, knew was there. "I'm sorry," he concluded, "but these boots are no use here any more."

Sadly I took the boots home, where my father patched the weak spot very discreetly and sent me up to Mr. Ellis's pawnshop at the corner of Parliament and St. James Place. Here they'd take in anything, for this was where the Negro-white-wife element did business.

I faced Mr. Ellis, who was still perspiring after a wrangle with a Negro pawning his stoker's shirt.

"I want two an' ninepence on these boots, Mr. Ellis."

Without looking at them too closely, he said, "I'll give you two an' threepence."

I accepted and went home with heart aquiver and explained my strategy to everyone. It was a pyrrhic victory, however, for instead of one pint my father appropriated for himself the price of two. We never redeemed the boots and continued doing regular weekly business with Mr. Harris until one Saturday night, with business at its peak, he dropped dead to the great joy, I feel I must say, of Mr. Ellis, his competitor, whom we had so unconscionably defrauded.

The Brick Street money lenders: When the pawnshop betrayed you, you could always do business with the "Fish and Money" people, who relied less upon collateral than upon their reputation for administering physical beatings to recalcitrant debtors. Polly Clark, Mrs. McKinley, Mollie Doran, Sissy Curlett, Mrs. Sweeney, Mary Ellen Grant, and Nellie Bowman were those best known around our neighborhood.

The technique went something like this: they would come up our entry with baskets of putrid fish and inquire who among the men had "got on" down at the dock. Thus if any of the men's wives were courageous enough to borrow four shillings in cash, they would also have to take two shillings' worth of this putrid fish. The debt would therefore stand at six shillings to·be paid on the following Saturday—or else.

My father was always in debt to the fish-and-money people but was also very discreet in paying them their debts. The fish, he would throw into the darkness of the entry, there to add to the general stink of the place and to be set upon by huge mangy cats. Only death and religious fear brought a sense of proportion to these women's minds. Mrs. Sweeney used to charge fourpence to the shilling interest in addition to the fish purchase, but when she lay dying, Father Wilson refused to give her absolution until she paid back all that interest to her victims—which she did very eagerly and, we assume, ascended into Heaven.

Mary Ellen Grant, the "Connaught Nigger" (white-Irish mother, west-coast-of-Africa father), and Nellie Bowman, her white partner, were a fairly good example of the type of money-lending women, tough, reckless, shrewd financially, abandoned morally. Together they went to the wake of a salt-heaver [i.e., a dock laborer who specialized in shoveling salt] who had died of smallpox, taking along with them some boiled potatoes and bread to eat during the long vigil. As the wake proceeded into the night, with the usual Celtic moaning and crying and joking, Mary Ellen and her mate, getting hungry decided to use the potatoes. They needed some salt for seasoning and, finding none at hand, on a dare from Nellie, the Connaught Nigger, dipped her potato in the salt that was placed on the dead man's belly to stop it from swelling, and ate it. On a like dare, Nellie followed suit. Shortly after the salt-heaver's burial both women, to the extreme satisfaction of their many creditors, were taken with smallpox and removed to the Brownlow Hill Workhouse Hospital, where the white Nellie Bowman died and the "Connaught Nigger" survived to tell the joke proudly wherever she went.

The priests frowned upon this fish-and-money lending practice and often went out of their way to try to stop it. Mrs. Mangan, a hard-working washerwoman, borrowed a pound from Sissy Curlett and found herself, after her husband had deserted her, unable either to meet principal or interest. The fact that her husband had deserted her saved her the beating; but from then on the entire Curlett family wash was sent to her weekly—to pay off the interest. One day, Father Corlett found Mrs. Mangan exhausted by the side of her tub, and when she explained that she would have to continue with this payless task to avoid a beating, the good priest's ire was aroused. It heightened considerably when she explained that this weekly washing had been going on for three months and had no definite time limit. In his spiritual capacity he commanded her to stop the washing.

The following week, when Sissy and her sister called with their basket, Mrs. Mangan, filled with spiritual righteousness, told of Father Corlett's order and her intention of complying with the divine command. The Corlett sisters set upon her and beat her into unconsciousness, after which they broke up all the furniture and prized religious pictures. Then Sissy very prudently got Dr. Walker, (the "tanner doctor", just dismissed as the head doctor from the South Dispensary and now on the down grade), to make out a certificate to the effect that she had been "wounded" by Mrs. Mangan, at the moment lying in the Southern Hospital. When the case came to court, Sissy, with the aid of the "tanner doctor", was winning hands down until Father Corlett put in an appearance and told his story. Sissy had to pay Mrs. Mangan twenty pounds for breaking up her cellar, the original debt was cancelled, and Sissy was warned by the court to be a little less primitive in the collection of her debts. It was a happy day for the debtors and a bad one for the creditors. Cancellations came right and left, for a happy precedent had been set. It was also a happy day for Father Corlett, a very somber, Anglicized and just man, as I recall him.

The church in Brick Street: As with everything else around our neighborhood, humor also sustained the church. It was always the custom to have the priest settle any intra-or inter-family conflict. The bobbies were too unreliable, never taking the slummies seriously, and making it a point to arrive always *after* the tragedy. Not so the priests, for their whole philosophy was to rescue. One day the Black Prince, naked on the roof, was doing his knife stunt so enthusiastically that we boys, at the behest of the astounded neighborhood, made the run for a priest. I got to St. Vincent's Parish house first and a moment later was galloping behind the cassock of that natural fighter, Father Toomey.

Up the entry we ran and, espying the Black Prince, the priest yelled: "Come down out of there, ye dirty mane lunatic, or I'll come up and bate the daylights out of ye."

"All right, father," said the Black Prince humbly, hiding his dagger and disappearing behind his favorite chimney pot.

Of the three priests in St. Vincent's Parish—Father Ryan the parish priest, Father Coffee, Father Toomey—I liked this fighter, Father Toomey, best. As sentimental as the country that bore him, he was governed entirely by his emotions. A child sent to the parish door for the usual "Me mother said could you let her have sixpence, Father" always would be told to try to get hold of Father Toomey. Father Ryan and Father Coffee, knowing the impoverished state of the church, could be more realistic and refuse—but not this young Fenian. He hated the English more bitterly than any Irishman I have ever known and was always a source of irritation to the more prudent and diplomatic Father Ryan.

The Toomey sermons from the pulpit were always looked forward to with intense glee from the congregation and with equally intense dissatisfaction by Father Ryan. When, eventually, the younger priest was recalled to his native Ireland (a surreptitious request by Father Ryan we all thought) our elderly parish priest threw up his hands and cried: "Thank God, he's going away from here!" It was ironic, however, that years later both should die on the same day—Father Ryan in a London nursing home and the younger priest dropping dead in his pulpit in his beloved Ireland.

Poor Father Ryan! How well I remember his big, florid, long-suffering face as he stood beside Bishop Whiteside, resplendent in pontifical robes and Crozier in hand, as the Bishop confirmed me. What a trinity here! The resplendent and grave English Bishop from elegant Sefton Park; the patient Father Ryan; the bitter Fenian, Father Toomey—there was Ireland!

I have dealt with Brick Street and its denizens at length because most of my early memories are rooted there. It was from here that Alice and I started our schooling together. She had attended school only spasmodically before this; because of our family history she had been allowed more latitude than most children. She was seven years of age then and I was five. St. Vincent's in Norfolk Street was the first school I attended. It was in here we were both baptised. More adept at lessons than Alice, I used to do her homework for her, but when I reached seven years of age I was transferred to St. Peter's school in Seel Street. That finished our walks together, but I still continued doing her lessons as best I could, considering the handicap under which both of us labored.

I liked school because it afforded me some sort of escape. I was the inveterate dreamer, and once absorbed in my dreams, reality could easily be forgotten. For instance, every Saturday, somehow or other I would get twopence, pack some bread and butter and go down to Lime Street to the Palais de Lux Cinema, where there was "continuous performance". Here, as soon as the place opened, I would repair to the gallery, pick out a comfortable place, and prepare myself for a twelve-hour vigil during which I would be regaled by cowboy films and the semi-classical tunes played by the string orchestra. Over and over again, until closing time, I would sit through the performance. As nightfall came, reality would break through this world of make believe and my mind would revert to the alley in Brick Street. Where was Alice? There was no escape for her, dour, loyal, little partisan of her mother that she was!

Sometimes I would fall asleep and remain in my seat until old Dan, the aged watchman with the stinking clay pipe, would wake me with, "Come on, youser! You're last out again. Eleven o'clock—it's in bed you ought to be, not looking at Injuns!". . . . But on my return home, up the dark entry the piercing scream of my mother or Alice or the roar of my father would bring me swiftly back to earth.

Small wonder that Alice was a bad scholar, for she always had her mind on what was happening in our shack. She never won a prize; indeed, except for me she would have never passed an examination. How that little mind used to torture itself over figures! One time we were working out at home a set of arithmetic examples, as my mother, just in from the Emigrant House and covered with sweat, prepared our tea. I had just asked Alice a question on numbers and she said to me quite blankly, "I wonder will daddy be drunk when he comes in, Timmy?" Small wonder that she was sometimes thought to be stupid at school.

School increased my mother's responsibility. Now that she was working regularly in the Emigrant House, my father extended his drinking to every day, thereby cancelling any midday lunch for us. To overcome this, my mother would risk her job by slipping away from her charing duties and meet Alice and me in Cornwallis Street with sandwiches and bottles of milk. In the street we would eat, our mother looking on admiringly while passersby wondered the reason for the picnic. To mother Alice was "poor little waif," while I was "me great big lump of love." Strangely enough, my father was cool to Alice but liked me intensely in his own apish way, while I despised him with equal intensity. On the other hand, despite his coldness toward her, my sister would never let anyone take advantage of him if she could stop it. But as we ate swiftly in the peaceful sunlight, I think the same thought raced swiftly through our minds: "What will the night bring?" Sometimes I would catch her eyes staring at me almost jealously as much as to say, "You're all right, Timmy! You can go out and play, but I. . . !" Sometimes she would beseech me not to desert her during a conflict and I would promise not to. But I broke many promises.

My most poignant memories of these school days were of meeting Alice after school about four o'clock and trudging home. The lessons were completely forgotten—especially by her—when we'd meet, and we would immediately begin laying plans how best to handle the prospective combatants later that evening. Sometimes, however, I would meet her and leave her, and her little face would drop and the big brown eyes would scowl as she continued on alone, I to the footy game, she to the hell-hole we called home.

Perhaps in those days the man I owed most to was my headmaster, Mr. McGinnis, a very sympathetic teacher. Mr. McGinnis, I think, partly guessed the nature of my peculiar problem and, though he often threatened to punish me with his ever-ready ruler for mental meandering, I seldom recall its landing. He never knew the true facts of our family, however. There was no way of his knowing and, like all good Englishmen, he probably would have refused to believe the facts even had they been before his eyes.

CHAPTER
TEN

ST. PETER'S school in Seel Street was, in a way, a new vista opening in my life. Here was an English school filled mainly with Irish-Catholic boys. But the tutors in this school, though all of them were Catholic, had been trained in England and all their teaching smacked of this English training. The Empire and the sacredness of its preservation ran through every text-book like a *liet-motif*. Our navy and the necessity of keeping Britannia ruling the waves is another indelible mark left in my memory—though the reason for this was never satisfactorily explained. Pride in our vast and far-flung colonies and the need for their protection and preservation were emphasized, as was the confidence that in any given crisis the colonies and the motherland stand as one.

The British always won wars—not the English, but the British—giving the impression that we were all more or less brothers under the skin, the Irish, the English, the Welsh and the Scotch. We were the kingpins; and we were always in the right—these are the straight, patriotic impressions that remain. And then came religion—and ah! that was something else again. Oliver Cromwell might have been a hero in Protestant St. Michael's but not in our school. And so, with forthright pastors like Father Toomey, it wasn't long before religion got to race, and from race to definite biases. . . . The best I can say is that what I derived from my elementary English-Irish schooling was an intense love for the British Empire and an equally intense hatred for England as opposed to Ireland.

Our mothers and fathers, of course, were unequivocal in their attitude—destroy England, no less! But we children at school, despite the intense religious atmosphere of the Catholic school, were rather patriotized and Britishized—until we got back to our shacks, where we were sternly Irishized. . . . The paradox has remained in my make-up for years—the sound of a patriotic Irish air will make me want to get out my shillalah for the old wrongs of Ireland; but the moment the music is over, common sense will warn me to put it back. My mental prejudices, today as an adult, work something like this; ferocious, sacrificial Irish-Catholic (die for Ireland's freedom) first; ferocious sacrificial patriotic Britisher second; and patient, wondering dreamer third. This three-way ticket may seem silly to more civilized people, but as long as it is true, open confession, as my poor benighted father used to say, is good for the soul. And what is true of me is true certainly of most slummy Irish-Catholic "Britishers."

Among the active members of our gang were Joe Manassi, a belligerent, stocky boy of Italian parentage; Harold May, Protestant, very English and quiet; Johnny

Mangan, heavy set, Irish, belligerent; Johnny Ford, the same; Henry Roche, wiry, belligerent, Irish but no relation to me; my cousin Bernard Roche, thin, quiet, a true fighter; Frankie Roza, half-caste Protestant Manilla boy, who played the concertina and was the favorite of the gang; Jackie (Quanito) Sanchez, fiery yet amiable Spanish boy, whose mother kept the big Spanish boarding house at the corner of Cornwallis Street and Park Lane; "Lepsey" Phillips, Protestant boy—mother, a very belligerent gypsy, and father, Irish—a quick tempered boy; Jackie Oldham, dare-devil and English; Freddie Seegar, comedian, of German-Irish parents, lazy and improvident; and a waif known to us all only as "Mickey"—an upcountry boy who had drifted into Liverpool and slept at the Working Boy's Home. The three Protestant members (Protestant only at the insistence of their parents) attended St. Michael's Protestant school in Pitt Street. This was our "gang", and our "corner" was the empty house in White Street at Pitt, opposite Mrs. Mallin's pub, until Aeroplane Joe, the bobby who wouldn't let us play pitch and toss, the war and death broke us up.

Of my pals, I liked Jackie Sanchez and Mickey best. Jackie was closer to me than Mickey, more because of his mother's Spanish boarding house which I loved to visit, and because of the fact that Mickey's connections with the Working Boy's Home made his appearance at the corner both uncertain and infrequent. I don't know precisely how Mickey came among us—via a Sunday footy game in Greenville Street; he was much younger than the rest of us, but we took him in.

In Jackie's boarding house it was pleasant listening to

the Spanish sailormen home from the sea, crowding around a table covered with luscious "continental" dinners. I used to like the stuffiness and informal nature of the kitchen, and in the men's tuneful language and swarthy complexions I could weave all sorts of adventures for gold on the Spanish Main. Actually, they were hard-working, very practical-minded stokers and sailors on the Larinaga boats. Through these boarders Jackie almost always could procure money either to go to the Cornwallis-Street public baths, managed by Ted Heaton, the Channel swimmer, or the Palais De Luxe Picture House. Harold May and I once fought over his friendship on account of this, and I was always at loggerheads with Freddie Seegar and the others over the same thing. I always dreaded any protracted separation from the Sanchez boarding house.

Joe Manassi, Johnny Mangan, and "Jacko" Oldham were the three toughest lads and usually had their way in any gang argument. We were all, however, more or less loud-mouthed boys, including dreamy Jackie Sanchez and myself, learning our habits from our elders—all, I should say, except boyish, sensitive Mickey, whose sadness of heart, combined with the rigors of the Working Boy's Home, dwarfed any youthful exuberance. I was, perhaps, the least belligerent of my mates, yet within me was a fierce pride to be just as tough as any of them.

This was illustrated by my fight with "Jacko" Oldham. We were playing football at the time and Jacko "charged" me very unfairly and I resented it. Immediately, as was the custom, he dared me to "have a try?" (The invitation to fight.) I demurred, of course. Johnny Ford called me a bloody coward; as also did Joe Manassi and Lepsey

Phillips. Johnny Mangan and Henry Roche pushed me into Jacko. Even my cousin Bernard, who was so close to me, as well as Jackie Sanchez and the timid Mickey frowned upon my hesitancy. I held up my hands as a gesture of combat. To the surprise of the gang (and delight, too, since I believe they liked me better than Jacko, the bully), I went after Jacko steadily, stalking him all the way up the long hilly distance from the base of Grenville Street to the top at Rowtowne House, assimilating a sound beating with each forward step, never hitting him once and wondering, no doubt, why I didn't hit him. I think I won the decision, since he got exhausted hitting me.

Fighting was then probably the greatest thing in the life of the British schoolboy. Fed almost exclusively in the school room upon the valor of the more obvious British patriots, the greatest stigma to attach to anyone was that of coward. This was the one thing I abjured most in Mickey—his apparent cowardice, for he would never accept an offer to fight. Also, his alleged Catholicism (while he stayed at the non-sectarian but pro-Protestant Working Boy's Home) always made me skeptical, to say nothing of the effect it had on Harold May, Frankie Roza, and Lepsey Phillips, the three unwillingly admitted Protestant members of our gang.

"To have a bloody try" meant that after school, if the invitation had been accepted by the one invited, both boys and those in on the secret would hie down to a lot near the school (in our case on Colquit Street near Parr), strip off coats and waistcoats and shirts and go to it. These were all fierce and bloody encounters; but there was always more of a thrill to it whenever a black boy and a white one hooked up. (It smacked of that encounter ever in the minds of all Liverpool slummy boys: the Jeffries and Johnson affair in America.) Most of the inviters "to have a bloody try" were not so brave as they made out, and almost always it was the boy who accepted the invitation rather than the inviter who came out victor.

I recall one exception of the rule, however. Myself. In an altercation at school recess while we played football, Jacko again invited me to combat and, without thinking, I accepted. All the preceding night I had been holding down my father and once or twice I had almost fallen asleep over my lessons. I went down to the lot, accompanied by a cheering crowd who predicted a swift victory for me. My performance shocked them. I stood up and made all the advances; but when Aeroplane Joe, the bobby, put in an appearance some thirty minutes later, my nose was bleeding and my heart was galloping so fast that I was afraid to run. I hobbled off with the gang, clutching my nose. A great pang of remorse came over me, too, for the new shirt my mother had bought me was torn. I thought it was beyond repair. She wouldn't like that, and I didn't like adding to her burdens.

Poor morose Mickey! I recall my victory over him. Mickey's life, guarded carefully by him, I think was something akin to mine, though not nearly so bad. I don't know what we fought over—I think I "picked on" him to consolidate my position with the gang, and I think he accepted my "will you have a try?" either because of contempt for my prowess or because he thought I was joking. At any rate, once the gang had heard the offer and the acceptance there was nothing either one of us could do to withdraw, and after much trudging in bare feet along cobblestoned streets to Parr Street, we pulled off our shirts and faced each other. It must have been really comical to see the two of us making vicious swipes intentionally sent awry. I think I scored a moral victory without a single blow being struck.

The most vicious fight I recall was between Jackie Sanchez and our comedian, Freddie Seegar. I was very glad of this fight because it definitely removed Freddy as my competitor for Jackie's friendship, which included the pennies to the pictures, the occasional feeds and the discarded boots of the Sanchez children. The Irish and the Spanish locked head and head and I think the result was a gory draw. Johnny Ford and Henry Roche, stocky loud-mouthed little fellows, fought several times. I think the line-up went something like this. Cock of the gang: Jacko Oldham; next, Joe Manassi; Johnny Mangan; Johnny Ford; Henry Roche; Harold May; my cousin Bernard Roche; Freddie Seegar; Jackie Sanchez; dark-skinned Frankie Roza; myself and Mickey. Lepsey Phillips was the true enigma of the gang. We all insisted upon our fighting superiority over him—but none of us ever actually hit him. I think at heart we all were afraid of this silent son of the mad gypsy woman and the even madder Irish father.

Along with this congenital urge to fight, the other recreations we indulged in were football, swimming and cricket—the last named very seldom, for it was played mostly by bourgeois English boys with uncles in Australia. Cricket was played in Sefton Park and Stanley Park, rather restricted territory for us of the no-boot brigade. But football (soccer in America) and swimming—these two were our favorites. Of the two, I think I loved swimming more, so well, in fact, that my over-indulgence in it —together with the conditions of my home life—had at one time a serious effect on my health. The gang was almost always together in these sports. Frankie Roza, the half-caste, was a fleet swimmer, but I think I could have beaten him had I had any nervous energy to call upon. I could lick him at forty yards, but after that something would seem to drop from within me and I was through.

In football it was the same way. Mr. Mooney couldn't understand why I could never sustain the brilliant game I almost always showed at the start when I substituted on the regular eleven. I recall one time, when we were playing St. Vincent's team, dribbling the ball all the way down the field and scoring all alone. It was a play that would have done credit to a regular on Liverpool's professional team, but after that I was ready for the stretcher. Thus, my dream of being photographed with arms and legs crossed as a member of the school's regular football team was never realized, and my games limited for the most part to those played after school hours— often with a ball made up of old rags—in Grenville, Cornwallis and Parr Streets. These were high-spirited encounters, with the bundle of rags dropping dead wherever it landed, or suddenly sailing through an innocent window when, of course, the game would be interrupted, a new rag ball made, and the game continued in the next street. After the game we would all be tired and repair gladly to our shacks—all except Mickey and myself, the former liking the frigid Working Boy's Home as much as I relished mine.

Our excursions up to Cob Hall were very frequent and a source of great fun. Cob Hall was a big, first-floor room at the corner of Slater and Leece Streets where, every Sunday evening at half-past six, Gypsy Smith and his Evangelical aides-de-camp yelled the furies of Hell-fire and damnation at a crowd of slummy children, all of whom were awaiting only the big bread cob to be distributed at the end of the sermon. Because of hunger, our gang attended regularly, but we had to be very discreet, for if Mr. McGinnis, our headmaster, heard about it, we would all get a severe spanking with the ruler. The purpose of Cob Hall was to save the Irish Catholic slummy children from a life-long devotion to the Pope.

Mr. Gypsy Smith (a very brave man) would send out Mr. MacNuff, a frail little man with two teeth, a peculiar-looking mustache and a strange light in his eyes, to garner us in from our corner to Sunday Services. Usually he came around our way on a Wednesday night, and we would take turns at pulling the tails of his swallow-tailed coat and in "kidding" him—all of which he would take good-naturedly so long as we promised to attend and join in the singing of the hymns "for great rejoicing in the Lord." When he would return up the road we would throw bricks at him; then duck around the corner.

But every Sunday evening we were among the first guests to take seats. We had foul parodies for all the hymns, but took care not to render our parodies too loudly. During a sermon, loud and unseemly noises would rend the place, and while the Gypsy or Mr. MacNuff were searching for a miscreant in our section, others of our gang planted elsewhere would blast forth only to be as tranquil as saints when the missionaries came their way. . . . Then, when the last hymn had been sung, we would all line up and pass out the door, each receiving his cob, the lads from the Park Lane School (a reformatory school for boys who had been truants from school) getting preference at the basket of cobs. But when we got out it would invariably mean a thrashing for the Park Lane boys and then as we munched the cob, we would chant:

> "King Billy's mother runs a
> whorehouse in Hell . . . ."

And we kept this sort of stuff up, but so also did Mr. MacNuff and Gypsy Smith keep up their hope that some day the light would come to us—highly improbable, since the cob was always in front of it.

But though "footy" and Cob Hall and the alleys were a big lure to us, I think the sea and the water held us more strongly. Practically all of us came from seafaring homes—that is to say, from parents whose livelihood was in some way or other tied up with the sea—and we took to water very readily. Here the placid docks were great for speed trials. Our big problem was in getting into the dock, for no children were allowed past the gateway unless with parents who themselves had to have some working connection there. We would wait until some wagon or float filled with merchandise was passing along and hide ourselves between the bales of cotton or the bags of flour and pass on into the docks in safety. Once inside, nobody bothered us, and we could always be sure of some good food and perhaps a penny or two thrown to us by generous sailormen.

These are among the few pleasant memories. The long straight pier head with the Mersey on one side and our placid speed course on the other, the Mersey containing ships in from all parts of the world and boasting men of every nationality—Madagascans, Lascars, Liverpudlians, Negroes, Indians, coolies, Cockneys leaning over the different ships' sides counselling us in their variant languages or in their broken English, throwing us foodstuffs and pennies, some luring the boys aboard ship, vicious ulterior motives in their minds. It is as though yesterday and I can see the whole gang of them—Joe Manassi, Harold May, Johnny Mangan, Johnny Ford, Henry Roche, and Bernard Roche, Frankie Roza, Jackie Sanchez, Jackie Oldham, Freddie Seegar, Lepsey Phillips and Mickey—standing on the ship's side of the Elder-Dempster boat *Lagos* ready to dive for the sixpence the jovial Negro cook was about to throw into the water, while I am already there, bobbing up and down.

Whenever we had money, Ted Heaton's baths in Cornwallis Street, in lieu of the docks, was our favorite spot. Here all the school speed trials were held; here the swimming team to compete with other swimming teams in the Empire was selected. As in the case of the twopence to admit me to the Palais de Luxe, I used somehow to corral twopence (most of the time from Jackie Sanchez) for these baths and stay there as long as my strength held out. It was a dirty place for dirty boys—

though not nearly so dirty as the Gore-Street baths in the south end. Sometimes this feeling of dirty water in our mouths and eyes would send us scurrying to the rear of the place where one could steal a surreptitious smoke.

In these impromptu symposiums the subject of conversation was almost invariably our fathers. Mothers were insignificant— it was the daddy that counted. Could he swim? Could he fight? Was he big? What was his history and background?

Joe Manassi would say proudly: "My daddy's an Italian and he can talk Italian!"

Lepsey, the dissenter, would retort, quietly vicious: "My mother's a gypsy!"

"Yes, but what's your daddy?"

"He's a gypsy, too—an Irish gypsy!" Everyone would want to laugh, but no one dared, for Lepsey, not realizing the humor of his statement, was there to back it up.

Somebody would ask Roza, "Frankie, is your father a Nigger?"

And Frankie would reply proudly: "No, he's a Filipino, and he used to be a cowboy . . ."

A question would be asked Jackie Sanchez whether or not there were cowboys in Spain and Jackie would reply proudly that there were—that Spain wasn't far from the United States and the cowboys often rode over there. Freddie Seegar bragged about the superiority of the Germans as sailors (his deceased father was German) and almost got to blows with Jacko Oldham who averred that the English were the best sailormen; but a few moments later, under the belligerent stares of us Irish risen now in a bloc, he tempered the English down to the

"British." Mickey wasn't at these swimming symposiums; he had to be out on the look-out for work during the day —his understanding with the Working Boy's Home.

The get-together usually ended with the St. Peter's Catholic gang turning on our three willing-to-be Catholic pals and asking them in bluffing belligerent tone whether or not they were I or O (Irish or Orange; the challenge to strangers on St. Patrick's Day), and although they invariably gave us the desired answer, "I", we would pick them up and throw them into the pool—religion forgotten.

I got my first taste of actual religious battle strangely enough not on St. Patrick's Day but on the twelfth of July or, as we were raised to call it, "King Billy's Day," the day on which the Protestant boys sung:

> "St. Paddy was a Bastard,
> St. Paddy was a thief,
> And he came to our house
> And stole a lump of meat."

Instead of confining our efforts to our own neighborhood this day, Joe Manassi suggested going down toward Netherfield Road to witness the Orangeman's parade and (bettering our elders) to do our bit toward making it a failure. Mickey had just put in an appearance at the corner and, upon hearing the suggestion, vanished— afraid of being ousted from the Working Boy's Home if discovered on such an errand. Harold May, Frankie Roza and Lepsey Phillips were, of course, kept indoors. It was a long way over, but the rest of us made it mostly by swinging on to the tail of tramcars and the back of floats pulled by galloping horses. I think we were all more or less tremulous heroes when we got within the enemy's gates and I know by the time we reached the start of the parade (George Wise's Protestant Reformed Church in Netherfield Road) and perceived just what we were up against, we rather repented our daring.

A huge crowd of our worst enemies (the "O's") with bands and banners carrying inscriptions that made our blood boil, surged around us. Orange everywhere and not a bit of *green*! I had never known there were so many enthusiastic Protestants. I had always been brought up in the belief that Protestantism was a dying cult, and its adherents cowards, easily frightened; but this mob up here, led by that magnificent white horse bearing a little boy dressed as a perfect duplicate of Prince William, didn't look frightened at all. Presently the bands flared up and the horde headed down Netherfield Road; we straggled along, in the rear, fearful lest we be discovered. Down Netherfield Road the procession marched, turning into London Road.

"Are they going to Scotland Road, Joe?" I asked Manassi, fearful and wondering what awful calamity must occur if they touched this stronghold of the "I's."

"I hope they bloody well do!" said Joe grimly, disclosing a brick hidden beneath his coat. "They'll get 'what for' then! I'm going to fling this brick at that bloody kid on the horse!"

But the parade very discreetly kept away from Scotland Road, executing a nice detour at London Road and Lime Street and heading then toward Parliament Street and Knowsley Park. Here we decided to leave them, for so far we had escaped detection and none of us, I think, was brave enough at the moment to continue on into the vastnesses of Protestant Knowsley Park. But just as we were about to escape into Lime Street, the parade stopped. The bands became silent. We pressed forward to see the nature of the trouble and, getting to the front, were astounded to see a little old chip-chopper we all knew from the South End holding her skirts sky high (disclosing a fine pair of green drawers), and shrieking defiantly: "Here's a 'Downey' bird!" (Catholic Bishop Downey of Liverpool) as she danced slowly and defiantly backward.

Our enthusiasm was inflamed to such a pitch that we yelled as one, "Good on yer, missis!" and instantly we were set upon by the Protestant youths in the parade. I never found out how the brave little woman of the green drawers fared, but our gang in its entirety was booted all over the place. I think before the boots stopped kicking they had us all singing with the rest of the stopped parade, "We are the sons of Billy and to hell with Popery!" But after the parade moved on and we gathered ourselves together, one by one we muttered the old refrain:

> "King Billy's mother runs a
> whorehouse in Hell . . . ."

I should add, in all fairness, that the Protestant paraders, unlike our crowd on the seventeenth of March, weren't really looking for battle; and if our crowd had only used half so much prudence as they, there wouldn't have been any. One day, however, the opposition did make a serious mistake. Instead of the usual route of march, which went across the Everton valley, they detoured into Shaw Street and past St. Francis Catholic Church where at that moment a very pious congregation of Irish Catholics were witnessing the ordination of three young priests.

The flaunting Protestant banners drew alongside the church at the very moment when the Catholic crowd surged out of it. Bedlam was the result. The little child who impersonated King Billy on his white charger had his head staved in with a brick, falling off the horse bleeding and screaming with pain. As long as it lasted it was a gruesome sight, with the women shrieking and the yell "Police! Police!" in the air and the poor bobbies being thrown helplessly from one side to the other. Our crowd did itself full justice, especially Jacko Oldham, who wound up with two "O" boys' shirts under his arm as souvenirs. We all had souvenirs, I think—watches, caps, handkerchiefs and other articles pilfered from fallen foes. The Rose Hill lock-up was overcrowded that night.

CHAPTER
ELEVEN

THE week following our King Billy's Defeat, I made my first Holy Communion—perhaps the most important event in the life of a Catholic Irish child. My sister had made hers two years previously, and I knew what to expect. It was a great event. Four of our gang was due about the same time—Jackie Sanchez, Joe Manassi, Freddie Seegar and I—and for a week prior to the actual event Mr. Mcginnis had been sedulously preparing us at school every day. At home, too, the preparation was just as breathtaking—each mother doing her level best to have her son look better than anyone else when he lined up at the altar. My mother, though she well may have been the most zealous, was the most handicapped in getting me a handsome outfit, and I felt quite sure that my first communion would be made in bare feet and my usual rags.

I had underestimated her resourcefulness, however. On the eventful Sunday morning, after the usual nightmare of Saturday night, I found myself being twisted into a homemade ensemble of white blouse, little blue knickers and—the most startling discovery of all—a brand new pair of boots! I asked her excitedly how all of this had been gotten but she pressed her finger to her lips as she and Alice and I hurried off to St. Peter's School, I, to join the boy's parade, they to gather with the other excitedly proud relatives awaiting the procession inside the church.

As we proceeded in the long wavering line of Eton collars from the school to the church, the four of us in the gang criticized each other's make-up and then speculated on how much each pair of our boots would bring in pledge on the morrow in Harris's pawnshop. Our mothers were all crowding around, sympathizing with the poor little innocents, never suspecting the subject of our conversation.

Then we went inside. I think I was much more impressed with the ceremony than were my mates, for to me then, as now, religious ritual was always a vital thing—childish perhaps in its external forms but behind it all something mystical and profound. When Joe Manassi and comedian Freddie Seegar kicked my shins and giggled and I paid no heed to them, they looked at me puzzled. They did not understand. First communion to them was simply play. But not with me. Perhaps it was Irish mysticism or my mother in me—I don't know. . . .

The long sea of Eton collars rises; sinks; the chant begins. Presently, in single file, the boys troop down the aisle, receive communion and return in the same manner, looking almost comical with their hands cupped in semblance of devout prayer. Now it is our bench and our turn. In a moment I'm looking at Father Corlett as he mumbles some Latin and places the Sacred Host on my tongue. He passes on, but something has happened to me. I come up the aisle behind the enigmatic Joe Manassi, my hands cupped and letting my mother (who I know is watching me very closely) see how pious I appear. . . . And then out in the street in the return procession to the school and the presentation from Mr. McGinnis of the Holy Communion certificates we are to carry for the rest of our lives. Then, a moment later, released to the chatter, the celebrating, the kissing, this to be followed immediately afterward by the usual spree. The following morning there was the wholesale rush to Harris's pawnshop.

My mother herself sinned that day but Alice and I did not admonish her, for this was *the* day. My boots were pawned the following morning, but it was my father who did the pawning and kept for beer the one-and-threepence that he got in pledge.

That was a particularly frightful night, for my father had gotten extremely drunk and, meeting my mother coming home from work, I stopped her in the rain and kept her from going into the house. She was very tired and her apron was filled with foodstuffs. I could see the sadness in her eyes as she understood my warning, and compared my bare feet and rags with the good clothes of the preceding morning. It was raining very hard and, hopeful of my father eventually going to bed at Alice's behest (she was inside coaxing him to go upstairs while I stayed on the look-out outside for mother), we walked around to the communal toilet.

It stank in this place as it always did, but the quietness and peace impressed me and I said, "Couldn't we put a

few shelves in here mother and live in it? It's so quiet
here."

She said nothing; only kissed me. Presently Alice came
out and reported that my father had gone upstairs, and we
crept in. The food was unbundled from my mother's
apron and we ate ravenously, my mother dozing off in
her chair. As I took her boots off I could hear her praying
unconsciously. Then the lion-like roar started upstairs.
Alice's face paled quickly, like chalk. Downstairs, my
father stumbled. It was the same old story. . . .

A little while after this, Alice and I, this time together,
suffered a very bitter disappointment. It was the occasion
of the coronation of King George and Queen Mary and
a gala sport carnival was to be held that day in Sefton
Park to commemorate the event. As few of the slummies
had ever seen their King or Queen, the preposterous rumor got about that they were to be crowned in Sefton
Park; and it was through believing this that Alice and I
were to suffer bitter disappointment.

On the morning of the great day, Mr. McGinnis handed
each of us schoolboys four shining halfpennies with the
dramatic announcement, "These coins are the gift of their
most gracious Majesties to you—see that you keep them
all your lives!" Mr. McGinnis was that unusual being: a
zealous British patriot of pure Irish stock. Then we were
dismissed for the day, and were warned to be sure to be
on hand in the park that afternoon to join in the hymns
and ballads.

Fortunately, that afternoon my father was in jail doing a fortnight for his usual petty thievery at the Docks.

Mother was toiling down at the Emigrant House. Excitedly, Alice and I washed our faces and in bare feet ran to meet our King and Queen. It was a lovely day in June and the park was crowded to capacity—with plenty of bare feet and satisfied stomachs, for a goodly number of the children were licking the greasy papers that had held chips and fish undoubtedly purchased with the King's grant. Bands blared forth with the more obvious national hymns—*Land of Hope and Glory! Britannia Rules the Waves!* and the one that ends with the roar, "Three cheers for the red, white and blue!" There is a great English streak in my sister and, though the news that this was a coronation by proxy was a keen disappointment to her, when the bands roared out and the lustier patriots screamed, her little face expanded with glee.

It was rather strange, too, to see the snooty bourgeoisie and their children for once mingling with the slummies —being Britishers one and all for the afternoon. Almost all the slummy element were drunk, and this drunken noisiness soon drove Alice and me out of the park and back home, there to get the fire started and have the kettle boiling for mother when she returned from the Emigrant House with that apronful of food. On the way down to the house I spent my four halfpennies for eccles cakes, but Alice kept hers and like a good patriot has them nicely polished to this day.

When there was no wood to start the fire our task was very clearly defined. We had two big bags which we would take down to the Cooperage, a barrel-making place in Bridgewater Street. Here we would join the many other barefoot children carrying bags, all of us awaiting the coopers who would call us into the yard in turn and give us the left-over wood. All slummy children had this task to do after school hours. Another we had was to go to Bank's meat shop and stand in the long line to get "two pennorth of pieces," (the wastes of the regular cuts of meats). It was always a source of irritation to my father when we would bring back pieces mostly of bone or fat, for he liked lean meat; and when he got it was less disposed to belligerency. One day (before my mother got on at the Emigrant House), when coming back from Bank's, I met Father Toomey, blood in his darkened eyes. He knew what I was about and, after throwing the pieces in the gutter, he handed me a shilling—the last I think he had in his pocket. "Now ye go back to that dirty English (his face would constrict here at the exigency of not swearing) . . . . and make him give ye some dacent meat!" But after Father Toomey had gone to the Parish House, I picked up the pieces, cleaned them on my pants and brought them, along with tenpence of the shilling (twopence deducted for my Saturday Palais de Luxe vigil) to my mother.

CHAPTER
TWELVE

JUST before I was to collapse physically my mother was dismissed from the Emigrant House; she was caught hurrying off to Cornwallis Street, with our midday lunch. It was a severe blow to all of us, for she got one and sixpence a day in addition to all her meals and that apron of stuff so eagerly awaited by us at night. Her job had had a religious implication for her too, for this big Cunard Line detention camp of illiterate Slavs, Germans, Russians, Poles, Italians—all future American Babbitts —had formerly been the "faithful Companions of Jesus" Convent. I can very well imagine my mother's surreptitious praying as she scrubbed the human filth from some darkened corner that once had housed the effigy of a Saint, and of the strength such prayers gave her to combat the torture awaiting her at home.

The night she came home with this sad news something seemed to have gone out of her—she had the same hopeless expression I had glimpsed on her face when we entered the Workhouse. My father, fearful of missing the apronful of food, suggested her going over to her sister:

"The 'big bale of hay.' She's the fancy woman down there. She'll get you back." My mother did this. But though Janie tried very hard it was no use, for my mother's physical condition was against her. My father was in an ugly mood when he heard this.

And there was additional trouble heading our way—my own physical condition, the first definite hint of which I got during one of my regular twelve-hour Saturday vigils in the Palais de Luxe Cinema. This particular day I had brought along a pair of scissors and tucked them obliquely down my pants ready for any redskins that might show up in Brick Street or thereabouts—but it wasn't redskins that were after me. Sweat poured out of my hands in the darkened gallery. The music I loved so well seemed strangely far off. All that I could do was cough and spit. I began to wonder where all the spit was coming from. It tasted peculiarly like dried bone, and every time I would cough it seemed as though something vital was about to crack within me. Many times before I had felt exhausted but never anything quite like this. I didn't want to eat my sandwiches or move or do anything, just sit there and dream while a strange melancholy happiness permeated me.

I lost consciousness and when I came to it was dark; the theater was empty and I was on the floor. Dan had missed me. It was a painful effort to rise, but as I made my way down the spiral stairway I felt a little strength come to me. The manager and the staff, just preparing to leave for the night, thought me an apparition; they didn't even speak to me but let me pass out into the rain.

On up darkened Lime Street I continued, straight

through to Park Lane, where a crowd of drunken rowdies headed by Big Irish Mary, the boarding-house keeper, and Georgie Bell playing his accordion, saw me. Big Mary knew my Auntie Janie very well and one time, when I was very young, they had quarreled over who should feed me their ale down in Threlfall's pub. They were all eating chips and fish from the usual greasy newspapers and, seeing me, Mary, in lieu of throwing of what remained in her paper into the gutter (she was quite drunk), thrust them at me. Then another paper full came my way, this time from a big Norwegian sailor. And another. When the parade had passed I was loaded down with the remnants of chips and fish and scallops. Aeroplane Joe, the bobby who was a nemesis to our gang, showed through the fog and rain, and, recognizing me, said proudly, "Sonny, we locked your daddy up again." Instantly I became apprehensive.

"Is my mammy hurt, sir?"

"Not much—not as bad as the last time." Then warningly: "And, young fellow, me lad, don't ever let me catch you or your mates on that corner playing toss! . . . I think this is your sister, isn't it?"

Yes it was—in her bare feet and on her way down to the Palais de Luxe to see what had become of me. Aeroplane Joe left us hastily; and after asking me if I was sick (the stock question to me for the last week) Alice took me home. In the shack I found my mother, her head bandaged, drinking a pint of ale and crying bitterly as her two sisters, Janie and Lizzie, endeavored to comfort her. Poor Aunt Lizzie, now a gaunt scarecrow, herself, took me on her knee and caressed me with the sympathetic intuition of one dying person for another.

"You'll not have this little fellow long, Polly," she said.

"Oh, leave Polly alone!" remonstrated Janie, "she's got enough to trouble about right now."

My mother tried to take hold of me, but she wasn't strong enough and presently Alice and Lizzie helped me upstairs where, upon seeing the spit-stained walls and floor, Lizzie, who lived in more elegant surroundings, became furious. After a bit she went downstairs, glancing back at Alice and me helplessly; then, as usual, Alice related to me the events of the evening. It always started the same way—she would look at me with her big brown eyes and berate me for having hid away all day and left her to the ordeal. Then, having gotten that off her mind, she would tell me the story, exaggerating everything to show how resourceful she had been. "I held 'im back until 'e got her down, then I ran up and got Aeroplane Joe, the bobby. 'E fixed 'im all right. Then I took mammy to the dispensary!" Then very proudly: "All by myself too! . . . Then apprehensive: "What's the matter, Timmy?" She could see with child-like intuition that something serious was wrong as I dropped back in the mattress on the floor, coughing and spitting more than ever before. "Are you *very* sick?"

Yes, I was very sick, and no clearer proof was necessary than that I couldn't raise myself from the floor. It seemed to me the end of everything; a floating off, as it were, into a more agreeable nothingness. Only the sorrow for my mother downstairs kept my mind working at all;

otherwise it was dead to all reality. Out the spit came, yellow, yellow, yellow, followed by blood, strewn all over the floor and the walls. Alice, distracted, covered me with the old clothes that substituted for blankets and suggested my holding my mouth shut as an antidote to the spitting. I didn't answer her, for I couldn't. Sleep came or unconsciousness, I don't know which, and after it had spent itself in the darkness I could feel two warm bodies beside me—my mother's and Alice's.

The following day, with the frenzy so characteristic of her when danger threatened her children, my mother brought Father Wilson from St. Peter's to see me. He took one look at me and the room and my mother and immediately got in touch with Miss Margaret Bevan ("the little mother," later Lord Mayoress of Liverpool, the first woman to hold that post). I was brought before her in her little social service room in Seel Street near my school. (Later the government purchased a huge social service establishment in Lowhill opposite the Adelphi Hotel and made her the head of it). I was examined by the government doctor, who recommended an immediate change of environment.

"Where is your husband?" asked Miss Bevan of my mother.

"In jail."

"Can you pay sixpence a week for your boy's board?"

The inference was clear and my mother, gratefully surprised, agreed. I was sent the next day with some other destitute children from the Landing Stage to West Kirby Sanitarium near Hoylake in beautiful Cheshire.

CHAPTER THIRTEEN

I was in the Sanitarium about four months, a pleasant interlude to remember. I was, at the time, eleven years of age but very precocious and fully appreciative of the loveliness of this strange, new place. All my life up to then had been lived between dock and alley and warehouse and dirt; to be suddenly removed from all this and placed in this pastoral setting close by the Irish Sea was a wonderful thing to me. Moreover, after the preliminary examination, the doctor decided that my lungs were not sufficiently affected to necessitate my staying inside the hospital during the day and that I be given as much open air as possible. (After learning something about my environment he must have assumed that the prime cause of my trouble was neglect and unsanitary living conditions.) Thus all I did in the ward was to sleep, the rest of the time I could devote to the sands, the Irish Sea and to my fantastic dreams.

The first few weeks I did not appreciate the sheer beauty and happiness of my surroundings. Separation from my mother, for the first time, brought intense loneliness. I knew, too, my father would be out of jail by now, and I could easily imagine what was happening up our entry in Liverpool. At night, I used to sit up in bed praying earnestly that no harm come to them, and sometimes I would even pray of a day alone on the sands. But gradually this fear and loneliness were replaced by that dreamy romantic spirit of my Palais de Luxe nights and I was very happy.

At the end of the first month, my mother and Alice visited me and brought over bananas and cakes and sweets. I asked about my father and both their faces clouded. "He's just about the same as usual," said my mother. "Doing a day now and again at the dock. But don't you worry about that." Obviously, they were keeping something from me, but as there were no physical marks of violence on my mother I was content to be so deceived. My mother was very happy with my appearance (I had greatly changed) and when Alice and she left me that evening I felt happy in the thought that they both were genuinely happy.

I always look back to the following month as one of those rare periods of unadulterated happiness in a person's life. I had little to do with the sanitarium itself, except to eat my meals and sleep there (in a clean bed). It was excellently conducted and nothing was spared in an effort to nurse destitute children, such as I, back to health whence, ironically enough, we would be placed right back into the danger again. I recall only once getting into trouble with the nurses there—that was when, in a momentary aberration, I started the old practice, learned from my father, of spitting surreptitiously on the walls.

A LIVERPOOL IRISH SLUMMY

Mostly, I was to be found on the beach. I would leave the sanitarium early in the morning with my bucket and wade out into the sea in search of fresh cockles. When my bucket would be filled, I would lie on the sands eating them and gazing out into the sea dreaming happily. Every afternoon the West Kirby life-boat crew, with their big southwesters and oilskins and boots and those lively big boats, used to practice. Gleefully I would watch them and sometimes I would help push their craft out into the choppy sea. Then one day the sun went down sharply and it got suddenly dark and blew and rained. I heard the signal gun go off and presently I saw my gallant crew going through the usual practice of launching the life-boat. But this time I was pushed away, and ran in from the rising sea. Then I paused higher up on the beach, panting in the rain. Out, out went the life-boat crew I used to play with, up, down, up, down, until their boat was but a speck in the swirling, misty distance. The speck never returned. Later that evening, as the storm raged, I heard that the Manx passenger boat *Ellen Vannin* from Port Erin to Liverpool had been wrecked just outside and had gone down with all hands, along with my gallant crew that had gone out after them.

I was very sad after this and for days after I would often sit alone on the exact spot where the life-boat crew had worked and would follow the imaginary wake of the water traversed by their boat, and I would picture what had happened to each and every one of them; how the waves had choked down their throats; what the big loquacious coxswain had thought as he saw the earth upturned about him and the water drowning out his life;

and all of the other men's last thoughts and where they were now, their bodies floating around down below and what was down below and all such strange stuff. . . . And I thought next of the sky above me so lovely, and of the quietness in the air and of this peace and—like a returning viper clutching at my heart—of what *this very minute* was going on in the shack in Brick Street across that stretch of water in Liverpool.

A strange love came to me at this sanitarium. I had secretly been admiring a comely, middle-aged nurse who seemed to admire me equally well. At night she would stop by my cot and talk to me and before long I was dreaming about her constantly. If she stopped and talked to any men about the place, I got very jealous and not a moment went by without my planning some day I would ask her to run off somewhere with me. Of an afternoon, out on the sands, I would imagine the two of us happily living together dreaming identical dreams, having identical thoughts; and of a night lying on my cot I would watch the movement of her hips and if she bent over a bed try my best to catch a glimpse of her legs, and when she stooped over to give me my goodnight maternal kiss, I would look down the cleft in her bosom and drink in the sight of her big breasts.

One time she was away for three days, and I got very sick worrying about her. I dreaded the thought of eventually having to leave the place and was constantly planning whether or not I should put my whole attitude frankly before her. She would understand and help, I felt sure, since I was convinced that her secret attitude toward me was just the same as mine toward her.

Then one day my mother came with my clothes and I was told that when the sun went down that day, I would no longer be in beautiful Cheshire. Instantly I left my poor mother, who was cheerfully talking to the doctor, and went in search of my love. But she had gone off to Birkenhead and wouldn't be back until tomorrow. Where did she live? I asked. But that wasn't at all necessary, I was told coldly. I pondered the idea of hiding in the place all night and of informing my mother of my intention. She would agree, for my mother would agree to anything I insisted upon. But when I got back to the bedside I discovered that one of the doctors was going to the station in his motor car and had agreed to drive us there. There was nothing for it but to go and later on scheme how best I was to return. Run myself into another breakdown, or something like that!

Over in Liverpool, with the dirt and smoke and stink once again reviving my sadness, I was scheming very fast when my mother stopped me just before reaching our entry. All around us were the dirty Gavneys and the Black Prince's children staring at my new boots and laughing at my clean collar. My mother herself was wearing the usual discarded navvy's boots. There was a tremor in my lips as she asked me:

"You don't seem happy, Timmy?"

"Yes, yes," I lied weakly, my mind torn between what awaited me in our shack and thoughts of the tranquillity and my silent love in West Kirby. We continued on up the alley, on up to the usual crowd of furtive men making bets with Mr. Brody, who stopped us, said how fine I looked, and gave me sixpence. On into the shack. My father was not wearing his flat hat and was sober and mending his boots; Alice was down with her bag at the Cooperage waiting for wood. My father kissed me without looking at my mother and we went upstairs to the stuffy bedroom. Here again my mother stared at me and asked the question:

"You don't want to come back home, do you, Timmy?"

"Yes, yes," I lied again, staring at the mattress on the floor and the spit-covered walls, only roughly cleaned, and the buckets.

Then suddenly she threw herself down on the floor in a more reckless abandon than I had ever seen before, and wept without restraint. Afraid my father might hear her downstairs and become angered, I closed the door and bent down beside her. All I could hear through the fierce outpour was a savage: "Me poor father! Me poor father! God have mercy on his soul! Oh, why don't you take me too. . . ?" Then it came out gradually, reluctantly. My grandfather had died while I was away at the sanitarium and had been buried, like his one-armed son, in unconsecrated Anfield. The news saddened me, for I had always loved these two. But there was another bitterness and doubt gnawing at my mother's heart, and though she wouldn't tell me then, I found it out later. It was my grandfather's books. When they saw him slipping, they brought in Father Ryan, but the good priest, though received by my grandfather with the usual deference, wasn't taken in the seriousness he desired. The following day, another hurry call was sent for him and, true to his faith, he came panting down to the barracks only to find my grandfather had passed away—without receiving Extreme Unction, a terrible thing in a family like my mother's.

That night my father stayed sober and we all retired early. He had worked a "half-day" down at the Cork boats and we were all attentive to his wants. My mother, of course, on our advice, made no mention of her father's death and we were glad, for assuredly it would have meant a sarcastic remark from my father—and the inevitable fight. Presently I went to sleep with dual thoughts of my dead grandfather and my beloved one in West Kirby, and a fierce determination to see her somehow on the morrow. I had two shillings with me, saved during my stay at the sanitarium, and this, combined with the six-pence given me by Mr. Brody, would see me over to West Kirby!

Next morning, after my father had gone to work and Alice and my mother were looking for wood, I put on my new boots, shined them, gave my Eton rubber collar a couple of extra rubs and started for the Landing Stage. I arrived in West Kirby at ten o'clock and at the sanitarium a few minutes later. The clerk was surprised—wasn't I discharged yesterday? I wanted to see Miss X, was she in? Yes, but—the clerk a very young, tubercular woman, went off smiling broadly and came back a moment later with my beloved looking bigger and better than ever.

She was very glad to see me, but even more anxious to know what brought me over there. Didn't I know it was very dangerous to come back here among consumptives now that I was cured? Now I must go right back to Liverpool and not come back any more. It was extremely dangerous and certainly not wise in any case, since I was not a congenital tubercular case but just a victim of neglect—and she was very busy and had to go now and for me to give her best regards to the little girl, Alice, my sister, and to run along and never, *never* to make such a silly and expensive journey. . . .

It was one of the major crisis of my life; a great sadness swept into my heart and stayed there all the way back to Liverpool. But the following day was Saturday and, with my Palais de Luxe interlude and all the horror in our house, I soon forgot all about this great love of mine and was once again at my post restraining my bellicose father.

CHAPTER
FOURTEEN

ON THE following Sunday morning my mother, with justifiable pride, gave Alice and me the weekly wash "all-over" in the baking pan mug. We were dressed up and taken over to the barracks to the family reunion which was being held there that day because of my grandfather's death. Two other reasons prompted her to go—my changed physical condition and the fact that my father had put in three full days at the dock so that the family's clothes had all been redeemed from Harris's pawnshop for the week-end.

As usual, my father did not join us, but saw us off with the customary parting shot: "Go ahead over to them bloody Molloy slummies! Not me! I'm an O'Mara. . . . Trace my people! The old slummy bastard shoulda died long ago!" "Yes, daddy," we had said, pushing our mother past the door before she exploded and started the inevitable battle. "Yes, daddy, you're right! Your people were the best: mammy's are slummies!" After which we went over to the Molloy barracks and he, resplendent in his clean white moleskins, joggered up to Walker's pub, to sup up there for the remainder of the day.

This was the most vivid family reunion I recall. My grandmother was there in her armchair with poor, tragic Lizzie and her Dutch playboy husband, Chris, seated opposite her—both women fast in the slowly tightening grip of death. Leisha and her husband, Johnny Roche, sat opposite Janie and her home-trained husband, Johnny Murray, his half-caste children now happily away, with Janie's love child, Katie, seated on his knee. Warming his bottom as usual in front of the fire was Janie's old lover, Joe Lonnigan, the alleged Irishman. My Uncle Jimmy, looking very proud and well-dressed (he was driving a cab then), was holding my elegant Auntie Katie's hand. She, clothed resplendently in a black coat, listened to him mildly criticize her elegant husband for not accompanying her from New Brighton.

"Is he too bloody good for my father, Katie!" he demanded testily.

"No, Jimmy," Katie defended, "Jack doesn't like sad things."

The children were whooping it up all around the place, munching stick-jaw toffee; jugs of ale and unwashed dishes were scattered over the table and everyone had a glass in hand, partly filled with ale; the air was definitely that of an Irish wake. My grandmother was crying softly; the loss was a little too much for even this stoic.

Well, there we all were; all, except Alice, sipping ale, we children getting ours by surreptitious offers from the sentimental womenfolk. As the ale was consumed and my grandfather's death was forgotten, the women continued with their marital difficulties. (It was at this gathering I first heard Lizzie, after a minor argument with her husband, jump up and make the allusion to the "Syph at nineteen!") Every time anything was needed, Janie would turn to her husband and say, "Johnny, do this" "Johnny, do that." If Johnny would show any resentment she would turn to Lonnigan and say with her usual oiliness, "Joe, would you mind movin' your bottom from the fire for a minute and go for a quart?" and if Joe would start to excuse himself—as he nearly always would in her case—then she would turn viciously on her husband and say to him, alluding of course to his deported half-caste children: "You go, Mad Andrew, or I'll be sendin' you with them leather-lipped childer of yours!"

After the argument had subsided and the ale again began to show its effect, everybody, except my brooding fretting grandmother, started singing, first, *The Harp That Once Through Tara's Hall*, and next, *Believe Me If All Those Endearing Young Charms*, Leisha's voice ringing high above the others. Janie asked my grandmother:

"Wouldn't you like to see Ireland again before you go, mother?"

"No," scowled my grandmother, "I remember nothin' in it but poverty!" The tears came faster. "I'd like to go maybe to St. Steven's Green where your father and me played as childer—but that's about all. Ireland! Don't talk to me about Ireland. Your father's an Irishman— see what he done! God have mercy on his soul!"

Then Lonnigan, wiping the beer from his mustache, said: "Mrs. Molloy, Ireland would be all right if she was left alone. It's England. . . ."

"What do you know about Ireland—born in Manchester as ye was!"

111

"That's all right, Mrs. Molloy, but I'm an Irishman just the same!"

"Arra g'wane! Shut your bloody mouth, Joe Lonnigan, don't argue with me now!"

And Lonnigan, the champion argufier, obeyed—for my grandmother when aroused could be very, very vicious.

My mother was very emotional when drinking, in a friendly atmosphere, and much, hitherto buried in her mind, would come to the fore. Alice dreaded this display as much as I did; rather we liked to see our mother sober and joining with us in attempting to solve our common problems. To see her getting "mopsed" (half-drunk) was something we dreaded, particularly Alice, whose efforts at preventing this had earned her a reputation around all the public houses. (In almost all the pubs around our way, whenever my mother would be drinking at the bar, the barman would always look forward to seeing Alice's face peer through the door entreating her mother to "come on home, mammy!" If and when she got her mother out —and she usually did—the job then would be to rush her up to the church to "take the pledge." I shared in this job many a time—a rather difficult task for us to accomplish, for my mother knew if she once gave the priest her pledge not to drink for a month, we could feel quite certain that the pledge would be kept. How she demurred and hesitated, poor wretched soul, when we would be lugging her up to the chapel with soft coaxings, for she knew full well that taking the pledge cut off all hope of escape from her mental torture!)

Now here she was quite drunk, and Alice and I both were beginning to worry about what would happen when eventually we had to take her over to our own shack. Sober, she would not offer resistance to my father, but drunk, she always did—and of course came off worse. Now she was disclosing everything on her mind, telling her sisters, despite their sullen objection to such stuff, how my father hated all of them intensely and what he said about them. The men sat in silence—they all knew my father from working with him at the dock and held him in contempt—and none of the women ventured anything until my mother hit upon Janie.

"Last night he called you the Bale of Hay—the Bale of Hay, that's nice for my sister, isn't it?"

Janie, incensed, rose and motioned Johnny to the door, returning alone a moment later to her seat. Late that evening, holding our mother as best we could between us and with our hearts beating furiously, we opened the front door to the shack and were astounded to find our father lying on the floor in a small pool of blood, groaning in his drunken stupor:

"Johnny—yah! Johnny—yah! Porridge-faced Janie's fancy man—Johnny—yah!"

It turned out that when my mother had informed Janie of my father's reference to her resembling a bale of hay, she had by the marvelous alchemy that was hers transformed her husband into a fighter and dispatched him over to our shack to revenge her hurt feelings. Johnny (I can quite understand his trembling as he approached our door) had knocked on the door and the moment my father opened it and disclosed his helpless drunken condition, had let fly with some sort of instrument.

Father hadn't much of a wound; the remarkable thing

was the transformation the incident worked in my sister. Immediately she started in bathing my father's head and after this was finished, we took him up to the Parliament Street dispensary and had his hurt dressed by Doctor Burns. I was for letting the thing slide by, but Alice, with her alarming British sense of justice, was adamant—she wanted revenge for her dear father! She took Doctor Burns's note to the Great George's Street Bridewell, where a bobby was dispatched in search of Johnny, the fighter.

Johnny was taken away from Janie that night and the next day charged with "wounding"; he was dismissed only after Janie had spent ten shillings for a solicitor and my father's terrible record as a trouble-maker had been disclosed. Shortly after this, I caught Janie up our entry threatening to beat the life out of Alice and calling her the foulest of names. Never very popular at the barracks, my mother became less so after this, and Alice was to be hated intensely, particularly by Janie and Johnny. My mother used to make surreptitious visits to the barracks and I would always be dispatched to get her out—but never Alice. It was about the only place into which she wouldn't venture after her mother.

CHAPTER
FIFTEEN

My RETURN to health was short lived, however; not long after my return from West Kirby, the old habits and unsanitary ways of living began to make their inroads. My bloated fat vanished; once again my clothes began to sag —and the fact I didn't die that year of rapid consumption, I think I owe to Tommy Brody, who, I am convinced, had us "put out." It was a case of Tommy's book-making business or us; so we went. From here we returned to the Bridgewater Street tenement of "Auld" Harris, who himself a few years previous had put us out.

The reason for this strange *volte-face* of the old musician-barber lay in the fact that during our sojourn in Brick Street my father and Mrs. Harris had been doing quite a bit of supping up together in their favorite pub— the drinks usually being paid for by my father. Contemplating a continuance of this charity, Mrs. Harris had persuaded her husband to let us in again, comforting him with the sophistry that "we were different people now." At any rate, we got in, renting the parlor and back room on the second floor for four and sixpence a week.

Most of the old tenants had died; this had given the house a nickname, "The Dead House." Those who greeted us were the Harrises occupying the back section of the first floor as usual; on the second floor were the Tars, a middle-aged couple living apart from their own children; Jack Hare, also on the second floor in a little back room; on the third floor was John Golding and his mother and in the two back rooms was old Kitty Daugherty, "the professional witness," and a sooty oldster named "Scrogy."

Mr. Tar was a galvaniser by trade and, unlike his wife, a rather sober and staid fellow and not given to her boisterous humor. He would give her so much money to run the table but, instead of expending it for food, she would drink up most of it—and then herself eat most of what food she actually would buy. I often compared the Tars to our mother and father, characters reversed. They were nearly always fighting, with Mr. Tar losing.

Living with the Tars was Willie, the illegitimate son of Mrs. Tar's sister ("tanner" Dr. Walker's wife), a simple-minded boy with one eye almost closed from the same mysterious ailment that had closed the opposite one of his mother. Dr. Walker's wife had had Willie by the son of Willie Porter, the undertaker on Stanhope Street, before her marriage to the "tanner doctor," or rather before she had contemplated marriage to anyone. He was shipped to his aunt (Mrs. Tar) immediately after happy-go-lucky Dr. Walker had proposed, to preserve the dignity of the doctor, of course. The question had once been put directly to him as to whom he liked better, his mother or his aunt, and Willie had replied naïvely:

A LIVERPOOL IRISH SLUMMY

"I don't like me real mother because she tried to poison me once."

Another time when Mrs. Tar was on a drunk, he took five shillings from her purse. His aunt frantically accused him of taking it, but he denied this. Whereupon, skeptical, she made him come up to St. Vincent's and stand in the church near the altar and repeat his denial. So Willie repeated: "I hope God may strike me blind ('drunk' spoken *sotto-voce*) if I took that five bob!"

This, of course, satisfied his aunt since it was unthinkable that any Catholic would perjure himself before God, and she went back to her room and slept. When she woke up sober, Willie gave her the five shillings she had missed. Mrs. Tar was delighted; yet the wound caused by his apparent blasphemy never quite healed. It was very comical to see them go to the pictures together, for neither one could see very well. Rumor had it that Darby (Willie) would look through his good left eye and Joan (Mrs. Tar) would look through her good right eye—thus balancing vision nicely.

Jack Hare was an elderly bachelor, a freight clerk, always in debt with the fish-and-money lenders and, like the rest of the household, a strong drinker. His life seemed to consist of starting to borrow from the money lenders on Monday and keeping it up until Saturday, when he handed his entire pay over to them. All the bad kippered herrings in the yard belonged to him.

The Goldings—mother and son—were really the humorous ones of the group. Mrs. Golding was an elderly woman who eked out a living by picking rags and other stuff from middens (refuse cans), and selling what was saleable to a cheap fence. Her son John was an indolent fellow whose chief boast under provocation was: "I don't have to work: my mother can keep me!" Mrs. Golding, too, seemed to take great pride in subscribing to this belief and always had him clad in boots though often going barefoot herself.

Kitty Daugherty, the "professional witness", was an adept, plausible old liar who made her living giving testimony in court at five shillings the day about something she had never witnessed. Lawyers liked her for her plausible lies and the apparent veracity with which she could report an assault or robbery. Though she lived in the south end, most of her material was garnered around Scotland Road, always a fruitful region for squabbles and fights.

The oldster Scrogy had just been put out of Victoria Terrace (ironic term, later christened "the Dardanelles",) and had come to the "Dead House" as a last resort. There was an interesting bit of history, too, about Scrogy. He, with most of his mates from our neighborhood, had been a member of the famous Elder-Dempster Liner *Matadi* that had been blown to pieces in Bonny River on the West Coast of Africa some years previous. Scrogy was the only survivor from this explosion, having been blown clear off the deck into the river. All of the widows and mothers got three hundred pounds each, most of which was spent with lively speed, while a shrewd few—like Annie Cummings—opened up as money lenders. But poor Scrogy, having been saved, got nothing; and what was worse, no one would ever believe, despite the evidence in his sailor's book to the contrary, that he had been on the *Matadi,* for at the time, the *Matadi* tragedy was so awful that people—particularly seafaring folk—forgot there had been a lone survivor.

Though there was much drinking and sometimes fierce fighting in the house, a general air of good nature usually prevailed; but with the advent of my father came the familiar dynamite.

"Auld" Harris, the barber-violinist, was perhaps the most civilized person in the house—I suppose because he was quite deaf and thus was spared hearing a great deal of what went on about him. In his varied undertakings, he was helped but little by his wife and his daughter, Emma, who took after her mother a great deal.

The day we came back the home-made barber pole, usually outside the parlor window, had vanished. It happened this way: my father gave a shilling deposit on our rent to Mrs. Harris, which they spent together immediately down in Walker's pub. Coming back intoxicated (Mrs. Harris was a very comical sight when drunk, what with her grayish mustache all damped and drooping), she entered her husband's room to find a young woman student there eagerly awaiting her violin lesson. Mr. Harris was in a back room groping for some music sheets and his wife, suspecting infidelity, immediately set upon the young student.

"What do you think I am, missy—a bloody whore!"

"I don't know," said the young woman, perplexed, "I only came to Professor Harris for a violin lesson."

Mr. Harris then came out with his fiddle and immediately chased his wife out into the hall, whereupon, furious, and eager to get another pint, she plucked the barber's pole out of its mooring and sold it farther up the street to an Italian vendor for sixpence.

Like our Brick-Street shack, the "Dead House" was a dirty hovel, but much bigger, yet since it was close by the docks and not sandwiched in a long court, much more healthful. Looking straight out at the street, it caught the breeze from the docks and the Mersey—not a clean breeze, but still infinitely better than no breeze at all. Just above us and below us and to the right and left of us were warehouses. Down to the left a little way lay the Dock Road (Chaloner Street), very noisy, by day, with the interminable flow of wagons and lorries and flats and steam engines and the screeching cranes and hissing winches—at night as quiet as the interior of a church, save for an occasional peal of a bell from some ship or the sharp toot of a steam whistle out on the river. I have always loved Bridgewater Street with the Queen's Dock at its base, so lovely and quiet of a night, so glorious of a summer Sunday in the quiet heat. I remember walking there with my father (on a sober Sunday of his) peering into the galleys of a foreign merchantman or standing on the Pier Head gazing up the river out to sea and listening to his fabulous lies of ships and sailormen.

On our second day in the Dead House, after we had settled our few belongings (carried under our arms and on a handcart from Brick Street), my father took Mrs. Harris down to the public house again. It was the first time I had seen my mother show jealousy—she decided to "have a bit of fun" herself. Her preference in the matter of "fun," of course, would have been to get drunk and to forget everything, but since she had taken the pledge for a month from Father Ryan just two weeks ago, this was out of the question. She looked at me and felt the bones of my chest.

"Would you like a sail to New Brighton, Timmy?"

New Brighton was the mecca of all children, and when this was mentioned both Alice and I were eager to go. So my mother prepared the supper table in case my father should come in—some bread and butter and jam and a piece of boiled meat—which wouldn't be eaten anyway, we knew. The idea was to have it there, thus reducing his wrath to a minimum when we got back. Then mother prepared some bread-and-butter sandwiches for us, and we were off.

There was something strange about my mother that day. I sensed it first in her suggesting this hazardous "bit of fun" for us; and I sensed it still more on the ferry boat plowing across the river to New Brighton as she held on to Alice and me, looking down at the waves made by the rapidly turning paddle. Then, inevitably, she turned to talk with me. (Whenever she wanted to unburden herself, it would always be to me, seldom to silent, dour Alice.)

"Timmy," she said, "your mammy hasn't got long to go, I'm thinkin'."

I looked up at her, for I knew just of what she was hinting; then I started to cry, saying:

"Mammy, I wish my daddy was dead."

A few minutes later, I noticed tears in her eyes too; but only amazement and fear in Alice's. Later, as the boat pulled away from the Egremont Ferry, she said in the same tone:

"Isn't it lovely and peaceful over here, Timmy? Wouldn't you like to live like these people over here? I'd like to die in a place like this. . . . "

I berated her mildly. "Don't talk about that, mammy—I couldn't live without you! Could you, Ali?"

Alice shook her head wonderingly: death, living, life itself—these mysteries seldom bothered her.

Arriving at New Brighton, we repaired first to the sands where my mother went over to the Ham and Egg parade, left sixpence on a borrowed teapot, and came back with it full of delicious tea. Then we stretched out and ate the sandwiches and drank the tea, my mother and I gazing to sea and Alice happily munching away at the sandwiches. People were all over the sands enjoying themselves very happily, but none of them was so intensely happy as we three—a happiness, the only false note of which was the impending grim reminder of what we must face before the night was over.

It was lovely lying there watching the thin specks of ships plowing out toward the Irish Sea. Birds were flying low and the sun was receding; soon my dreams were returning. When the wind came up and the crowds started to go, I was nudged back to reality and we went up to the Tower and there mother gave both of us a turn on the Joy Wheel [merry-go-round]—perhaps the only time she ever deliberately hoodwinked me. New Brighton had Pierrot shows, a ballroom, opera shows, donkey rides, sail boats and almost everything else in the way of amusements; but the American Joy Wheel was about the only thing that could divert us children from our mother—a point she well knew.

Over it Alice and I were flung again and again, and later, when we looked for our mother on the sidelines, she was not there. Then a woman took hold of my arm.

"Sonny," she said, "your mammy's just gone over to get you some eccles cakes. She told me to watch you two."

The woman drifted away, her mission accomplished, and Alice and I stood there wonderingly. Presently my mother returned, strangely optimistic, and our spirits drooped, for we knew well what had happened.

"You've been to the pub, haven't you, and broken your pledge!" I challenged bitterly.

"No," she lied, pulling out two big eccles cakes from under her shawl.

Alice stared up into her face. "Yes, you have, mammy; you've broken the pledge! Now you've gone and done it!"

"But I'm all right!" protested our mother. "Leave me alone—I'm all right!"

We watched her critically and the more we watched the more confused and uncomfortable she became. Presently we relinquished our questioning, but the happiness had been taken out of our holiday by this breaking of the pledge. We insisted that she go back to Father Ryan that night and retake the pledge—a promise she gave us solemnly after we'd agreed to another pint of ale for her.

Later, in the darkness of the returning boat, she tried to comfort us, but we would not listen. A breach of faith like this was unforgiveable and we tortured her all the way to the Landing Stage and from here clear up to St.

Vincent's Parish House in Hardy Street. Here we ushered her into Father Ryan's study where, in utter abjection, she took the pledge for another month. Much happier now, arm in arm, we walked down to our rooms in Bridgewater Street. There was no light in the back room when we got there and, striking a match, we saw our father lying on the floor in a drunken stupor in a pool of what obviously was his own water. Instantly we pressed lips and tiptoed around and silently cursed each other when the slightest noise was made. The table lay undisturbed and we gathered up the sandwiches and the tea-pot and the oil-lamp, closed the door behind him and crept upstairs—the three of us intensely happy at finding him asleep.

CHAPTER
SIXTEEN

HARRIS's shack was little changed from when we had last been there, with the exception perhaps that Emma, their daughter, was beginning to show galvanic signs of life. She was about the same age—twelve—as myself, with my sister Alice two years our senior. Music, running fiercely through her father, "Auld" Harris, seemed to come to focus in Emma. She loved to sing, and the fact that she was an abominable singer only increased her desire to let fly. My father, with his usual brutal sarcasm, likened her singing to "a Clan boat's whistle"—the loudest ship's whistle in the noisy River Mersey. Saturday night, about nine in the evening, was the signal for Emma's recitals, with her parents and Jack Hare to admire her. The fire would be roaring in the grate, the oil-lamp burning on the table with three or four quarts of ale upon it.

When there was ale to be had gratis my father would be sure to be on hand, with his customary ingratitude and sarcasm. His invitation to these gatherings came from Mrs. Harris, and quite naturally it was she whom he insulted.

One time, in a particularly ebullient mood, Mrs. Harris, wiping the ale from her mustache, started a solo dance around the floor, the while smilingly surveying my father. Eyeing her critically, he asked:

"Do you want a Pick?"

"Pick, Jimmy?"

"Sure; you've got a whisker and you feel like doing a bit of graft [work], don't-cha?"

"Graft, Jimmy?"

"Sure, you're a bloody navvy, ain't-cha?"

Whereupon Mrs. Harris—insult proof—burst out giggling.

Sometimes Mrs. Tar, either en route to her room or to the pub, might drop in impromptu; but if she did, she was almost always put out, there to lie in the hallway until someone came along and assisted her upstairs. Along with her sister, Dr. Walker's wife, she had just come out of jail; they had served three years for cashing the "death policies" of people not as yet dead—a not-too-difficult procedure in those days. She was very glum, probably because her indiscreet doctor brother-in-law was now reduced to a clerk for the Birkenhead railway.

But usually she would be kept out of these Saturday-night gatherings; and if my father ever discovered her or the "professional witness" lying drunk in the dark hallway, he, knowing the Harris's attitude toward them, would promptly kick them to one side. The songs that Emma would shriek were usually religious in spirit, the overture almost always being "Thy Will Be Done!" Sometimes, tiring of this theme, she would, to the great shock of her father, burst out with *When Irish Eyes Are Smiling, My Kathleen Is So Pure and Bright* or some other Irish ballad.

A fine strapping girl, Emma had all the cunning of her father and all the recklessness of her mother. Her greatest thrill, I think, was in playing "Shop-keeper and Purchaser" with Willie Tar, or "Daddies and Mammies." Willie was nineteen then but not quite so mature mentally and, when her father would be out, Emma would dispatch him down to the dock to get a bucket full of sand, this to take into the kitchen (barber shop, music conservatory, etc.). The old man's barbering tools would then be used for weights and measures and they would stand opposite each other in the role of seller versus buyer.

"Give me twopennorth of sugar, please," Willie, the customer, would say very formally, and Emma, the worried shop-keeper, would weigh it out with equal formality, commenting idly on the weather and the prospects of a fight in the house.

Then the tone would change quickly and Willie would say very skeptically, "How much a pound is this, missis?"

"Four and six," Emma would reply tragically. "That's on account of the bloody conservatives, Mr. Tar. The country will never be any good till we get Auld Asquith out!"

In the "Daddies and Mammies" game, Emma with her shieking voice would predominate. I'll take off Mrs. O'Mara and you take off Mr. O'Mara," she would say.

Whereupon Willie, like a good trouper, would pick up one of the Harris's barber tools, grimace horribly at Emma and go at her. Emma in turn would shriek for the bobbies amid cries of "Murder! Murder!" Due to this game, with the accompanying screams, it was always difficult to know what real or imaginary violence was occurring, and no one became alarmed until the ambulance or the Black Maria pulled up to the door. If "Auld" Harris came in, all merchandising apparatus, with the exception of the shaving tools, would be thrown through the window by him, and Willie dispatched upstairs amid much cursing.

There was always great consternation whenever anyone took the barber pole seriously. One time the Black Prince, in a very belligerent mood, dropped in for a shave, while Mr. Harris was giving a violin lesson. The pupil was kindly asked to step out into the backyard for a moment and the can was put on the fire to heat some water, and after it was heated, the right side of the Hombre's face was clipped of its whiskers. While this was going on, Mrs. Harris came in quietly and took the can out to heat herself some water, to make the morning cup of tea. Now the left side of the Black Prince's face was ready, but there was no can. The Black Prince fumed at the untoward delay. A ship's whistle blew the signal for the docker's "muster." Mr. Harris was thrown ruthlessly into the corner and the Black Prince, with one side of his face shaved, left quickly (without paying), after which Mrs. Harris was kicked out by the professor and the music student called in from the yard. Presently the raucous strains of the violin filled the conservatory. . . .

As with the rest of the shacks we had lived in, Harris's also only had one toilet receptacle in the yard. To evacuate the bowels, one took the line on the right, but to evacuate the kidneys one simply stood out in the yard and let go. My father with his genius for originality would, if he was up in our room, stand at the open window and furnish a shower bath for anyone passing below in the darkness. "Give 'em a bloody wash!" he used to say.

After a week in our new rooms, my mother finally broke down. She came home one windy night from the Dock Road, her apron full of wet wood for the fire, and sank down upon the floor, gasping to us: "Come to me, my two little chicks!" Her face was green and I thought that she was about to die. My father was down in the public house with Mrs. Harris and the "professional witness," scheming some "compensation" job; and, without further ado, I raced in my bare feet all the way to Dr. McConnell's house on Park Road, the scissors (six-shooter) jammed into my pants, in emulation of a cowboy effecting a rescue.

The doctor had treated me once before, and I felt he was a good man. He came right down and, after taking one look at my mother, immediately ordered the ambulance, which came a few minutes later and took her to Brownlow Hill Workhouse Hospital. Alice went along with her, and I stayed at home, the glow of heroism now gone and my "gun" cast aside, awaiting my father to tell him the news. Alice got back first, crying bitterly, and my father came in later from Gordon's pub, floundering all over the hallway and, as usual, furiously cursing my mother and her people. When I confronted him and told him my mother had been taken to the hospital and that she might die (at the time Alice and I believed she would), he said:

"She ought to die, the dirty, bloody, slummy Molloy! Her pitcher ought to be in the Wax Works! The Chamber of 'orrors! The Molloys are no good and never were!"

Very angry, I ran into the kitchen, but he called me back peremptorily: "Here, user, take my boots off!" Then to Alice: "Get me summick to eat, you!"

As I knelt down to undo his boot laces, the stench from his white moleskins and the darkish stain told me that he had unburdened himself in his pants—not an unusual thing for him when drinking. A moment later, he swept the table with his hand, dropped into the chair nearest him, and, when it crashed to the floor (a job for me the following day, tying it up), lay there singing his usual imbecilic songs.

CHAPTER SEVENTEEN

I was fourteen years of age at the time and Alice had turned sixteen. On the second day of my mother's sojourn in the hospital, my father went out with everything pawnable or saleable and did not come back for a long time. My mother was desperately sick and when the doctor told him he thought she would die, I think he decided it would be best to leave us. When the third day had passed, Alice went up and applied for Panel relief, which was due my mother, and with this seven shillings and sixpence per week she managed to pay the rent and keep the two of us in food. She said nothing about my father absconding, because we knew that any moment might see his return.

Seven shillings and sixpence wasn't very much, and I was at that age when pauper children are usually freed—if they can show their headmaster they have a job to go to. Moreover, all my pals had now left school and were working in Read's Tin Works or in Appleby's Flour Mills or the Phoenix Oil Mill—all around the neighborhood. This meant that school held little charm for me.

Moreover, I was very eager to show my mother what a dutiful son I could be. I was still very weak and "chesty" but my spirit was dynamic, and so, with the fear that any day might see the death of my mother, I went up to Timothy Seddons, the fish merchant in Leece Street, who needed an errand boy. This represented a last gamble to achieve my mother's life-long dream, a room of our own, away from our father.

Mr. Seddons was a kindly man and after skeptically feeling my muscles he agreed that I wasn't quite ready for warehouse work and hired me at the amazing sum of ten shillings per week. I thought I'd go mad with joy, and when I confronted Mr. McGinnis for my exemption from school the following day and he demurred, I got very excited. He couldn't see the logic of my leaving school before my time was up. But I pleaded earnestly and finally he released me. I started the next morning on my first paying job.

That evening, when I reported at the corner, the gang minimized the phenomenal nature of my ten-bob-a-week salary. Those working in Read's Tin Works proudly showed the calluses on their hands—and talked of "fifteen shillings with overtime," or "almost a quid with Sunday." We all compared muscles, and I fared the worst. Then they started criticizing my long trousers and the men's boots my mother had handed down to me, and my pants, made of an old pair of my father's moleskins. Jackie Oldham divined that they had been my father's and I resented it with heat. Immediately he invited me "to have a try?" I agreed, but at that moment our old nemesis, Aeroplane Joe, showed through the fog. We fled. When we returned to the corner, panting, the next one to be picked upon was the "kid" of the gang, Mickey. After this, we all bought packages of cigarettes and compared our resistance when it came to smoking. Inhaling was the thing, and I did my best. But again I fared the worst, for the smoke set me coughing and made me very sick.

Next we played pitch and toss for halfpence under the lamplight on the empty lot and talked and took turns in keeping douse again for our common enemy. Presently darkness came, and it was difficult to see the coins. Jacko suggested climbing into the empty house for the usual dare-devil roof display. Presently, like wraiths, we were up three stories gliding about the roof. There must be show-offs, of course. Lepsey, Harold May and myself were astride one of the big eaves, staring down some sixty feet to the street below. The door of Mrs. Mallin's pub opened and cast a ghostly flicker over all of us. Then suddenly the big stone the three of us were astride started to turn outward to the street. There was a quick scramble, and when it was over, Harold and I were clutching the body of the building while Lepsey had gone down with the huge segment of ledge. I saw the whole thing complete: Lepsey's body hurling first, impaled on the railings and then the huge stone smashing in the head—and the squirt of human blood. It was the first actual death I had ever seen. I crawled back on the roof and with the others made our escape. . . . That night, from neighboring mattresses, Alice and I talked of nothing else.

All the gang and a good many of the relatives attended the funeral of our pal. The "Professional Witness" was there. The gypsy woman went mad at the sight of her son in the bier and made a fierce attack, first upon her husband and then upon everybody else. It was a terrific scene with all the nice cakes and things prepared for the guests swept off the table and the mother forcibly led away for observation. Later, when she recovered and the tragedy lost its tang, Kitty induced the gypsy woman to seek redress. I am not sure, but I think the case was thrown out of court despite the expert eye-witness testimony given by Kitty, who had been asleep at the time of the accident. All we knew when everything was settled was that we had one Protestant less in the gang.

CHAPTER EIGHTEEN

AT THE end of my second week at Timothy Seddons's, my mother, contrary to the doctor's orders, left the hospital and came home. She looked very badly and I was afraid for her. Sheer desperation kept her going. She went down to Peter Williams's factory, the old sweatshop she had worked in as a girl, and got in as an operator. Her task this time was sewing navvy's heavy moleskin trousers, four shillings per dozen and buy your own thread. This was very meager pay and extremely hard work, and it became necessary to bring Alice in as a helper. Here the combined earnings of both of them would not come above thirteen shillings a week. The moleskin trousers my mother worked on would stand straight up, they were so stiff. Williams used to stand at the top of the stairway watching the women stagger up after dinner and if they showed signs of collapse he would taunt them: "Come on, you auld drone [cow]!" It was a decided change for the worst for my mother, and although happily freed from my father for the time being, she was much more exhausted when coming home at evening than when returning from the Emigrant House. Moreover—and what hurt Alice and myself very much—there was no big apronful of choice food on the table at night, a luxury missed greatly.

It was heaven to live away from our father, even though fear of his imminent arrival did destroy much of the pleasure. We had heard he was staying down at the fourpenny doss-house; all we hoped and prayed for was that he would continue to do so. At night, at every noise outside our door, our faces would constrict and the words, "It's him!" would be spoken by all three of us. But as the weeks went by our apprehension waned a little, and when we locked the door we felt a reasonable degree of safety. The bobby had told us not to let him in, and we were going to take him at his word. There was no home for my father here any more!

But six weeks after he had left us, after hearing tales of Alice and me both wearing boots and working, Enoch Arden returned. We were in the kitchen drinking tea with Mrs. Tar, just a little past midnight, when there came a knock at the door. In the instant I think all of us, save Mrs. Tar, knew "Who's there?" I asked. "Open this bloody door!" came the command. We refused. Then, amid fuming and cursing, he crashed it in and charged in among us very drunk and with murder in his eyes. He made straight for me, leering: "You wouldn't open the door, would you, little maneen, eh?" Then he struck me a hard blow in the mouth, throwing me in a corner. Next, Mrs. Tar was thrown out and Alice swept aside; then he made for his constant quarry, my mother, falsely accusing her of all sorts of sins.

Mother, exhausted after a hard day's work, was in no condition to withstand anything like this and, lying in the corner with blood pouring from my mouth, I felt that a severe beating now would be the end for her. I saw her face whiten as he took her throat in his hands and I heard her scream as they fell to the floor together, with him uppermost. Alice had fled in terror. I rose and picked up the big iron kettle and brought it down on his head with all the force at my command, and as he sagged I brought it down again and again and again and undoubtedly I would have killed him had my mother not grasped my arm and commanded me in the name of God to stop.

I don't remember exactly everything that happened that night. The bobbies came, as they always do come, after the fight, and my father was taken away in the ambulance, my mother over my protests assuming responsibility for his condition. She was taken along to the Argyle Street lock-up, where the following morning Magistrate Stuart Deacon, knowing of our awful history, released her. The next day she applied to Dale Street for an official police separation from my father (this would make it criminal in the future for him to bother us) and cast about for another place to live, for the Harrises, like everyone else, now demanded that all, or at least half of us, leave. A kindly woman, Mrs. Andrews, who lived two doors farther up the street, had two rooms that would just suit us and, knowing my mother, she consented to rent them to her, if my mother got the legal separation. This being produced, she let us in.

By the time my father was released from the hospital, his head swathed in bandages, we had comfortably established ourselves in our new domicile. My mother and Alice, however, were thoughtful of his welfare to the last. We took only what we absolutely needed and left his rooms very clean and with utensils for bachelor house-keeping if he cared to do that. The night before he returned, Alice even saw to it that there was bread and some tea and corned meat on the table. But live with him—that was a thing of the past. Finished!

It was the greatest possible relief to get away and stay away from my father. It was a hot August night, and while Alice was down the street fixing my father's table, I excused myself from my mother. I couldn't quite explain to her: I was so transcendently happy at the knowledge that at last there was to be a permanent armistice in our family strife. I strolled up Bridgewater Street in the darkness. As the lights of Park Lane drew near, I saw frenzied activity among the newspaper boys. A man standing outside Cain's public house dropped a newspaper, and ran wildly up the street. I picked up the *Echo* and read "ENGLAND DECLARES WAR," and wondered. Then I continued up to the corner.

The gang were all there talking in whispers about our mate's death and occasionally pointing up at the wall of the empty house. I envied the physical appearance of Joe Manassi and Johnny Mangan; and when they showed the size of their muscles under the lamplight, I began to think that perhaps the mill was the place for me. Freddie Seegar had on Yankee shoes and Jackie Sanchez was chewing gum; Harold May was proudly rattling the five shillings his mother gave him out of his wages. Frankie Roza had brought out his concertina and was getting ready to give us all a few uncertain chords, while my cousin Bernard and his namesake Henry Roche and Johnny looked on. Mickey had just gone to work that day and was talking about buying long pants, leaving the Working Boy's Home, and going to the doss-house. But though it was to mean so much to them, they were too much interested in other things right then to trouble themselves about the war, and when colored Frankie finally got his concertina going we all hurried to John the Greek's fish and chip shop in St. James Street.

CHAPTER NINETEEN

THE slums from that night on seemed to change. The old lethargic deadness and dullness of the dank alleys seemed to vanish, and instead of the desolate quietness at night, there would be lights and gayety and, paradoxical though it may seem, a strange new-found happiness. The days that followed saw the streets full of exceedingly happy soldiers, young and mature. I was still doing my errands for Timothy Seddons and when they would take me to the neighborhood of the Lime-Street Station or the Central Station on Bold Street, I would forget all about fish and listen to the loudly blaring bands at the heads of the various contingents. There were all kinds of soldiers, with many of the faces well known to me and from my neighborhood—Connaught Rangers, Scotch soldiers vary hilarious in their kilts, Liverpool's own pride, the Eighth Irish, and many others, all happy and in distinctly holiday mood.

Inside the stations as the trains pulled out, there would be tears for departing husbands and fathers, but the general tone was one of hilarity and new-found happiness. The end of dullness! Such scenes as these, watched by me for hours while the fish in my hands grew less edible, eventually cost me my job. However, I was glad, for I never liked the errand-boy stigma, particularly since it left me, with the exception of Mickey, the only member of the gang not working like a man in a warehouse. So that when Mr. Seddons discharged me I was pleased and came home to my mother in that mood; I warned her that henceforth nothing less than a warehouse career—or the cherished sea—would suffice for my ambition.

My mother thought me very silly. "Some day," she said, "you might have been manager of that fish shop."

"Yes," agreed my sister, "and you could have brought home lots of fish, like mammy used to do from the Emigrant House." However, I had decided differently, and my decision was gradually shaping in favor of a career at sea.

We found Mrs. Andrews's house much better conducted than the Harris's, but occupied by the same sort of jetsam. Mrs. Andrews had the front parlor. Very English, she reacted kindly to honesty and the opposite to skullduggery. The back parlor went to "Auld" Mrs. Mitchel. We had the back kitchen and the top back room. "Auld" Mr. Harford had one rear second-floor room and Mickey Boyd and wife and young baby had the other. "Auld" Mrs. Mitchel was a gentle, deaf old lady, and all she seemed able to say at any time was, "Yes, my dear!" Supported entirely by the old-age pension, she was more or less a recluse. I think the only news she ever heard was the awful doings of my father; from the moment she glimpsed us coming into our new quarters, her face whitened and she retreated into her room muttering fearfully. "Auld" Mr. Harford was an old dock laborer, with no relatives, who lived almost entirely in Gordon's pub parlor down the street. Sometimes, however, he would share a bottle of stout with Mrs. Mitchel and this was a pleasant sight to see. Mickey Boyd was a graduate of my school, St. Peter's, and a dock laborer, a sickly young man following the slummy's usual uneventful passage across life; his wife was as shiftless and as ignorant as he. None of these people was disturbed by the war; all of them were too old for the army except Mickey, who, as his wife would say sardonically when in her cups, "was neither fit for 'ome service nor abroad!"

When, after due deliberation, I told my mother that my intentions were not to fool with any cheap land jobs but to get away to sea (and give her the big advance note) she was crestfallen. She had seen too much in our home of what usually happens to sailormen (Otto, for example) and she didn't want anything like that to happen to me. She pleaded with me and offered what she thought were some very sound points: we had at last attained the happiness we had always prayed for; there were the three of us together at last; was I going to break her heart after all she had endured for me? But my mind was set upon the sea. For many nights the entire gang, encouraged by the ease with which greenhorns could get ships now that the war was on, had pondered the thing deeply. I reasoned right back with my mother. It would make a man of me for one thing, put some flesh on my bones, strengthen my lungs and chest (I knew that would go big with her); also, it would make us rich, give me a real profession, and so on. The opportunity opened by the regular merchant sailormen being called to the Navy or the Army might never come again! My mother, very sickly at that time, gave up. "Do what you like," she said, "only if you go to sea, be sure you go to Holy Communion first—that's all. And see that you always wear your scapular."

How happy I was the evening I told the gang of my sea-going intentions. They all agreed one after the other to desert their mill jobs and join me in my search. How thrilled I was on the morning I awoke with no school to go to and no job to go to, nothing to do but to strike out with the gang in search of—ships! Ships! That magic word is everything to your Liverpool waterfront youngster, and I think as we set out that morning to scour the line of docks, every heart was aquiver at the important role the war had made possible for us.

It was a damp, chilly day for August, but we all had on good solid boots, buttressed by the inevitable steel protectors, and—with the exception of my cousin Berny —long trousers. Moreover, we all had money in our pockets—a dangerous thing right then, addicted as we were to pitch and toss. As we walked down Norfolk Street we pondered over to what part of the world we'd best like to go. Almost unanimously we said South America, for there was something glamorous about the name—and it always meant a long voyage. The Lusy (*Lusitania*) and the Maury (*Mauretania*), commuting to New York, though more easy to ship on by a novice, were entirely too businesslike and the trip was over too quickly. We wanted a cruise, about eighteen months, so that when we came home it would be as outstanding sailormen and with a real pay-off. South America, or the West Coast of Africa, offered the best inducements, or else the Banana boats going to Spain. So when we reached the Dock Road, we struck south, walking for a while, then finally jumping on the tail end of a lorry.

At the gates of the Coburg Dock, we jumped off. This was the Houston Line headquarters, and there were two of their boats tied up here. We hesitated, and very seriously Joe Manassi suggested that we first go across the street to the pub and all get a pint of ale. None of us was of age and none of us had ever attempted to line up on our own hook in front of a bar. But hadn't most of them been doing *men's* work in the mills? So across the street we went, the crowd of us in the rear giggling softly as Joe Manassi and Harold May and Jacko Oldham led the parade. The bar was filled with dockers and sailormen of all nationalities, and all talking about the new war. (Quite a number of them were German sailormen befuddled and wondering and as yet not seized as enemies.) We lined up at the bar and, amid the quizzical gaze of the men, Joe truculently called for "ten pints." The barman looked at him skeptically, for eighteen is the deadline for serving at the bar. Then he looked at my cousin Berny and laughed, saying: "We don't serve kids in here!"

We were all mortified and could have murdered Bernard for we knew very well it was his short-pants (his long ones were still in Harris's pawnshop) that had cooked our goose. As we were trooping out amid the jests of the men, the barman took the customary bottle of water held on every bar and sprinkled it over us generously. Outside, laughing our ignominy away and forgetful of the Houston Boats, we raced aboard the rear of the first wagon we saw heading south.

We went on every dock that morning and aboard every ship that sufficiently appealed to us. But the day ended in failure. Most of the ships still had complete crews and where there was a vacancy they weren't anxious for "first trippers." It was decided to call that day a failure and the following morning to converge on the proper place to get a ship—the Sailors' Home On the way back we dropped into the Gore-Street free baths, among all the tough kids from the South End, black, brown, and white. Our clothes and boots were left on the benches without fear, for our gang was large, and in we went into the putrid water. When we came out an hour later, it was discovered that my boots were missing. I had made the mistake of putting them on top of my bundle and they had been swiped. Everybody, save Mickey, gave me a great laugh as I walked disconsolately back to the corner in my bare feet. When a game of pitch and toss was started, I saw a chance of retrieving enough to buy another pair of boots and took part in the game—anything to stop my sickly mother from worrying.

Then we made a fatal mistake. Ordinarily there was always a destitute member to keep douse for Aeroplane Joe; but now everyone had money. Result: no trustworthy "douser." Secondary result: our old friend, blowing his whistle fiercely, swooped around the corner and collared all of us, but after much scrambling and ducking held on only to me. Sadistically he smiled with the satisfaction of a man long frustrated. After my new address was taken, he muttered: "This'll put a stop to you when your mammy gets this here summons! You thought I was kidding you t'other night, eh? An' I'll get every bloody one of them yet, you see if I don't."

He was right, though not in the way he anticipated.

CHAPTER
TWENTY

I WAS indeed a sad boy trudging home that evening without boots, with the Law soon to be after me and with two of my three shillings and sixpence gone in the game. Standing in front of my mother and Alice I sputtered out a cock-and-bull story of having had both my boots and money stolen in the Gore-Street baths and that while coming home I had (while walking beside a crowd of boys) been mistaken by Aeroplane Joe for one of the pitchers and tossers and had had my name and address taken too.

My mother never doubted my story a bit, and after she had promised somehow and sometime to buy me another pair of boots, the immediate prospect of the police summons was discussed. Here I assured her everything would be all right, for I had already made up my mind about that. If I could possibly get a ship, the summons could go hang. The next day, when the gang assembled at the corner, my plan of evading the answering of the summons found ready support in the rest of the gang, most of whom swore not to assist the police in finding me should I get a ship. We all went down to the Sailors' Home, myself in Alice's boots, all cursing our mutual enemy, Aeroplane Joe, and at least one of us praying silently that we get a ship.

This particular morning we had better luck than the preceding day. In the first place, Joe Manassi had boldly gone into the Flag of All Nations pub and came out wiping his lips (though all of us had doubted his getting served) and that phenomenal success had given us the impetus to mingle with the older men at the Sailors' Home. In the second place, this business of transforming oneself from a landlubber into a sailor seemed much easier than when we had gone direct to the ships in the docks. The Arcade was crowded as usual, but the sailors seemed very choicy and the demands for their services greatly exceeded their requests for ships. I had been there many times before with my father (in search of a homeward-bounder), and the sights of burly ship-mates and engineers examining sailors' and firemen's books rapidly over the heads of others anxiously holding up-raised books was not new to me.

Now, this day, it seemed the other way. One big engineer, hairy arms akimbo and very wroth, was shouting: "Does anny of yis want a bloody ship—or don't yis?" Over on the other side of the arcade, Scandinavian-looking ship-mates were beseeching sailormen in like tone. In this hullabaloo, I think all of us boys sensed the imminence of the realization of our desires—that we would get a ship that morning—and discreetly we deserted one another to apply at the point of most vantage to ourselves. After the separation I found myself hemmed in among a crowd of mature North Enders staring up at a big square-headed ship's-mate yelling at us, "I want fourteen ordinary seamen that ain't afraid of work!"

I raised my hand. "All right," he said without asking for my book, "step over there."

One by one the North-End boys (regular sailors most of them) had their books examined and passed over beside me, who had no book. Later, as we signed on inside the Board of Trade office, I confided this to the mate and, caught in a dilemma, he said that if it were all right with the Board of Trade Official to start me off as an Ordinary Seaman, it would be all right with him. I was passed and signed on as an ordinary seaman at six pounds per month—the greatest sum of money I had ever dreamed of earning in my life. A few minutes later I was given my advance note of two pounds and was a member of the crew of the S. S *Restitution*.

Outside in the archway, my heart aquiver with delight, I sought out my pals and picked them up one by one. Despite the optimistic outlook, I was the only lucky one. I listened to their explanations for a while, then left them to continue their efforts at duplicating my feat. For myself, I was intensely excited at what great news I had for my mother and there were many pressing things to be done—the cashing of the advance note and the purchasing of sea paraphernalia.

The thing for me to do, then, was to go home and give the advance note to my mother. But the war spirit had gripped me and I had begun to feel I must show I was a "man." I could not bear the stigma of being called a "mammy's lad," so I went it alone. In the Board of Trade

149

offices I had heard that the *Restitution*, which was lying in the Nelson Dock, was going on a voyage to Cuba and we had signed up for three years (a mere formality if the ship came to England again). The fact that I was going to a mysterious place called Cuba and had signed on for three years definitely gave me the edge over the other members of the gang.

I made my way down Paradise Street to the spot where I knew Jew Grossi's Sailors' Outfitters' shop stood—he would tell me what I needed and cash my note. But Mr. Grossi, a like parasite a few doors down told me, had passed from the scene, dying from a broken heart when his Trocadero was done away with. But *he* could fix me up quite as good as Grossi—in fact much better and on the same old terms. He was very jovial, this little lynx-eyed fellow, recalling several hypothetical trips he himself had made on four-masted barques. Yes, he knew *exactly* what I needed for my first trip on deck! My two-pound advance note must go, seventy-five per cent stuff and the remainder cash. Standard contract. He was very attentive to my wants (harping always on his alleged trips on the barques) and when I walked out of his place I looked like a life-boat man putting out to sea. Very proudly I staggered homeward along Paradise Street, sweating under the weight of seaboots, oilskins and South-Wester, with ten shillings cash in hand—the residue of my two-pound advance.

My mother and Alice not only were heartbroken at my sea-going intentions but they almost collapsed when I checked the price of each item purchased from my advance note. "I could have bought it all for two shillin's from the sale!" averred my mother. "And the dirty robber never even gave him a sailor's bag!" So a pillow-slip was gotten for me. I became furious myself at this anticlimax. Here I was signing on for three years at six quid per month, and at the very moment when I should have been the center of much rejoicing they were making my life miserable!

This was on Thursday and I was due to sail on Saturday, leaving me the entire Friday to meditate and celebrate and bask in public commendation. Unfortunately the war had begun to seep into the Liverpudlian consciousness and whereas formerly the sight of a neighborhood boy putting out on his first jaunt to sea would have been the signal for calling out the accordionist, Georgie Bell, my going away didn't cause even the slightest fluster. Indeed, most of my hectic Friday prior to sailing was spent by me up in Jones's Coffee Rooms gazing at Edna, the counter girl, to whom I was very much attached.

I bought and ate twelve custards that day and tried to impress her with the gravity of what I was undertaking. But she couldn't see things my way, and so I left about six o'clock after putting in seven hours, and went down to the corner. Here, since they hadn't been near the mills, the gang was all on deck early, and I came in for a little of the adulation for which I yearned. It was something to have tough Joe Manassi call me by my first name, or for Jacko Oldham to stop kidding me or my apparel. And the news spread to the older women inside Mrs. Mallin's pub. Mrs. Seegar, whose second husband (she was now Mrs. Fox) had just left for France, kissed me; some other women celebrating the departure of their army or navy husbands also kissed me; later in the semi-darkness came the usual game of toss; then a fond good-by to the gang.

On the way home, desirous of doing the farewell job right, I dropped into the Molloy barracks, at 83 St. James Street, to say good-by to my grandmother and whomever else I might encounter. My Uncle Jimmy was there and the Murrays (including Mr. Murray, ill-at-ease in a new pair of home-made pants). My grandmother, as always, was in her armchair. Lonnigan, hoping Ireland would embarrass England in her new war, was still warming his bottom in front of the fire and absorbing all the heat. I came there for congratulations; but the air definitely was one of pity. I said something about going to sea "for three years," but nobody seemed moved by this portentous news. Embarrassed at the silence, I offered my grandmother the price of a pint; but she refused this and also forbade me buying anything for anyone else present. Subdued, I kissed her good-by. I saw her only once again.

Down at the house, both Alice and my mother had taken the day off from Peter Williams's and were busy packing my pillow-slip sea-bag. I had arranged after the bag was packed that what was left of my two-shillings pocket money would be spent in taking the three of us to the pictures. Aeroplane Joe and that police summons were very much in my mother's mind however, and as I found it difficult to convince her that once on the high seas British justice was scotched, I left her to ponder the problem with Alice and went out into the hallway to think over something that had been bothering me all day.

A LIVERPOOL IRISH SLUMMY

It was whether or not I should say good-by to my father. Two reasons made me hesitate: first, fear that he might try to get back at me for the kettle incident and, second, I didn't know whether he was worth it. However, sentiment had its way, so down into Harris's dirty old place I went falteringly. He was very friendly and when I told him I was going to sea, he broke down crying, slobbering all over me so long and seemingly so genuinely that I began to think that perhaps my mother had been unjust in deserting him.

I could see he was broke, so I gave him a threepenny bit to get a pint, and when we reached the door he kissed me again, continuing to the pub while I made my way back to our rooms.

And so that night went—the pictures, a long supper, confession, my frenzied dreams stimulated by this, my first venture to sea; in the morning Holy Communion, after which a sumptuous breakfast of bacon and eggs, the scapular pinned around my neck, the proud carrying of my pillow-slip sea-bag down the unnoticing street, the kiss of my sister at the Nelson Dock gates and that fierce embrace of my mother's farewell.

CHAPTER
TWENTY-ONE

THE *Restitution* was a broken-down old whaler commissioned by shipping agents, Votch & McGuire, to bring molasses from Cuba to Liverpool, and the main task of the fourteen ordinary seamen she hired was to transform the whaler into a molasses carrier while en route to Cuba. This was to cause much disillusionment among the regular sailor lads who, when signing on, must have wondered why a small boat like the *Restitution* should hire so many ordinary seamen and so few A. B.'s. I didn't mind it so much, for I knew little of regular ship's work, save what I had picked up at the docks. True, I knew how to tie all the stock knots and I could splice ropes and run winches (as every dock ragamuffin can), but I didn't know how to steer a ship, nor to box the compass nor anything of the technique of sea "watches" and the general routine of the forecastle. Many other things I didn't know, but these were to be hammered into me very shortly.

The *Restitution* was perhaps the dirtiest ship I have ever known, and when I first glimpsed her lying at the farther end of the Nelson Dock, blanketed with the barley-like hail that had begun to fall (it almost always hails, rains or snows when a sailor must carry his bag to his ship), it looked to me like some fantastic ogre that had risen for a moment from the deep and was about to sink back into it. There was whale oil all over her which could be smelt for miles around and it stuck in hard lumps around her bulwarks and on the rickety ladder stretched down to the quay. This greasy dirtiness extended to the decks, up the companionway to the bridge and skipper's quarters and back aft on the poop under which stood the sailors' and firemen's forecastle. Standing on her wooden deck, she seemed a huge piece of greasy, barley-covered wood a mile high and slanting as though about to capsize. As I lurched along with my pillow-slip sea-bag, I was already wondering whether or not I should desert. Then I saw the other boys I had glimpsed in the Sailors' Home, standing in the darkened passageway leading to the forecastle looking around them critically, and I decided to go through with it. They nudged each other when they saw my home-made sea-bag, confident I was a "first tripper."

The forecastle of this old whaler was even more disappointing than its general appearance. When I entered the sailor's compartment on the left, the mustiness of the place and closeness of room space gave me the impression of climbing into a greasy old orange box. The typical "old-scow" forecastle, the bunks, long eating-table, the deck—all were filthy. Some of the bunks had mattresses and bags thrown in them (the signal of occupancy) and some were empty. I picked out a lower one and felt around in the darkness before depositing my clean white sea-bag. There was whale grease all over it. Wondering, I stood there while the other men poured in and out, many of them drunk, cursing their new ship.

Then a big fellow, obviously a Scandinavian, loomed in the doorway, and after disclosing in broken English that he was the new boatswain, he began checking up on his crowd. Gradually they drifted in until he had them all: five A. B.'s, two Russians, two Danes and one Liverpudlian. The fourteen boys had all made an initial trip on the "Lusy" (the *Lusitania*) as deck boys—a point that did not add much to their prestige with our "sailing ship" boatswain. One of the boys asked:

"Do you keep the lookout up in the crow's nest, Boats?" And the big fellow replied sardonically:

"Don't you worry about that, kid; what you're here for is to clean out that whale oil down below; the sailormen'll take care of the lookouts."

Then he came to me.

"This your first trip, eh?"

I nodded.

"Then you be mess boy here. When you get straightened out, get some water and clean this fo'c'sle up a bit."

He turned to the men:

"You fellers fix your watches up to suit yourself. Hans here (one of the Danes) he be Chips (carpenter) on day work. We sail as soon as the tugs get here!" He pulled a bottle from out his pocket, took a draught of the whisky and handed it good-naturedly to the nearest of the men. "You fellers go along with me, and you'll be all right."

"How's she feed?" asked the Liverpool A. B.

"I don't know," said the boatswain, "this is my first trip on her. She's no worse than that Houston boat I just got off. . . . Well, get busy, fellers. . . ."

The boatswain was right: We sailed in half an hour. I don't remember very much about it, except that after he had apportioned the men and boys to their tasks of helping get the ship off, he handed me a brand new bucket and scrubbing brush and left me alone in the darkness. It seemed he had, in his gruff manner, taken pity on me and, contrary to what I thought at the moment, was really giving me an easy task. Well, where was I to start cleaning? Up on deck I could hear the men scurrying about and the whistle of the tug alongside us blowing and the straining of the ship's beams as its old engine started to rumble, and the noise and hiss of the winches. The big new oilskin I was still wearing was almost choking me. What was this I was tackling? Where now was the thrill of "looking for a ship" of "signing on" of "cashing the advance note"?

I played around with the brush and water for a while; then a battered old face with a piece of sweat-rag clinched between the teeth peered in and, seeing me scrubbing, inquired of me what I thought about the boat and when I told him it was my first trip he took sympathy on me. He was the firemen's "mess boy" across the passageway and he too was cleaning his forecastle out. "I fired on the Monkey boats for fifteen years, but this bloody thing's got them skinned a mile for dirt! If you go to sea all your life you'll never see a packet like this again."

He took the bucket from me and poured the contents over the table and started to scrub. "Go ahead and get another bucket full." And so it went, with him doing the scrubbing and me bringing the water, not thinking of the forecastle or anything else, only of Liverpool and how every minute I was drawing farther away from it. Then the fireman over in my benefactor's forecastle awakened from a drunken sleep and began cursing, and my new friend left me. I had caught a glimpse of the "below" crowd as I passed the doorway to their forecastle; some of them were white, some black, but all dirty and nondescript, and their hovel, it seemed to me, was even dirtier and more smelly than ours.

Then presently, when we had cleared the dock, the crew came tumbling down one by one and helped me get the place cleaned up. The big boatswain's name I recall as Ollie and, though very tough in his manner, he was like most Scandinavians, kindly at heart. He called me aside and put two big pans in my hand. "Go on to the galley and get the grub." One of the A. B.'s went with me—the big lanky fellow from the extreme South End of Liverpool, an expert curser and natural radical—"To see what kind of bloody chow this lousy bastard (the cook—he hadn't as yet met the man) was going to give us."

The cook was one of those dark-complexioned, mysterious foreigners, of no definite nationality, so common in Liverpool. He looked almost comical, standing there half-drunk with his second cook, a vacuous Spanish boy; the cook had on a dirty white apron and a chef's hat and was ladling out bacon and eggs into a vast dish, held there by the elderly coal-trimmer who a moment ago had helped me clean up my side of the forecastle. As soon as my companion saw the bacon and eggs his whole demeanor changed and he tried to become friends with the cook. Here, however, the latter stood upon his inviolable dignity and insisted that the sailor remain outside the galley. But he seemed to take a liking to me, kidding me about my first trip.

As the lanky fellow staggered up to the forecastle with the bacon and eggs (picking and eating pieces of bacon and eggs en route to his destination) the cook handed me the dish with the potatoes and bread, tucked the pot of coffee under my arm, and patted my back fondly and said he was going to be my friend and for me to come to the galley or his room any time and see him. I reacted very favorably to this kindness and determined to take advantage of it. I told him of Sanchez's boarding house and he said he knew of it and indeed had stayed in it many times when ashore. Did he know Jackie? Yes, he knew *Quanito* very well. His name was Alonzo Don Alverez and he had been going to sea forty-odd years, he said proudly, along with a great many other things the relevancy of which I couldn't quite see at the moment, but which I was to discover later on.

After I left him and came out on the short strip of deck before reaching the well-deck, I looked across the river. We were then abreast of the Landing Stage and were still being towed by the tug, which puffed away desperately under our bows. Away to the right I could hardly make out the Queen's Dock and I stopped and peered closely, trying to decide the specific spot where our house lay, and wondering what my mother was doing at the moment. Over on the left lay Seacombe, Egremont, New

Brighton, Hoylake—all places that I cherished. As the *Restitution* plowed along, my mind went back to that eventful, tempestuous day when I sat on those sands there and watched the life-boat crew pull out to where we now were, and then to sink. Again my heart fell, and the only friend I thought I had in the world was the old Spaniard in the galley.

Down in the forecastle, the crews of both departments had come together over the first meal. As I passed the fireman's forecastle, I saw them all seated around the dirty table, some eating out of the old tin plates they had brought with them from a previous voyage, and others desperately looking for their new plates amid the clutter of stuff in their sea-bags. They were of every nationality and color, and almost all were tipsy and talking, cursing everything, particularly the ship. One tall, thin fellow was examining the contents of his sea-bag dubiously; another was examining himself at the far end of the room, while a third, watching him, commented critically: "You got it all right, all right. I told you about that two-penny bitch, didn't I?"

The air was filled with pipe smoke; I passed along and into our own forecastle. It was pretty much the same, except that here a petty row was in progress. One of the fourteen tough lads from the North End had irritated the lanky radical South End A. B., and the latter, his dignity hurt, was admonishing the younger man:

"When you made as many bloody trips as me, sonny, you can act like that. You hain't stopped s . . . yeller yet, and you're giving the older man sass. . . ."

A LIVERPOOL IRISH SLUMMY

"I didn't say nowt to you!" said the lad in a surly manner. The tall lanky fellow leaped erect.

"Another bleedin' remark out 'o you, and I'll knock your bloody . . . jaw out!'

Silence, then, with the lanky fellow vindicated and more surliness on the part of the fourteen ordinary seamen. I placed the pan of potatoes and bread on the table and the coffee near the humiliated lad's elbow. Instantly, he leaped erect and wanted to do to me what the lanky A. B. had offered to do to him. I drew away perplexed and was dispatched without ceremony after more bacon and eggs. But Alonzo Don Alverez, after showing me the nice dish he had reserved for me, sent me back with an empty pan.

"They keed you because you are new. They know there ees no more eggs until next Sunday."

I came back with his message and drew a great laugh. Another big lad, striving for notice, dispatched me this time for some "plum duff." When I came back empty-handed again, they had all forgotten the joke and were now clearing away their bunks and "fixing in." The men were commenting on the shortage of A. B.'s.

"That's a bloody lie, he couldn't get 'em!" said the lanky radical fellow "They want to work our bloody hides off—that's what!" The Russian A. B. agreed with him; but the Danes merely smiled and said nothing. I wondered what to do next. Eating was out of the question; so I turned to one of the Danes, the one named Gustave who had the bunk above mine, and asked him what I should do with the remains of the meal. Instantly he left his task and before he was through with me, I had a pretty good idea of what a mess boy's duty should be aboard a boat like the *Restitution*.

And so it went all the time the old whaler was plowing out to the mouth of the Mersey. I wanted to get on deck to see the sights along with the rest of the crew, but there wasn't much chance. Intent upon getting the forecastle into some sort of shape, the boatswain, despite his friendly attitude, had piled task after task upon me. First the table, then the floor, then the lockers, then the alleyway.

Most of the time, in spurts, he helped me, and when dusk began to fall and the watches had been set he told me to quit and further informed me of my duties. Like my grimy little friend in the other forecastle I was to be part-time mess-boy. I was to get up at five bells—six-thirty in the morning—lay the table and bring the grub from the galley, after which when, the day men had finished their meal, I would clean up and in about half-an-hour report for work down the hold with the men I had served. At one bell (quarter to twelve, midday) I would come up ahead of the gang and repeat what I had done for them at breakfast; and the same thing at supper time. He hinted that there usually were tips given the mess man at the termination of the voyage. Then he left me with the advice, "You better turn in and get some sleep; tomorrow you'll be pretty busy."

I went up then on the forecastle head, more for some fresh air than for anything else. All the members of the crew not busy at their respective tasks were there loung-ing around on ropes or the windlass or just walking, the firemen easily identifiable by their singlets and sweat rags hung around their necks. On the bridge amidships I caught sight of two squat figures, one of whom obviously was the captain and the other the man who had given me my job at the Sailors' Home. I looked over the rail; it seemed a great way down to the water, for we were, save for the ballast, sailing "light." Ahead of us the tug pouted away, its own crew looking very contented as, seated on coils of rope, they leisurely smoked their pipes. Again I looked southward, but there was no sight of the Queen's Dock now and the land was getting dimmer and the water wider. Over on the left, too, the sand and the New Brighton Tower had disappeared. I went down below. Here the lanky fellow was lighting an oil-lamp. "Lamp trimmer on a bloody scow like this!" he muttered drunkenly as I made my way over to my bunk.

After the lamp was lighted, he went out and I was left alone. The big Dane who bunked above me came in, nodded to me, got his pipe and walked out again. One of the Russians came in and suggested that I open my bag and get my bunk ready. "When we get out a bit it's liable to get rough and you'll be fallin' all over yerself," he said in surprisingly good English.

After he had gone, I took him at his word and explored my pillow-slip sea-bag. My mother had put in there almost everything I owned and quite a number of things to which I had never paid much attention—my rosary, for instance, and my scapular. There were blankets and socks and new boots and all the other things she deemed necessary—knife, fork, spoon, plate and cup, etc. I arranged them as best I could in the darkness, then rolled in with my clothes on. I was weighed down by the deepest despondency I have ever known.

CHAPTER
TWENTY-TWO

I SLEPT fitfully that night. All night long, I could hear the lookout on the forecastle head walking to and fro, and the watch changing, both down below and on deck. The occasional clanging of the ship's bell or the cry from the lookout man on the forecastle head, "Lights are burning bright, sir!" usually awoke me, or the low murmuring of the watch relieving each other as two went to the wheel and lookout and the other two smoked and turned in.

But an unfortunate thing happened that was to plague me all through the trip. About two o'clock in the morning I leaped up from my bunk crying: "Mammy! Mammy!" striking my head on the Dane's bunk above me and awakening almost everybody in the forecastle. Growlingly, they protested and went back to sleep; but from then on "Mammy!" was my nickname, starting on the morrow down in the hold. They thought I was crying for my mother; what had actually happened was that I was reliving one of those murderous assaults of my father and was leaping to my mother's rescue.

164

A LIVERPOOL IRISH SLUMMY

When I came up on deck that morning a different scene greeted me. Liverpool was gone and so, too, were the pilot and the accompanying tug, and much smoke was coming from the top of our dirty yellow smoke stack. Land was but a dim outline to the left. There was a strong ripple which threatened to break into genuine waves at any moment; the air was more salty and my stomach didn't feel any too certain of itself. The hatches had been thrown off number one hold and I gazed down there and became genuinely sick. Away below the grease was swirling around in a sickening mass; and it dawned on me then just why this boat that ordinarily would hire three boys had hired fourteen.

I had guessed correctly. As the boys, still twitting me over the "Mammy" business, were eating their first breakfast of porridge, meat balls, coffee, and bread, the boatswain came in and warned all the ordinary seamen to wear their new sea-boots. The A. B.'s (very rebellious now since they were three short of their regular quota) were to turn-to on deck. After breakfast and after I had cleaned up the table (each man cleaned his own plate and "tools" and put them in his own locker), I reported at the top of the hatch and followed the boatswain down the greasy steel ladder, away down to the bilges where the other boys, standing up to their hips in whale oil grease, filled buckets that were hoisted up on deck by the clean A. B.'s and dumped overboard. I was dumped into a bilge with two boys and given a huge ladel and a bucket, and pretty soon my new sea-boots looked very old and messy.

When the boatswain had gone up on deck, the "Mammy" pantomime started. The North-End boys, about equal in toughness, needed a victim, and with seasickness fast coming on me they found it in me. And so with the creaking strains of the old boat as she labored from side to side and with the whale oil smell and with the good-natured taunts, I tried as best I could to look the part of a sailor. But it was too much. I hadn't eaten any breakfast and wasn't feeling too certain of myself when I had followed the boatswain down the hold; now, with the putrid whale oil smell, I was about done. Down came my pan; my stomach began heaving. This gave the boys more zest for taunting, but when blood came out of my mouth, the joking stopped for a minute and I was helped on deck very sympathetically, and from the deck to my bunk.

How I suffered with belly, chest and headache in that dirty little forecastle that morning as we plowed slowly across the buoyant Irish Sea! Another boy was commissioned to do the mess-cleaning for me, and that night, dipping into the Atlantic, the boat started rolling and pitching more violently, and I got worse. One had to hold on to the bunks to steady oneself—at least I had to, though many of the older seamen were quite sure of their legs. After that night, however, the ocean became placid and remained so most of the distance to Cuba.

It was an uneventful voyage and of practically no maritime consequence to me or to the other ordinary seamen. Every day it was the same old routine—turn-to, down the hold all day, up for dinner, then down again until five o'clock that night. For the entire three weeks it took us to reach Cienfuegos, Cuba, we were never entirely rid of whale grease. It was in our hair, and in our bunks, on the table, everywhere.

About a week out from Cuba, it was estimated that we wouldn't be able to finish all the hatches unless some overtime was put in. So we were worked until eight o'clock each night, and the final night before entering the harbor we labored all night long to complete the job.

With the job completed now and lying at anchor in Cienfuegos harbor, life was a little more bearable for us. The weather was tropical and the bugs soon ran us out on deck. A few of the A. B.'s, foreseeing these conditions, had brought hammocks along with them and these they took up on the forecastle head. Until then I had only caught glimpses of the Captain, sometimes in midday on the bridge with the second mate looking through his sexton, or of an evening in his shirt sleeves peering out of his cabin below the pilot house. But one afternoon as I painted away on one of the life-boats, he touched me on the shoulder.

"Ain't your father's nickname 'Plunger,' son?"

"Yessir," I said.

"You know Sarah Acte's boarding house?"

"Yessir," I said. "Do you know my father?"

His face clouded. "I ought to. I remember you, too. He robbed me one time when I was mate on one of the Cork boats."

"I'm sorry, sir," I said.

Then he patted me on the shoulder.

"That's all right, me lad—only don't grow up and be the bloke he is." Then he passed along.

I never saw much of him after that, and I wish I had

never seen him in the first place. Whenever I'd see him and the mate together, I'd imagine they were talking about me, and that he knew everything distasteful pertaining to me and my early life.

The old cook was very nice to me and used to save me little tit-bits made for the officers. One night he made some tea, and I became very drowsy and fairly fell into the spare bunk in his room. But with that suspicious instinct so well developed through my early family life, I never entirely lost consciousness. Presently he locked the door and climbed into the bunk beside me and I realized the nature of his friendship. I fought him off, biting and scratching, until he pleaded very suavely that I had misjudged him, and that he was very sorry. But now I had quite regained my senses, and though I was quite certain he had put some drug in that tea, I said nothing and he said nothing and we remained outwardly friendly to each other. But no more tea parties!

Little of interest occurred while we lay at anchor in Cienfuegos harbor, loading with molasses. One day the hole of the sailors' toilet, looking down on the brightly painted, spotlessly clean barge that was "feeding" us the molasses, was stopped up, and the only way it could be cleared was from the deck of the barge. Being more or less the goat, I was dispatched down the Jacob's ladder onto the barge to probe the hole with a big bamboo cane. Had the Cuban skipper of the barge seen what I was about, he undoubtedly would have stopped me, for it was obvious to everyone except me (the smart boys were all on deck having a good time laughing) that if I cleared the hole with my bamboo cane, the stream of accumulated human refuse must land first on me and next on the barge.

That is exactly what happened, and the only reason I am alive today is that I was so covered with the refuse that I dived headlong into the harbor and left the angry Cuban skipper brandishing his knife as he danced in fury, watching the stream of human refuse spreading all over his clean barge. Undoubtedly he would have killed me had he caught me, for as I swam around the bow of the *Restitution*, he continued brandishing the knife and cursing me violently in Spanish. However, I reached the other side in safety and crawled up the Jacob's ladder. A number of the boys were later sent down on the barge to clean it up, but the mate very wisely kept me aboard.

On the last day in harbor, the skipper brought word aboard about the war. Some of the men got letters, but I got none. Up to then nothing much had been said of it, for there was a strong suspicion among the younger element that at least one of the Danes (the big fellow who slept above me) was German and, anyway, no one realized the magnitude the war eventually would reach. Now the skipper came aboard with exciting talk of the pillage of Belgium and of the raping of women and children; of the brave stand the Belgians were putting up at Liège; and of the French and British and Russians closing in to swift victory. This was new stuff to us all. We had read or heard about wars, but the proximity of an actual one was something else. The old-timers in both forecastles recalled the Boer War, pointing out that *that* was a war. This thing—it would blow over in no time, what with the size of the British Navy, etc. When we pulled anchor and sailed for Liverpool that evening, the consensus of opinion was that we all would be robbed of the excitement and that the whole thing would be settled when we got to the Pool.

Now on the return trip things were much better for us ordinary seamen and we came in for some real sailors' work. The mate had figured the whole thing out very nicely. The A. B.'s would be undermanned going out, but they would have it easy coming back. We whale-oil cleaners were equally divided between the port and the starboard watches and day work. As mess boy, I was put into the latter category, although I was anxious to get on watch, for it seemed so much more exciting. There were so many things I wanted to do: to steer; to have the responsibility of the lookout; to shout dramatically in the middle of the night, "Lights are burning bright, sir!" or the parody I learned later on "*Your* eyes are full of . . . sir!" However, I learned things much faster by being on day work than I would had I been put on a watch. Strangely enough my best friend in the tuition was McCarthy, the radical. He would take me up on the forecastle head with him and to the crow's-nest away up on the foremast to show me how best to keep a lookout; and when it was his wheel I would go into the pilot house and he would explain things in detail for me, while the officer snoozed standing up in the lee corner of the bridge. How vast and mysterious and awful that ocean looked when first I glimpsed it in the quiet of an early summer night from the crow's-nest! And yet—how *beautiful*!

The voyage back was almost as placid as the one going out. It was lovely weather and, moreover, a full cargo weighted us down, below the water mark. We had no wireless and, of course, got no news about the war. There were dreary days plowing along counting the hours when the big event in my life would come—the moment when I would set off for home with the pay-off!

It was in the Irish Sea that we first sensed the nearness of the war, for there was great activity here among the warships. Almost every hour a British destroyer would spurt across our bows, and once a signal went up from one of them followed by a blank shot aimed to attract us. Immediately after, the mate blew for me and I had the honor of pulling up the Union Jack on the poop, and there it remained until we entered the Mersey. How I thrilled when I pulled up that flag and observed the low-lying mass of steel with bristling guns close beside to protect us! This was war! This was great!

Now, Gustave, the poor fellow above me, became suspect and nobody talked to him. Prior to our starting out, someone had seen his papers and they registered many departures from Hamburg; he might have been a Dane but we gave him the worst of the doubt and, I believe, had he not been such a quiet-mannered fellow and our ship so close to home, something very tragic might have happened to him. (I learned later that he was a German and was interned right after getting paid off at the Home.) Poor fellow, he must have suffered damnably from the realization that his nation was at war with Britain and that his real country and only love (true of all sailormen), the sea, was to be taken from him.

Nevertheless, nothing was said or done to him and I think even thoughts of the war were subsidiary to thoughts of the imminent pay-off—the big thought of all sailors homeward bound. It was good to see the Bar Lightship and New Brighton Tower and the Sands and Egremont and Seacombe ferries, and then the Landing Stage and the Royal Liver Building and the Cunard Building and all the other sights so full of nostalgia for me. The pilot had come aboard buzzing with war talk, but we paid no attention to the stuff that came down from the bridge. The firemen lined the rail with their bags all packed. In the sailors' forecastle all bags, including my torn pillow-slip, were packed and waiting only the throwing in of the working clothes being worn by all hands now on deck, ready to make fast.

We were going into the Brocklebank Dock, and from the forecastle head where I stood holding a manila hauser I could see my father down on the quay, searching among the crew for my face. With him were some of his cronies. Obviously he was down here to cadge from me.

I faced the boatswain, himself partly drunk now and pointed to my father. "Boats," I said, "that man is my father and I want to get away from him. Will you go down and tell him I've just gone up the Dock Road?"

He stared at me wonderingly for a moment. "That's a fine bloody way to treat your daddy! But I'll do it for you." Then I saw him go down and explain rather contemptuously to my father, pointing to the Dock Road; and apishly my father and his mates followed quickly in that direction. A few minutes later, as the overhead train whizzed me home, I saw my father and his cronies ambling along the Dock Road eagerly looking about to see if they could catch a glimpse of me.

CHAPTER TWENTY-THREE

MY MOTHER and Alice were delighted with my improved physical condition. I couldn't be quite so enthusiastic over theirs. Alice was thin and sickly and mother had collapsed at the overall task and was now charing in the Chicago Building on Paradise Street. Alice, making use of what she had learned with my mother at Peter Williams's sweatshop, had gotten a job in Davis's clothiers in Great George Street. One cause of my mother's condition was the death of my Aunt Leisha that had occurred shortly after I had put out to sea. There were a large number of Roche children, and it was this brood, now to be without a mother's care, that worried her so.

The report on my father was what I expected. Drunk all the time; except for Alice, he would probably have starved to death. She used to go down to his room in the Dead House, clean it, empty his bucket, and put food on the table.

Everything was discussed in one breath. How did I like the sea? Liverpool had changed almost overnight— all the men were leaving their regular jobs for the Army or Navy and bits of lads were stepping into their shoes and at big wages, too. All my mates—despite their alleged preference for the sea—were making good money in the mills. Mr. Fox, Freddie Seegar's stepfather, had gone to France with the Eighth Irish; so had Billy Johnson, who lived next to Jackie Sanchez; so had Johnny Calvey and Willy Hasty and Peter Thomas and Johnny Flaherty. Had I heard what the dirty Huns had done to the brave Belgians at Liège? And just look at these sections of the *Express* and the *Echo* filled with lists of Dead, Wounded and Missing! But with Auld Asquith out and Lloyd George in command it would be different!

And the enemy in our midst. All of those unnaturalized Germans living in Freddy (Frederick) Street had been rounded up and sent to the Isle of Man detention camp— including "that dirty auld Jocob Brone who used to sing them German soldier songs!" There were some others around the neighborhood, but they had their British Naturalization papers—cute rascals! I tried to reason with mother that perhaps it was a bit unfair, interning German sailormen, like Charlie Thomas, for instance, who had raised big families and had forgotten all about the Fatherland. But my mother had been stung by the patriotic bee and was beyond reasoning. "Sure it's right to break up the families—they'd do it to us, wouldn't they?" she'd ask. Yes, I supposed they would. Then to prove her point she showed me reports of the latest German atrocities.

The big news for me, however, was when they confided to me that my dispute with the Law had been settled (eight shillings it had cost my mother) and that I could look the gang's constant enemy, Aeroplane Joe, squarely in the eye, without fear of arrest.

Just as I anticipated, the following morning my father was down at the Sailors' Home at the hour of the *Restitution's* pay-off. He was very glad to see me, but I was not very glad to see him. Dogging me like this disgusted me. I tried to get him to go away, and presently my insistence upon this point made him show his true colors. To prevent a scene, I gave him two shillings. It wasn't enough and reluctantly I gave him another and, after endeavoring to kiss me, he slunk off, growling contentedly. With the rest of the pay-off—four pound seven—and declining a second trip on the *Restitution* and an invitation from the North-End boys to the Flag of All Nations pub, I hurried off homeward, alone. Here all the neighbors, sensing a pay-off, tried to crash through to our kitchen. But frigid Alice, detested by the merrymakers, met them all and waved them away.

That evening, after the inevitable bacon and eggs for "tea" and a rather unsatisfactory split of the pay-off had been made (three pounds for mother; one for me), I made my way hurriedly to the corner to bask in the adulation of my mates. I found them all except Mickey outside Mrs. Mallin's pub like a committee of reception, and all apparently very content with their lucrative mill jobs. After the usual volley of maritime questions had been asked of me and answered adequately with a like number of maritime lies, we made our way up Park Lane for the inevitable nightly treat of fish and chips, myself in the honorable vanguard, since I was now a sailorman.

It was about the last time I was to see so many of the gang together. The warehouse, mills and the big money drew them now, and although we were to meet almost every night outside the pub and certainly every Sunday for the regular "footy" game, from then on the *esprit de corps* of the gang waned.

This frenzy to make money conflicted with my holiday spirit—the prerogative of every returning sailorman. Everyone was making money; no one wanted to play. Walking past the mills day or night, men could be seen stretched out in the street snatching bits of sleep (a waste of time to go home), to return quickly to fatten the pay-envelopes. Along the line of docks arch lights glared over ships-holds and winches ground out all night long. But, of course, there are some boys congenitally lazy. So that it wasn't long before playboy Freddie Seegar and tubercular Jackie Sanchez and I were thrown together, and this holiday mood continued for about a month.

These were happy days indeed, which didn't end until the three of us started out from the Spanish boarding house to search the line of docks for a ship—made to measure, of course. What we wanted was a mess-boy's task—the attraction being the better food that went with this job and the white coat to be worn. One day Freddie confessed a yearning for the Orient, and immediately we took the ferry over to Birkenhead, where Alfred Holt's Blue Funnel China boats docked. Failure. For the Blue Funnel boats fed their sailormen and seldom needed any help. Late in the evening, as we turned for home, I struck ice on the *Caledonia*. The *Caledonia* had an Indian crew and I had a little difficulty getting to the Steward, a big glum Scotsman. He wanted to know had I been sent from the Shipping Office. I shook my head and handed him my sailor's book.

"But you've been on deck," he said. "What do you know about the mess?"

"I worked in the Adelphi hotel," I lied. He looked at me quizzically.

"How old?"

I was fourteen, but I said seventeen. Then he took my name and told me to meet him at the Home at ten o'clock the following morning when the *Caledonia* signed on. I was so elated to break into the mess-boys' game, I forgot to ask him what the job paid.

All the way over to Liverpool I jabbered quite happily—a mood not shared by my jealously sullen mates. Nor did my mother and Alice find it easy to share my happiness, for the sea to them was an unnecessary gamble with death. Now I told them the deck-hand paraphernalia would have to give way to the mess-man's—two white coats at least. Was the ship going to hot or to cold weather, mother asked. I didn't know. But the following afternoon, after signing on at six pounds per month with the title of Second Steward, I brought home a two-pound advance note and the news that our destination was the Mediterranean and warmth. I was apportioned five shillings pocket money, and two second-hand white coats were bought for me in Harris's pawnshop—always stocked with unredeemed maritime pledges.

Ordinarily, with five bob and the portentous news that I was off to sea again, I should have gone very proudly to the corner that night. But I didn't, and for a very good reason. Two nights before, while I was passing Brick Street, I espied a quasi-colored group congregated in the middle of the street laughing to their heart's content in the darkness. I pressed forward and, ducking underneath many legs, I saw two bobbies holding a couple of Negroes while another bobby was down on the cobblestones trying to revive a young white woman. I recognized her as a "Nigger's bit." Her clothes were up over her neck: she had been sexually ganged. The view of her before her dress was pulled down had caught and clung to my imagination. . . . Now two days later, I wanted a woman myself!

That is why, instead of going to the corner, I went to Lime Street that last night ashore. For hours I trudged up and down this windy thoroughfare to no avail. Many obvious prostitutes were there, but all of them had escorts and were not the fawning alley-like creatures I had thrown bricks at a few years previous. Under the eaves of my Palais de Luxe Cinema, I saw three men stand beside me and (out of deference to each other) take turns in picking up the first unescorted woman that chanced along. Now I was alone, but though I looked intently at the few unescorted ones that appeared, they smiled at me and passed along. I knew the inference—they thought me a mere kid with a few coppers in my pocket!

Silently I prayed that I could see Helen Reilly or any of the other girls from our neighborhood—I'd offer her the whole five shillings, so determined was I! Then an old hag hobbled down the street, caught my smile and motioned me to follow her. Down John's Lane she went with me after her, away down to an alley behind the Royal Court Theatre.

"How much?" I asked when I faced her.

"A bob—to you."

It was probably the hardest shilling she had ever earned, and though she was very patient and industrious, she finally came to the conclusion that most of my desire was in my head. After she left me trembling stupidly in the doorway, I turned to read a poster just behind me. The O'Mara Opera Company (no relation of mine) were doing *Romeo and Juliet* right then inside the theatre!

CHAPTER
TWENTY-FOUR

MY HAPPINESS at obtaining the messman's job on the *Caledonia* was to be short lived. As soon as the big Scotch Steward discovered I had lied to him, he began to be-devil me. Moreover, he was a strict Presbyterian and there was my name, which didn't help matters much. Alone after the first meal, when my ignorance of pantry technique became apparent, he leered at me: "You're just like all the bloody Liverpool Irish scum—liars and parasites! Want somebody else to do the work while you get the pay. Well, we'll see who's goin' to be kidded!"

From then on this voyage to and from the beautiful Mediterranean was for me simply a matter of dishes and tongue-lashings. All that I recall now in retrospect was strict deference of our white officers for the habits of the Hindu crew; the sharp cleaving of few whites from many browns; the beautiful blue of the "Meddy"; our arrival in Leghorn; and the anticlimactic meeting with my boss in a brothel and the mutual embarrassment when Madame tried to jolly us into an introduction! Here came the letter from home aboard, telling, among other things, of the death of my once beautiful Aunt Lizzie and of the horrible inroads of the war—and the inevitable postscript: did I say my prayers regularly and wear my scapular, particularly when in the danger zone? Then the return from the Blue of the "Meddy" into the green of the Irish Sea, the Danger Zone and the huddling of the Hindus by the lifeboats; the old familiar landmarks, darkness in the river, happy packing of the old pillow-slip—the felicitations and the pay-off the next day.

That night, after the usual controversial division of my pay, and clad in the American tailored suit and block-toed shoes I had bought that day (much to my mother's deep chagrin, since much better second-hand things could have been gotten from Harris's pawnshop), I went over to the Sanchez boarding house to see my old mate who now, my mother confided, was "makin' almost two quid a week as a regular docker! What you ought to be doin' instead of goin' to sea. . . ."

I found Jackie there, just in after doing a "half a night." He was very glad to see me and, after comparing the size of our muscles, he told me the news about the gang. Not like the fellers we used to know—they all had girls now. "They come around the corner once in a while," he explained, "but not every night like they used to. They're all tryin' to join up—before the War finishes. . . . Last week we all tried to join the Army and the Recruiting Sergeant ran your cousin Berny out the room by the pants!"

Then the most portentous news of all—he was actually dancing! In fact all the gang were. How had they learned? Why, they had simply gone into old Harry Graves's *Balfe* on top of Lunstrom's pub, the *Nook,* and when the Velita was called they barged their way through it! "I'm goin' up there tonight. Come on with me." Then, very proudly flaunting his docker's hook as he put it into a drawer, he led the way up the street.

The piano, the only music Mr. Graves would tolerate, was banging away under fat Mrs. Todd's direction when we entered. A huge crowd of soldiers, sailors and "civvies" were participating in and watching the dancing. All of my mates were there, but they didn't see us enter. Then the dancers disbanded and presently were called to order again by Mr. Graves—"Take your partners, gentlemen, for the Velita! . . ." I don't know what I did but I did something, and that something I liked even if my partner did not. Here was a new thrill!

At the intermission my mates, who had been very attentive to the girls when I entered, all came over and congratulated me on my second trip—but not nearly so enthusiastically as I had anticipated. Their felicitations smacked more of deference than of envy. They seemed more mannish than I, and when we repaired downstairs to the bar they mixed more easily with the soldiers, sailors, and womenfolk, and spent with alarming generosity. Johnny Mangan, in colloquy with two Royal Navy men, seemed very much interested in what they said; while my cousin Berny and Johnny Ford engaged in like conversation with two soldiers, back from France on brief leave. The Bar and Parlor was crowded to capacity and the talk was all about the War and "them bleedin' 'Uns!" In the rear of the place, the sharp click of billiard balls could be heard; in the parlor off to the right, women's

voices laughed and cursed, sometimes in a painful wail—
" 'E's gone—the 'Uns got 'im!" Sadness, gayety, ribaldry
—this combination dance-academy-pub was just such a
place. How happy and carefree was this mob of young
men, most of whom very shortly would be floating in the
sea or lying dead in Flanders! Now intermission is over
and it is old Harry Graves's voice sounding the return
upstairs to the dance: "Gentlemen, please take your
partners for. . . ."

CHAPTER
TWENTY-FIVE

I LOAFED for some time after this, in general self-indulgence, and attended the Daulby Hall, a cheap dance hall at the top of London Road and Daulby Street. Once I dropped in at the barracks. It was as I had been told by my mother—the elegant Pattersons emerging slowly but surely from the economic morass; the German Hazemans, since Lizzie's death despised by the Clan; the Murrays salting it away; Lonnigan and my grandmother still at it. Outside the barracks the Roches, with father and mother dead, were in a state of confusion. It cost the returning sailorman ten pints of ale on that visit: I never made a second one.

One afternoon, by arrangement, I met Jackie Sanchez and we went in search of a docker's hook and a Union card—for me. I had partly succumbed to my mother's insistence that I leave the sea until the war stopped. This, combined with the stories of the immense pay-envelopes paid to dockers and my newly awakened interest in the dance, had been the deciding influence. I couldn't very well dance at sea; therefore, to stay ashore, I must look toward the docks. The hook we obtained from Harris's pawnshop; the Union button from the Docker's Union. Then a week later I bought a truss to support me; I had strained myself hauling huge bales of cotton out of a ship. We were on equal terms now, for Jackie had definitely ruptured himself sometime previous.

One night, while the rain pounded outside in the alley and all three of us huddled at home in front of the fire drinking tea, Mrs. Tar, very drunk, rapped on the door and, peering in, whispered fearfully:

"Mrs. O'Mara, I think the 'Shelterin' 'ome' lad's outside after you."

My mother rose and said, "Well, I'm workin' and I'm not afraid of the Shelterin' 'ome lady! I'll go out and see her." So my mother went out, leaving us wonderingly by the fire, and presently returned with a very aristocratic-looking lady staring at us and everything, it seemed, down her nose. She was my father's sister (*our aunt!* Alice and I thrilled together) and she was here to inform us that our father's brother (we'd never heard of nor seen him) had died intestate and that if we'd take this letter and show it to the eminent Mr. Thomas, Hamlington Square, Birkenhead, solicitor, the next morning, we'd get our legal share of our uncle's *estate*.

"I'm giving you the letter," she said, "because we can't trust James. But you'd better take him along with you."

Then the door opened and my father stood there, very abject. Instantly we realized the subtlety of our elegant relative and her trickery—she had come around to pave the way for his getting back with us. But he was sober and my mother, her face suddenly pale, said nothing as he sat down; and the elegant lady continued to talk. Every time she would hint about us getting together again, however, my mother would shake her head dubiously and I know she must have been suffering terribly, because here apparently right in front of her was the realization of the dream that had first made her marry my father— the legacy! True, it was not the legacy he had hinted about in his brief courtship days, for that was his mother's and when she died she had never even mentioned him. The reason he was being consulted at all in this legacy was on account of the unhappy fact that there was no will—a misfortune quite obvious from my superior aunt's every gesture.

My mother listened, and when the lady's obvious contempt for her brother and her desire to foist him upon us once again showed itself, my mother ended the proceedings by consenting to accompany my father over to Birkenhead on the morrow but only to protect his interest. (I think mother had a feeling she could cop a pound or two for herself.) But his rejoining us—that was out. Then, as my father apishly tried to persuade his sister to speak up for him and even offered to take the stump in his own behalf, my mother opened the door wide. She would accompany him over the water on the morrow and see that he got his rightful share of his brother's legacy—but there was to be no reunion! Never!

He left the letter with us and slunk off crying. My sister Alice said very proudly to the stately lady, "Good-by, Auntie," only to be ignored as the lady swept outside to her taxi. Later, we scrutinized every character on the envelope of that imposing introduction to the Birkenhead solicitor and I think all of us went to sleep that night dreaming of riches—especially mother who, no doubt, was wondering whether or not to gamble anew.

So the next day we all got dressed up and took turns washing in the bucket and reported down the street a little fearfully to the Dead House. "Jimmy's up in his room; go on up," said Mrs. Harris above the screeching of Emma's voice and the maestro's violin.

"No," said my mother. "Tell him we're here. We'll wait for him."

"Isn't it wonderful to fall in luck like Jimmy—getting that legacy?"

"Yes," said my mother, knowing as we did that my father with his usual loquaciousness had already spread the news around the neighborhood. "He'll never be sober now."

Presently my father came down the steps in the dirtiest white moleskins I had ever seen him in, but with his boots, as always, nicely polished. He kissed both of us children, but when he attempted to kiss mother she drew away. He said nothing to this and we struck off down the street for the overhead railway. Down at the corner of the Dock Road he hesitated outside Gordon's pub and suggested amiably to my mother that she go in. But here Alice, suspecting as I did a subtle plot, objected (if the authorities heard of intimacy between them, the separation order was revoked) and my father's eyes flashed angrily. We waited outside and presently he came out, wiping his lips and filling his clay pipe, and in a little while we were seated on the overhead railway speeding toward the Landing Stage and the boat to Birkenhead.

Solicitor Thomas's office in Hamlington Square was in a very select section, the parlor of a very genteel home; and I think three of us had slight heart palpitation when the eminent solicitor faced us. My father, however, with his usual obtuseness, wasn't a bit abashed and as this Birkenhead was his boyhood playground he must, of course, wax sloppishly sentimental. But Mr. Thomas was in no mood for sentiment and, after giving my mother and her two children the usual look of pity and contempt, immediately got down to business. It seemed he was desirous of getting rid of us as soon as possible and made no bones about it. After opening and reading the letter handed to him by my mother, he began questioning my father, at the same time making a notation on a big legal document he had gotten from a cupboard. The catechism went on, with my father answering most of the time "Yes,"; the questions had to do with whether or not he was a rightful heir. It was here I heard for the first time the vastness of my father's family.

"Are you James O'Mara?"

"Yes."

"Are you the brother of Cornelius O'Mara?"

"Yes."

"Are you the brother?" and so on, naming many brothers and sisters, to Alice's keen pride and joy.

Then came the reading of the division according to law, and it was here my poor mother's face dropped. All my father was to receive was five pounds. Standing there listening to the solicitor droning away, I knew from my mother's blank expression that another mirage had vanished. *This* was the legacy for which she had sacrificed her life! Then the solicitor handed my father the five pounds and led us all quickly to the door.

I have only the haziest recollections of my father's antics that day with the remainder of the five pounds. My mother got nothing and Alice and I got nothing. But my mother was offered (very loudly in the middle of the street with a goodly audience), "Two bloody quid, if you'll come back an' behave yourself, like a *white woman,* not like a bloody slummy Molloy!"

On the boat my mother tried to temporize with my father to get some of the money from him, but with his usual cunning not a penny did he give her, knowing full well, I think, of her determination never again to live with him. Alice wanted to get away from him but my mother, knowing he was going to squander the whole thing, hung on to him. Along the Dock Road we straggled, with my father placing one of the gold sovereigns in his eye like a monocle and all the docker bums who knew him following us in droves and singing his praises as he returned proudly: "This is only *one* of them you see in me eye!" Finally, nearing Bridgewater Street, we became tangled in the mob and my mother gave up in disgust, threw a few quiet curses at him, and led us away, leaving him with the mob that followed him inside Gordon's pub. Two days later he was pawning his hook and button in Harris's pawnshop for sixpence.

CHAPTER
TWENTY-SIX

MY MOTHER'S insistence that I stay ashore prevailed, and for the next twelve months I was dock laborer, teamster, sign-painter, and dance man at the Daulby Dance Hall. And what was true of me, was true of the rest of the gang, with the exception of comedian Freddie Seegar, who fell down rather badly in the matter of work. Yet, despite our youthful gayety, sadness and tragedy were in the air. There was hardly a door in our neighborhood without a crêpe, particularly in the "Dardanelles"—not as yet christened that until the tragic Turkish venture. The streets were pitch black, and though the *Echo* and *Express* tried editorially to bolster the people's courage, the terrible lists of killed, wounded and missing in the papers could mean only one thing—we were getting licked. The unthinkable was happening: Britain was getting licked.

Then a bright star was shut out. One evening, on my way to the Daulby Hall, a medley of newsboy shouts sounded behind me. Unable to believe my ears I listened again "Lord Kitchener dead!" "Death of Lord Kitchener!" The paper told the tragic story: he'd been blown up in the S. S. *Hampshire* while en route to bolster totter-ing Russia! Crowds gathered around, among whom were many of my mates, some half drunken women and sooty dockers, all staring blankly at each other. Kitchener of Khartoum; the Kitchener of the glass eye, who abjured politics, rebuked Princes, feared God, avoided women— this legendary figure was a sort of god among the slummies. Now *he* was gone!

Everything seemed tinged with tragedy that sorrowful night. I ran into Mrs. Fox (Freddie's mother) coming out of Mrs. Mallin's pub, crying drunkenly. Kitchener dead? Had I heard of *Mr. Fox's* death in France that morning? No, I hadn't. I passed on. Next it was quiet Mrs. Hasty, who used to share our shack in Pitt Street, drying her eyes as she came up Nelson Street. Had I heard of Mr. Hasty's death in France? Willy Hasty's death— amiable Willy Hasty, who had given me the pennies and saved my mother many a beating? I passed on. Next it was Mrs. Thomas telling of Peter's death. Husbands, fathers, sons—that night was awful in such revelations. Mr. Fox, Mr. Hasty, Peter Thomas—I could still see them as they had swirled off but a short time before, look-ing very clumsy in their new khaki, down to the Lime-Street Station. Now they were dead: they would never return to our neighborhood.

Drama came in spurts like that—usually four or five neighborhood "casualties" reported at the same time. The next day a fellow I knew as "Bucko" was taken from hiding down on Frederick Street and was shot. He had come home from France on leave sometime previous and had decided not to go back. But they discovered him, thanks to his wife whom he used to beat and who now gave him away. Our milkwoman's son, John Heapy, a very timid boy, when notified he'd have to join up, took poison and died in his mother's arms. Johnny Calvey came back that day with a "blighty wound" in his chest, and when he saw the blinds down for Peter Thomas's death next door to him, he very nearly fainted. Peter had bade him good-by a few days previous in France! Every pub parlor that night was a chamber of woes. Every dank "court" had its quota of crying, drunken women.

Then a few days later, the most startling news of all: ale, that happy escape, that Nirvanna of the slummies, was to be curtailed! More of that dirty, bloody Lloyd George, the food rationer! Barley, sugar, etc., needed for food, was to be limited among the brewers—three barrels of ale per pub per day. A new and stranger cry was soon to be heard—the barman's "Sold out! No more —sold out!" And in the next pub, the same. And the next. No ale!

One Saturday afternoon, Jackie Sanchez and I awaited the appearance of Johnny Mangan at the corner, to continue on to the football game in Sheil Park. A half hour later he joined us and said very quietly: "I can't go, mates—Ted McNally's dead." Gallant Ted, Johnny's brother-in-law, of the Connaught Rangers, dead! Then Johnny told us of the peculiar way his mother had come by the news. She and Ted's wife, Johnny's sister, were in St. James Picture house when a flash came on the screen: "If Mrs. McNally is here she's wanted at the manager's office." Fearful, they hurried out there, and the fatal War Office letter was handed them. Kitty went stark mad and tore her hair out, while Johnny's mother screamed and screamed. . . . It was from this disturbance he had run. . . . The football game was postponed that day.

The next day another War Office letter came to the Mangan house, now tragically quiet, this one insisting that either Johnny, who had now come of age, or his elder brother Frank, who was thirty, would have to join up on the morrow. Johnny volunteered gladly, but only after his choice of the Navy had won over his mother's insistence upon an army career. His job in Read's Tin Works was given up immediately—a resignation that reacted upon the future of the entire gang.

All of us were younger by months than Johnny, but the evening he confided to us his intentions, the desire to emulate him, despite age, became obvious. My cousin Berny and Johnny Ford wanted very much to be seen in the uniform of the Eighth Irish. Henry Roche, still a paradoxical Irishman, wanted the plaid kilts of the Liverpool Scottish, no less. The rest of us, it seemed, wanted the Merchant Marine, the Yankee suits and the big advance notes One thing was certain—shore jobs and at least the majority of us were definitely parted. The five dissenters, it seemed, were Jacko Oldham, Harold May, Frankie Roza, Joe Manassi and Freddie Seegar, particularly the last named who knew leaving home and working were synonymous terms. An argument started and terminated with Harold's averring that "Anyone who wants to join up, go ahead. . . . I ain't made up my mind yet."

"Nor me, either!" seconded Joe beside him.

However, if these two dancing men hadn't made up their minds, someone else had done it for them. We were, at that moment, in the middle of a game of pitch and toss, with that very unreliable dowser Freddie Seegar at the corner. Around through the fog charged our old nemesis, Aeroplane Joe, blowing his whistle for all his worth, and when the excitement died down, his catch, strangely enough, consisted of Joe and Harold.

After he had taken their names and addresses and departed and we had all assembled again, the two dissenters changed their minds and decided that perhaps a short trip, say on one of the Cunard boats, might be very helpful—this after I had lied to them about the success I had had with the Law when on the *Restitution*. Indeed, before we disbanded that night, it was decided that all those intending to join the Army and Navy or to go to sea should chuck their shore jobs right then and report early tomorrow morning on the corner for concerted action.

The following morning, Joe, Harold and I struck out from the corner and saw Johnny Mangan down to Cannon Place, leaving him there to sign up with the Royal Navy. The rest of the gang hadn't shown up as scheduled and though we were pretty nearly certain (with the possible exception of Jacko Oldham, Frankie Roza and Freddie Seegar) that they hadn't suffered a change of mind, we were much too impatient to wait for them. The plan had been to accompany Johnny Ford, Henry Roche and my cousin Berny down to the Army Recruiting Office, then to continue on with Johnny Mangan to Cannon Place—the remainder then to cast about for a Merchant Ship. With Johnny now safely inside the Navy Station, the three of us slouched over to the Sailors' Home.

It was something to have these two leading members

of the gang look up to me for the maritime advice that was to scotch Aeroplane Joe's knavery, and as they followed me in among my fellow sailormen I felt very important indeed. We did not stay long, however, in the bustle and excitement. Any ship appealed to me, but Joe and Harold wanted only a short trip—just long enough to be away when the summons fell due and to have the Court (as I had mislead them to believe) strike it off the docket the moment it learned of the warrior status of the defendants. Someone mentioned that the "Lusy" (*Lusitania*) had just gotten in that morning. That gave my mates an idea —let the three of us go down to the Langdon Dock and breast the boatswain before the Lusy signed on. I didn't want to go, but they insisted and presently we set off at a slow gallop for the North End Docks.

Tramcars, wagons, floats—between these three methods of transportation, we finally got to the Langdon, and there, as predicted at the Home, was the big greyhound, just tied up and with the long line of sea bags standing around the crew's forecastle. As we clambered aboard, I knew there was to be no *Lusitania* for me. I liked the old scows that plowed leisurely through the ocean, touching strange places and—what was of more importance—staying there long enough to get to know something about them. A beautiful ship certainly, bespeaking, whenever one looked, lean strength. But not for your sailorman! In my mind, as we walked the long clean deck toward the boatswain's quarters, I thought of the old four-masted barques that used to tie up in the Queen's Dock and up whose masts I used to shin so happily—they were the ships! This gigantic contraption so strong, so beautiful, so amazing—this was no ship; it was a floating hotel. Perhaps it was the rumbling of winches and the numerous artisans scrambling all over her that gave me this hotel impression; cutting through the seas with battened hatches undoubtedly she would make an impressive sight.

I did not need to ask Joe and Harold their reaction to the biggest ship they'd ever seen; their glowing eyes told me the story As we ducked through the companionway leading to the boatswain's room, I hesitated and let my two mates shove through with the crowd of sailormen already there seeking jobs and friends home with the pay-off. Then, when they were lost among the crowded alleyway, I turned around and quickly retraced my steps toward the Sailors' Home. I wanted a smaller boat; a longer trip. It wouldn't be hard finding excuses at the corner that night. I could say I had missed my pals in the crowd on the boat. If they wanted the *Lusitania*, there it was for them—not for me. I did not learn until much later that they did not ship aboard the *Lusitania*.

At the Flag of All Nations I lined up boldly in front of the bar. "A pint!"

The barman looked at me skeptically. "How old are you?"

"Nineteen," I lied, and he served me, confident, I believe, that this was my first public pint.

A few minutes later, in pretty much the same manner that I had signed on the *Restitution*, I obtained an Ordinary Seaman's berth on the *Lowtyne*. What the *Lowtyne* was I neither knew nor cared. All I did know was that we were going to Salonika, Greece (then expected to come in with the Triple Entente) with "munitions;" that

she had the same type crew as the *Restitution;* that she
sailed that night from the Herculanean Dock. This I didn't
like, for at one stroke it took away all the thrill of spending the magic advance note. . . . Still, it was a ship, obviously from the size of her crew a tramp, and Salonika
sounded romantic. . . .

Before taking my advance note home, I dropped into
the Spanish boarding house to tell Jackie the good news.
But Mrs Sanchez, who spoke but little English, waved
me away No, Quantio wasn't home. "Him and other
boys . . . gone . . . corner . . . gone." At the corner I
found them all except Mickey and they had just as
portentous news to tell me as I had to tell them.
Johnny Ford and my cousin Berny had joined the Eighth
Irish; Henry Roche had joined the Liverpool Scottish;
Johnny Mangan was now in the Royal Navy. The rest of
the gang apologetically decided to stay at their respective
mill tasks until they could reduce parental opposition.
This was a satisfactory explanation, for we knew, with
most of us under age, if a zealous parent so decided he
could get us out of the service after we'd lied to get in.
Those who had joined up, with the exception of Johnny
Mangan, had apparently overcome parental objection. As
a matter of fact, I think the stay-at-homers secretly envied our importance. Frankie Roza got out his concertina
and gave us those tunes he knew best. Then came the chips
and fish and a few pints from Walker's up the street.
Finally I had to leave, for the time was passing quickly
and I had to pack my sea-bag and be aboard the *Lowtyne* before midnight. Yet I did not leave before making
it clear to Freddie Seegar to tell Harold and Joe, when

they got back to the corner, that my missing them on the *Lusitania* had been quite accidental.

My mother and Alice tried to take this sudden going away to sea as stoically as everything else that had happened to them. My poor mother was terror-stricken, of course. Though I paid scant attention to the newspaper headline "Only sixty ships torpedoed this week" it was a grim reality with her. I tried to offset her fears by telling her how Johnny Mangan had joined the Navy and how Johnny Ford, Henry Roche and my cousin Berny had joined the Army. But it was with me she was concerned, and before anything else was done I had to go to Father Ryan in St. Vincent's chapel and make my confession. She saw to it that I did this, accompanying me to the church, and then returned with me for bacon and eggs and the packing of my bag.

My mother never gives up hope. As the late hour approached and she was helping fill my sea-bag, she kept up an incessant barrage of objections to my going away, clear up to the point where, in order to get out of the house at all, I had to promise that, if the *Lowtyne* turned out to be a ship like the *Restitution,* I wouldn't go aboard. "To hell with the advance note!" she said. "They'll be here when you're dead and gone. . . . Go along with him, Alice, and *see* that he comes back. . . ."

The bag was hoisted on my shoulder as Alice put on her shawl; there were many frenzied kisses and we were off, scurrying down the street in the darkness. On Harris's steps sat my father, in his cups, with the Midden Picker and Mrs. Harris in like condition.

"Better kiss daddy good-by," warned dutiful Alice, and I did.

"Good-by, dad, I'm going to sea," I said. Had I a bob for the Poor Auld Man? I gave it to him and, to offset any further sentimentalism, I pushed off down the street. Presently we were on the overhead railway, droning slowly southward to the Herculanean Dock.

It is a curious thing that this sister, whom I love intensely, is never at ease with me, nor am I with her. We, who have endured so much together, are antithetical natures. So we sat in silence, I looking out at the rain showering the docks while she just sat and stared, no doubt cogitating on how best to fulfill her mother's request to *see* that I returned home. Presently, she started adducing reasons why I shouldn't go through with this thing—very naïve and humorous. Then she said nothing, knowing my mind was made up. So into the darkened gate at the Herculanean Dock we trudged and were intercepted by the sleepy bobby. What ship? The *Lowtyne*. He pointed away down in the rainy darkness and as Alice started off with me, he stepped between us. I could go, but not the girl, for the Country was at war.

"But he's not going!" said Alice stupidly. "He's coming back!"

The bobby looked perplexed; then suggested that she await me at the gate. Alice kissed me frenziedly, confident now that her last hope was blasted. "Timmy," she pleaded, "please don't go on that ship now, will you?"

"I must!" I insisted. She stared at me hopelessly; we kissed again; I left her. . . .

A hulk of a ship, not unlike the *Restitution*, loomed

to the right and the name was there on her starboard bow
—*Lowtyne*. She was loaded to the scuppers. Up the rickety ladder I staggered and on across the well-deck toward
the forecastle. On the forecastle-head I noticed a group
of shadowy drunken men awkwardly fiddling with ropes
and the windlass in the darkness, and on the bridge there
was a like activity. The stink of the forecastle sickened
me. The windlass rumbled out overhead and the fumbling
with ropes increased. Across the hall in the fireman's forecastle came the usual stifled drunken yawns and curses.
I had to get out into the air, and as I came out upon the
well-deck again, I saw that the companionway lantern
amidships had been taken aboard and that the ladder was
rising from the quay and—we were moving from the dock.
Poor Alice—we were heading out to sea!

(Later I learned she had waited patiently, hopefully,
outside in the rain, until the bobby came out and told her
the *Lowtyne* had pulled out an hour ago. She must go
home, he told her, and as the overhead railway had
stopped she'd have to run for it. That whole four miles
of Dock Road she galloped, stopped, galloped some more,
with the Coolies, Negroes and other nocturnal slummies
assuming her a rapable alley waif. And when my mother,
who, in alarm, had come out to the Dock Road seeking
both of us, met her, she fainted dead away. Little stoic, it
had been just a bit too much for her.)

CHAPTER
TWENTY-SEVEN

THE only difference between the *Lowtyne* and the other ships I had been on was the addition of multi-colored camouflage paint, now used to befuddle the submarines. But in everything else she was the *Restitution* all over again, especially as regarded the crew The "Black Crowd" was made up almost exclusively from Scotland Road and, of course, so soon as we had cleared dock a terrible brawl broke out. In our forecastle things were a bit more peaceful; the members of the crew, too far gone to "turn-to," were snoring drunkenly in their bunks.

I hadn't been asked on deck, and I didn't volunteer to go. Through the portholes I saw a darkened ship occasionally slide by or a smaller tug puffing away; the feet rumbling overhead stumbled and then there were curses. Sometimes the half-drunken boatswain would give an order and be answered with an obedient, "Aye, aye, sir!" and sometimes, when his command would be a little too peremptory, the answer would be a sullenly quiet, "Ah, go an' . . . yourself!"

I picked out an empty bunk and threw my sea-bag into

it. We were going to Greece, but where was that? I tried to recall my geography under Mr. McGinnis. There was Australia, Canada, New Zealand, Africa—but no Greece; I couldn't quite place that as part of the Empire. I was still in my meditations when the rumble of feet overhead ceased and the forecastle quickly filled—boatswain, A. B.'s, ordinary seamen and behind them all, not too sober himself, the Chief Mate checking on his crew. They were all there except one A. B.

"He's in my room, Mr. Mate," vouchsafed the boatswain. "He'll be all right tomorrow."

Then the mate went out and the boatswain took charge. He was a big, swarthy fellow, an Anglicized Russian, I think, and he turned his attention to us ordinary seamen first. There were three of us: two stocky boys from Manchester making their second trip, and myself. He read out their names, Dallas and Thomson, I believe. Then, to show off before the A. B.'s who were drunkenly settling into their bunks, he had at us apropos our seamanship. How many of us could box the compass? Tie a bowlin'? Splice rope—eye, short, and long splice? And wire splice —how many could do that? What he was trying to do, he confided when he saw the painful nature of our smiles, was pick out the greenest boy for the sailor's mess. I kept quiet about my experience on the *Caledonia*, and the task fell to the boy named Dallas. Then he took the names of the A. B.'s, a polyglot gang of six, and apportioned the watches, after which he told us three important items: despite the way she looked the *Lowtyne* fed good; she was on her way to Cardigan Bay to pick up a convoy; and "if we get it with all these shells we have aboard, we might as well say our prayers." This last was no news among the older men who, from experience with torpedoes, seldom missed a trick concerning the ship's cargo.

Then the cook and his assistant came in and put a bottle of whisky on the table and talked about the cook's boy over in France with the Black Watch, almost precipitating an argument as to the relative fighting merits of the Scotch and the Irish. A compromise was reached by roundly condemning the English. And so it went, on and on through the night, talking mostly of non-maritime things, of the different boarding houses, of the various whores, their sicknesses, capacities and ingenuities. Presently, one by one the men turned in to their bunks to snatch a little rest before going on deck to relieve their mates, now suffering drunkenly at their routine tasks. The boatswain left; the cook left; the day A. B., appointed lamp-trimmer by the boatswain, filled the lamp with oil and staggered into his bunk. The two Manchester boys, obviously mates, were holding colloquy up forward as I opened my sea-bag and started to arrange my bunk.

This was the task that always made my mind revert to my mother. Invariably when opening the sea-bag I looked forward to finding some little surprise meant for me, and this time, along with the inevitable rosary, there was a big choice piece of Cooper's candy marzipan. Then out came my sea-boots, the heavy oilskins and south-wester and the dungarees and mattress. I was very tired then and, after getting these out, I lay down on top of the cumbersome straw mattress that had filled one half of my bag and fell into a sound sleep.

I was awakened in the darkness by the rough hand of

one of the A. B.'s "One bell!" he whispered hoarsely, the stink of his drunken breath repulsing me. I had been dreaming of my earlier life and a fight was in progress—the sudden wakening made me sit up and stare straight at the man. "One bell!" the man commanded again, wondering at the stare I was giving him. "What the bleedin' 'ells up with you?"

Then it came to me—I had been asleep almost three hours and it was now quarter of four in the morning and my turn on watch. The A. B.'s of the watch were growling out of their bunks, and as I hurriedly changed from my American tailored suit to the dungarees, I wondered where I was to fit in. Two A. B.'s and I composed the port watch. One of them, noticing my hesitancy, growled to me: "You on this watch, kid?"

"Yes," I answered.

"Well, hereafter, see that you got some Java on that table instead of sittin' on your. . . ."

I rose willingly, but he demurred:

"It's too bloody late now." The twin bells started ringing out from the forecastle head.

"There's eight bells. Go ahead there and take the first lookout." The other fellow was already scurrying up to the pilot house to relieve the wheel, and quickly I followed him. In the well-deck I became confused as to where the lookout was being kept; then a drunken voice came from the forecastle head:

"Up here, kid, up here—and let me get down to that bleedin' bunk!"

I quickly walked up the steel ladder, but not quite as quickly as the older man I relieved walked down it. "All's well!" he growled to the officer on the bridge as he staggered uncertainly down the ladder and disappeared into the forecastle.

My first actual lookout! I knew from my experience on the *Restitution* all about the technique of the thing, but this was the first time the actual responsibility was mine. We were hugging the coast and searchlights were flashing constantly; it all seemed to me pretty much like the realization of a dream—this fantastically painted ship gliding along through the night with the coast on both sides of us. Intermittent searchlights spread faint paths of gold across our bows. The ship itself was in darkness, save for a dim light emanating from the chute for ashes; the only sound was the grating noise of the ashes being dumped overboard. A dwarf-like figure, in singlet and biting a sweat rag, occasionally moved across the well-deck, and up on the bridge the head of the officer on watch showed over the canvas awning, disappeared, then showed again as he did his sentry walk.

We were moving very slowly and deep in the water; as I turned and looked aft, the movement seemed almost slower. One time, stopping in my sentry walk, staring down into the black water and engrossed in some fantastic dream, I was brought back to reality by the shrill whistle from the bridge and the mate's peremptory challenge: "Lookout! Are you falling asleep?" Then the muffled bell from the bridge would sound and I would leap to the place behind the windlass and repeat the ringing. One time, after ringing seven bells, the mate again admonished me: "Not too loud there, sonny! You want us to get it?"—"it" meaning a torpedo.

Then came my relief—the gruff A. B. who had spoken to me about the coffee business—but, having imbibed his coffee, in a different mood now. An Irish Cockney, he had been boarding in Bob Acte's sailor's house some time and he knew most of the slummy people with whom I had been raised. He didn't know my father, however, and that was a relief. This *Lowtyne* was the lousiest bloody scow he'd ever been on, and he only signed on her because they were after him for skipping the *Adriatic*. I asked him where Salonika was, and he answered "Somewhere up the Meddy—I've been there before, but it's been a long time ago. I know the bloody place—I got a blue-ball (venereal term) there once. Takes about three weeks in this tub—if we get there. . . . All right, kid, go on down the galley and get a cup of Java."

I left him and went amidships to the galley, but this atrocious mixture of burnt bread and chickory was a little too much for my stomach, and I left it there. This was the "easy" end of the watch—attending to the officer's whistle. If there was no whistle, there was nothing to do but loaf. Presently, however, the whistle sounded and I hurried up on the bridge. The mate was a squat man with a paunch and he had the air of a scholar surfeited with books. Without looking at me he said: "Son, after you've had your own coffee, always come up here and ask the officer on watch if he'd like his."

I nodded, and he said again without looking at me: "Now do as I told you—ask me."

"Do you want any coffee, sir?"

"Yes." Then he walked to the pilot house and brought out a cup and handed it to me along with a key for the pantry. "Just put one teaspoonful of sugar in it and if there's a sandwich there bring it up." Then he left me again without noticing me and continued with his walk.

Down on the pantry, the plates and other things were so very nice and clean that I helped myself to a cup of coffee (vastly different from that which I tasted in the galley) and ate one of the many sandwiches left on the plate by the steward. The mate's tone of voice had been very severe; but nevertheless I liked it. It smacked of authority and intelligence—a happy contrast to that drunken recklessness of the forecastle. With such a man as the mate aboard, one felt there was someone with intelligence to whom to appeal in a crisis. . . . A little while after serving him his coffee the starboard watch relieved us and once again I chucked myself on top of the straw mattress to dream of Alice waiting outside the Herculanean Dock, my mother, Salonika, and my mates.

We reached Cardigan Bay (I think this was it) the following day and joined about a dozen other camouflage-painted ships, of like size and tonnage, already anchored there. About a half-dozen destroyers stood like specks on the water at the mouth of the bay. Our anchor rumbled out and once again everything was silence. The crew were sober by now and intensely industrious, as is the case with most sailormen after a protracted drunk. Wash lines were being strung around the forecastle head and clothes washed out in buckets. The firemen and trimmers off watch sat on the hatches watching the sailors working and kidding with those they knew. The boatswain, stern and peremptory, was a much changed man as was the cook, who now stayed strictly amidships with the "quality." Our watch was on deck with the day men, at the time, battening down the hatches more securely, and the boatswain, under the observing eyes of the mate and captain (they looked like twins), was making himself very officious.

I don't know why it was nor how it was, but all that morning as we worked around the deck the figures of Joe Manassi and Harold May were constantly in my mind, seeming to beseech me not to go away to sea. This was superstition pure and simple and came, I suppose, from the fact I had imagined—quite wrongly—that they had missed getting a ship and I had succeeded. Nevertheless, rationalize as I would, the thing had persisted clear up until the convoy was completed and the signal from the destroyers and the answer of the ship's whistle told of our leaving. I was dispatched down the "chain-locker" to help in the back-breaking task of "stowing away" the anchor chain as it rumbled in slowly and jerkily from the windlass up above. When, perspiring, I came back on deck we had cleared the harbor and were out at sea.

I stood on deck amazed at what I saw, for this was the first "convoy" I had witnessed proceeding to sea. Twenty-odd ships, in four lines of five ships, were steaming slowly ahead at a designated speed. Around us swirled the protecting destroyers. Ours had the left outside front position—the idea being to keep the more expensive cargoes in the middle of the convoy and in appreciably less danger from torpedoes. The procedure, I knew from maritime conversation, was to continue this way until the Danger Zone was past, then to disperse and go our separate ways—the Houston boat on our right, for instance, to South America and ourselves to Greece. When those swirling destroyers left us they hung around there and picked up an incoming convoy or proceeded at a radioed order to a spot where one would be picked up.

Outside the harbor, the sea became very choppy; the clouds gathered and it rained hard. When the boatswain came up to me at five o'clock and indicated that so far as "work" was concerned the day was ended, I was doing all I could to hold on the deck, the weather had become so boisterous. I fumbled along the passageway into the forecastle, there to eat and await my next lookout. I had seen the gruff A. B., who had berated me about the coffee, ascending the rigging. Up, up he went, clear up to the topmast crow's nest, binoculars by his side—the topmast lookout for submarines. At six o'clock I would be up there!

At supper seasickness gripped me and I felt that I must get outside of the stuffy forecastle, regardless of the tempest. As I stumbled along the passageway toward the now closed passageway door, the ghostly figures of the pals I had left on the *Lusitania* came before me, this time again admonishing me in no uncertain voice. Opening the iron door, I almost broke my hand, so great was the force of the wind; and as I stepped out on the wave-ridden welldeck, the officer on the bridge, snug in oilskins and southwester, observed me wonderingly. The sea was running high and wild and beautiful. I had never seen such vast waves and I had never heard the song of such a savage wind. The other ships in the convoy were tossing about and, like our ship, trying desperately to keep in line, while around and around, bobbing up and down, under the water and over it, encircled the racing destroyers. Every few minutes, one of them would blow a signal blast on its whistle, to be answered in turn by all the boats. Occasionally a fireman, watching his chance, would dart from the engine-room amidships along the well-deck to the forecastle, a grim, sickly smile on his face.

The wheel was relieved, and the big fellow, who had told of living in Bob Acte's boarding house, blustered through the well-deck and told me the mate said I better go inside the forecastle if I didn't want to be washed overboard. I nodded and paid no attention to him, my mind now torn between the seasickness and wondering how on earth I was going to get up to the crow's nest to relieve the lookout. Well, it *had* to be done.

I don't know yet how I got to the rigging, and the lofty ascent was an even more difficult task. Stop—hang-on—stop—hang-on. It continued thus to the cross-trees; from there up it seemed the mast was swaying almost to the snapping point. Then out on to the more fragile rope ladder and a wild swinging in a maddening arc. Sometimes the sea and the mast seemed to touch each other. Too awful to look below, it seemed the ocean touched my back, then swung me upward and outward. . . . I could see now the oilskins of the shadowy figure hanging inside the crow's nest, still doggedly peering through his glasses for subs! Up, up, abreast of him now and he helped me in, handed me the glasses quickly and descended as though it were no feat at all.

But I was so sick that all I could do was to collapse right inside the crow's nest. . . . If submarines were about in that swirling madness no one would have learned it from me! For two whole hours I lay there without once looking out at the sea, only rising to repeat the bells rung from the bridge. Then, presently, another figure loomed outside and shouted for my hand to help him get in. Cautiously I got out. It was a little easier going down than it was coming up.

When I reached the foot of the rigging a cry came from the bridge, but it was too late. A wave swept over the well-deck and I had to jump; another followed it and went over me, tossing me in the scuppers. I opened the forecastle door as best I could and stumbled through the darkness to the toilet.

Here I vomited and listened to the sea swirling at the bottom of the stool. Every few seconds the closed port-hole quivered as the sea hit it. I don't know how long I sat there but when I came out and again entered the fore-castle, the boatswain and third mate were in seeing that all the covers were on the portholes and advising the men about lighting matches.

"We'll be out of the danger zone in a couple of days," advised the youngish officer very unconvincingly, "then you can smoke as much as you want." They did not see me, and as I had no particular desire to see anyone just then, I crawled into my bunk in my wet clothes. Completely exhausted, I fell asleep while my watch mates huddled over their coffee and smoked.

Events now moved swiftly. I was awakened sometime in the middle of the night by a terrific impact and a terrible cry: *"All hands on deck! All hands on deck!"* This meant only one thing to us—we had been torpedoed! We'd *got it*! Only three of us were in the forecastle, and we did not wait for clothes or anything else but raced madly for the dark hallway and the deck. More shadowy figures joined us in the alleyway—the "down below" crowd. The ship was rolling terribly and outside the storm raged. The night was pitch black; the wind hissed; some brave soul on our bridge was giving the usual signal of the torpedoing—eight short blasts, I think, meaning, "we're torpedoed, look out for yourselves!"

Beyond in the darkness the sea was racing high and gleaming beautifully. From the well-deck one could see the stark outline of other ships racing madly away from us. Dull reverberations sounded—perhaps another ship had "got it"; maybe they were the guns of the racing destroyers. I stood in the well-deck petrified, while hazy figures swept around and about me. I noticed we had listed to port. We were going to plunge beneath the whirlpool. A wave surged aboard and hit me from the rear. From then on I remember nothing but rushing water, mad prayers, the figure of my mother and towers of water . . . and blackness.

Then my vision cleared. I was still in the scuppers of the well-deck with the night and the sea just the same and a paralyzing pain across my back. Our ship had listed away over, but we were still afloat and under our own steam. Shadowy figures still flitted about the deck, and to one of these I shouted for help. It was a fireman and he helped me into the forecastle. "What's up?" he asked. "I don't know." More terrified figures came into the forecastle, staring at each other and wondering. An engineer barged in—"You bleedin' cowards get back down the bloody fireroom!"

There was a grim silence and no one moved. The engineer roared: "Come on! Gawd blimey we're not sunk; let's get her back into the harbor!" Then the mate came down—no one knew precisely what had happened—the *Lowtyne* was still afloat; listing, but afloat. The mate thought the cargo had shifted and we hadn't been torpedoed, and he offered as proof the fact that no submarine could possibly live in this storm. But we had to keep her nose to that gale—or else!

Presently all hands were out doing anything asked of them. All I could do was lie down; something had cracked down to the right of my back. I lay in the nearest bunk wondering and hoping and thinking. I couldn't stay here and die like that. I staggered out through the forecastle doorway and again looked at the wild sea. Hope surged in my breast when I saw human activity on the bridge and the smoke going the opposite way from that I last saw. We were alone—the convoy, thinking us torpedoed, had left us. But we were heading back to harbor, listing pretty badly but groaning ahead under our own steam. And still afloat!

CHAPTER
TWENTY-EIGHT

WE GOT back to Cardigan Bay all right and here ended my voyage on the *Lowtyne*. The mate's theory about the cargo moving turned out to be right. The storm had shaken many of the boxes of shells and now they would have to be righted. I was taken off in a boat, examined by a doctor and put in a hospital for X-ray examination. Three ribs were found fractured. Two weeks later, I was on my way home.

A curious thing happened here. From the hospital in Wales I had written home to my mother telling her to expect me at any time, but the letter, through the chaos of war, had not been delivered. What had been delivered, however, was the news in the paper that the *Lowtyne* had gone down, torpedoed, with all hands—a fact after she put to sea the second time. Later, my mother received a government letter stating that I was all right and en route home. They didn't know which to believe—the paper or the government letter. . . . All this was disclosed to me breathlessly when I got home.

Every few minutes Alice and mother would stare at me

as though looking at a man suddenly come back from the dead. "See," vouchsafed my mother, "it was your Scapular that saved you!"

"And I prayed for him, too," Alice would say breathlessly.

I was thinking of the intelligent mate and his coffee and the two ordinary seamen and the other jetsam floating on the sea. It seemed so strange and swift that I couldn't think coherently. They showed me in the *Echo* the lists of ships torpedoed, pointing to the *Lowtyne,* but I pushed it away.

"I hate to think of it—and them," I said.

Mother felt my hands and stared at me. "You're sure your ribs are all right?" she asked.

"Sure," I said, shrugging my shoulders. "Why look at me like that. Everything's all right, isn't it?"

Then Alice stopped pouring out the tea and exchanged looks with my mother. Something was wrong, I could see, and I asked the nature of it. Neither spoke and this time, suspecting something the matter with my father, I sought an explanation.

"It's your mates," said my mother, her face paling quickly.

"My mates?"

My mother sat down ond her face got very white. "Johnny Mangan was blown up just two hours after he left the Queen's down the street—on a destroyer."

"And Harold May and Joe Manassi," added Alice tensely. "They drowned too."

Once again I was back in the forecastle of the ill-fated *Lowtyne,* the strange vision in front of me. I gripped my mother's arm and she nodded in affirmation. "That dirty Aeroplane Joe!" she muttered. "He summoned them, like you, and they ran away and got a Harrison boat—the day after you left. It was torpedoed; they went down with her."

A swift, benumbing sense of guilt swept through me. There came a knock on the door, and Alice, fearing it my father, asked: "Who is it?"

"Berny."

It was my cousin Bernard, come in to see how I was and also to let me see how wonderful he looked in his new khaki suit of the Eighth Liverpool Irish. He looked very pale and young, but the Liverpool Irish air of braggadocio was there very strong. He shook hands with me. "Wasn't he bloody lucky, Auntie Polly?"

"Yes," replied my mother. "I was just tellin' him about your mates. You know more about it—tell him. Tell him about Mrs. Mangan."

Then Berny told of leaving Johnny at the Queen's Dock at three o'clock the day the other was assigned to a destroyer and how, two hours later, it was blown to pieces in the Channel (torpedo or mine it was never ascertained), going down with all hands. (He said this as though it were a mere nothing.) Then came a poignant part; At eight o'clock the next night, Johnny's elder brother, Frank, sitting alone in the house, got the government message. Fearful for his mother's sanity, he kept the news from her for a week, during which time his strange behavior made Mrs. Mangan think that the neighbors were at him again for not joining up with his younger brother.

Then one day Mrs. Tully came to the door and said to Mrs. Mangan: "Wasn't that awful about your lad, Johnny?" Frank heard this and pulled his mother indoors, where, after trying to convince his mother that Johnny was only hurt and in a hospital, he finally had to admit that he was drowned.

"She carried on like Hell," concluded Berny in matter-of-fact, mannish spirit.

"Tell Tim about Joe and Harold," said my mother, eager to throw a sea scare into me for all time. "And how Joe went back for his sea-boots. Poor Mrs. Manassi! She was half-cracked before this; now I know she's hopeless."

Then Berny, in the same objective tone, related how Joe and Harold had shipped on a Harrison boat—to get away from Aeroplane Joe—and how they had been torpedoed the second day out. "A trimmer who lives in Gerard Street said Joe could have been saved if he wouldn't have gone back for his new sea-boots. . . . He was in Joe's life-boat. They were all saved in that life-boat. . . ."

Aeroplane Joe and his summons—myself assisting Joe and Harold to get a ship—their outstretched hands to me on the *Lowtyne*—they were dead now—it all seemed too strange! Berny was looking at his new khaki suit in the glass. "I left Harold and Joe in the Lusy—that's the last I saw of them. . . . It seems so funny. . . ." I wouldn't tell them of the mirage on the *Lowtyne*—such things often led my mother into protracted drinking.

Berny was leaving with his regiment for France the following morning and wanted to know if I could accompany him to the Lime Street Station. I wanted to go,

but my mother excused me. "His back's still weak, Berny
—after what he's been through. Next time, when you
come on leave maybe. . . ."

He kissed my mother and Alice good-by and shook
hands with me. My mother said something sentimental
about his always remembering his mother (her sister;
my Aunt Leisha), dispatched Alice upstairs for the Scapular I had worn on the *Lowtyne* and placed it under his
tunic and around his neck. He looked very uncomfortable
while this went on, but my mother, confident of its great
charm, was happy that he had it. "You're flesh of my
flesh and bone of my bone!" she muttered. "You're my
sister's son—poor Leisha!" She kissed him again and he
was off, a pale but cocky figure in his new khaki suit.

CHAPTER TWENTY-NINE

THERE was a new caller in our kitchen, a young soldier named Jorgensen, who boarded with his father down near the Dock Road. None of us knew anything about him, for he had enlisted in the Army at the outbreak of War straight from training school and had been preserved to this day. It seemed that one day while on leave he had met my sister and had visualized in her a respectable post-war wife.

A frail boy, he looked even more absurd in khaki than my cousin Berny. But he had a very pleasant disposition and it was easy to like him. I saw much of him during his two weeks' leave from France, and when I settled my accounts with the *Lowtyne's* agent, we did quite a bit of "supping up" in the pubs together—to Alice's deep chagrin. Most of it was on his money, for all I got from the *Lowtyne* trip was actual pay up to the time I landed in Liverpool—altogether about three pounds. I felt inwardly sorry for Austin, because I believed that Alice's early life would not make her an agreeable wife for him. I think I touched on this once, but he thought otherwise, and on the day before he left for France he got a tacit promise from my mother that Alice would accept him when and if he ever returned from France.

When he was gone, I felt rather alone, for our corner now, due to the deaths of Joe, Harold and Johnny and the departure of others for France had lost its charm. Jacko Oldham, Frankie Roza, Freddie Seegar, Jackie Sanchez, and myself were the actual members still at home. Mickey, "the kid" from the Working Boys' Home, had drifted away in the same mysterious manner that he had come among us. Perhaps he had gone off to the colonies, as so many of the Working Boy's Home lads do —no one seemed to know. Perhaps what was chiefly responsible for breaking up the gang was the fact that we were accepted around the neighborhood as "men"—in lieu of real men away at the War. The old codgers, cadging from us, encouraged this vanity. So that the only time we got together was at the Saturday afternoon "footy" game or the pitch and toss affair. For the remainder of the week, Jacko Oldham and Frankie Roza served their time in Davidson's Engineering Company in Grayson Street! Freddie Seegar, Jackie Sanchez and myself hung around the docks working whenever the whimsy struck us.

The dock catechism went something like this:

Foreman: "Will you go to work mate?"

Worker: "Naw."

Foreman: "Will you go to a wedding?"

The hoofs of fine English draught horses beat a continuous rumble on the Dock Road as they pulled wagon load after wagon load of merchandise and munitions to and from the ships. Winches ground out all night; flash-lights glared from their holds; men like Auntie Janie's husband, Mr. Murray, scarcely ever ceased working.

But further in town was deep darkness and gloom and tragedy, interspersed here and there with the glowing rapture in the eyes of sooty artisans now making more money than ever before. There were few Saturday night celebrations in the streets. Flukey Alley's Flukes, Sparling Street's Negroes, and the Chinamen of Pitt Street—even into these un-British sections tragedy and gloom had seeped, for many half-caste boys had lost their lives. It was the same up the Courts, where the tragic inroads of war were worse than anywhere else. "Wiped out" could be placed against most of the raggedy young manhood that, when war beckoned, had rushed eagerly from these cess-pools.

The Black Prince no longer paraded naked, but staggered through the streets, face eaten away with cancer. Sometimes I would stand at our door watching these hopeless creatures, scrawny children who had grown up exactly as they could have been expected to grow up—rowdies one and all, toughs or wrecks and duplicating the sordid, half-savage lives of their fathers and mothers. The money-lenders still lent their money and foistered their stinking fish upon the dupes. Mrs. Golding still picked her favorite *middens*, vowing now that the thing was traditional: "Me mother before me had these middens for years. . . . There's no loiterers allowed around *these*." A sooty couple named Bob and Leah (that's all they went by) took up where my father and mother had left off. Leah's husband had been killed in France and she married Bob with the government money the week after the news of his death. Then started another thirty years war—and they were still at it. Harris's pawnshop, despite the war affluence (which barely affected many slummies—their ritual being, earn so much, then loaf) was doing a bigger business than ever. I met Leah coming out of the Dead House one Saturday, very gay and tipsy, and on her way to procure the services of Mr. Levy, the cut-rate furniture dealer in Mill Street. "Timmy, I wonder 'ow much 'e'll give me for the sofa and two chairs? Oo! Then me and Bob'll 'ave to sleep on the bloody floor again. . . ."

I would watch the Black Prince's son, Jimmy, as he helped his mother chop chips; I mused on his life story more than the others because it was so like my own. His head used to shake continuously and suddenly, for no apparent reason, his eyes would dilate and his mouth froth and he would subside to the pavement in the grip of a fit—his father's handiwork undoubtedly. And there was a little half-caste harlot living in Sparling Street, whom I used to see as a child in the dispensary and whom I now saw as a young woman in the same place. She was one of the many offshoots of West African Negro-Irish wife combinations. The more brazenly attractive of her mates, after working all day in Read's Tin Works up the street, would reappear of a night in Lime Street or in the dive that had taken the place of Mr. Grossi's Trocadero. But not she—the darkened Courts sufficed for her. The professional witness, Kitty Daughtery, was still mooching around for "cases" in which to give her expert evidence. That sturdy old rock, St. Vincent's church, still stood, despite its economic plight, and Father Ryan's big worried face had at last assumed an aspect of quietness, for in Father Toomey's place now was a quiet, unassuming little Irish scholar, Father Dee, a professor of Theology from Dublin. This little academician—how strange he looked when, capped and gowned, I'd see him walking down Sparling Street, among all the Negroes and whites and half-caste children!

Down in the Dead House my father was up to his old tricks with a new foil—Mrs. Harris. Up in the barracks, with the deaths and the general dismal effects of the War, there were few signs of any of the old activity. My grandmother, of course, sat in her rocking chair in silence, cogitating, cogitating and scowling at pro-German Lonnigan, while he gave out his latest explanation of why the Germans shelled Rheims Cathedral. Perhaps my Uncle Jimmy, now acquiring a beautiful red-nose by virtue of his job on the Guinness's stout boats and a nicely dyed hair by reason of something else, would drop in and buy his mother a pint; and as like as not my lugubrious Aunt Janie would drop in and (after complaining how terrible economic conditions were) duplicate his feat.

Then the dynamite hidden underneath all this was touched off. It was five o'clock one evening, and I was watching the home-coming dockers when a newsboy came racing down from Park Lane, yelling: "Sinking of the *Lusitania*!"

The men stopped short; women peered from doorways. I joined one anxious group, poring over the fatal news. It was right—the "Lusy," the fine boat I had left Joe Manassi and Harold May aboard not two months ago, had been torpedoed! The news was only brief—she had "got it" in the Irish Sea bound for Liverpool "with terrible loss," the paper concluded. Later, another edition of the paper gave more tragic details.

My mother was shocked by the news, especially as a very good friend of hers when she worked at the Emigrant House, a steward named Alfred Gilroy, was on it. She berated me when I touched her for entrance money to the Daulby Hall. "Here you are loafing around here and good men being sunk and shot and your poor sister and me working our hands off. . . . Here, take it!"

It took about two days for the names of the drowned among the crew to be published. They were appalling. That night Freddie Seegar and I, clad in our American tailored suits, started for a dance over Paddy's Market in St. Martin's Hall. We never attended it, however. Before entering the Hall we walked around Scotland Road listening to the cries of the women whose husbands and sons had gone down in the "Lusy" and we heard the bitter threats made against Germany and anything with a German name. We walked down Bostock Street, where practically every blind was drawn in token of a death. All these little houses were occupied by Irish coal-trimmers and firemen and sailormen on the *Lusitania;* now these men who, barely two weeks ago, had carried their bags jokingly down the street, were gone, never to return.

Some of the women, drunk, were laughing—laughing as mad people laugh when the border line had been passed. Freddie, usually a very light-hearted boy, turned to me with whitened face and said: "Listen to all them women crying!"

224

On the corner of Scotland Road ominous gangs were gathering—men and women, very drunk and very angry. Something was afoot; we could sense that and, like good slummy boys, we crowded around eager to help in any disturbance. Suddenly something crashed up the road near Ben Jonson Street; followed in turn by another terrific crash of glass. We ran up the road. A pork butcher's had had its front window knocked in with a brick and a crowd of men and women were wrecking the place. A little higher up the same thing was happening—everything suggestive of Germany was being smashed to pieces.

Up the road the crowd surged, some cutting into Sawny Pope Street; others going into Ben Jonson Street; others continuing up the road. Down Scotland Road in the opposite direction the window crashing was more terrific— clear down to Bryon Street. Everyone had a brick or a stick or something tucked under his or her coat or apron and there was much pilfering. The police themselves, imbued with bitterness, were the most passive guardians of law. I recall one stout little Irish sausage dealer pleading with the crowd that her husband wasn't a German; but the name was too suspicious and in the windows went and the place was wrecked.

Freddie turned to me: "What about all the 'uns up our way? I'll bet they're having some bloody fun up there now. Let's go up there." So we left the Scotland Road mob and took the tram up to our own South End.

Freddie had guessed correctly. As soon as the tram got near Charlie Beech's pork shop, opposite St. Vincent's Church, a dense mob caused it to stop. Mr. Beech had been living in Liverpool thirty odd years, but there was a faint suspicion that years ago, anticipating just such a riot, he had changed his name. His big shop was in shambles when, running from the halted tramcar, we got to it; Mr. Beech and his son had made their escape.

Someone in the mob mentioned Bob Acte's sailor's boarding house in Nelson Street. Mr. Acte was a retired German sailorman, now a naturalized Britisher, and married to the popular Sarah Doran, as Irish as a leprechaun. "Ah, lave thim alone!" said a Joan of Arc who was leading the mob. "Sarah allers hilped the church. Let's get after Yaag—that's the bloody 'un!"

So instead of Acte's we raced on to Yaag's pork butcher's in Great George's Street, most of us boys in the vanguard and anxious to be the first to crash the enemy's windows. Mr. Yaag, a big, wholesome fellow allegedly had been born in Germany, but I don't think he remembered much about it. Two of his nephews at the time were with my cousin Berny and the Eighth Irish over in France. I always liked Mr. Yaag, but not quite so keenly as I liked to break his window without fear of molestation.

As we converged on the big shop, Mr. Yaag, arms akimbo and thinking some urchin was fleeing from Aeroplane Joe, came out, pipe in mouth and with his usual broad smile; this vanished instantly as someone kicked him in the belly and a volley of bricks sent in the huge windows. From the sawdust floor the astounded man had the pleasure of seeing his choice sausages kicked and thrown about and the furnishings reduced to shambles. "You'll sink the bleedin' 'Lusy,' will you!" yelled our Joan, waving a shillalah over his prostrate form. "I'll give you sinking the bloody 'Lusy'! 'Ere, bust that up;

kick that out; smash that whole bloody business!" We left Mr. Yaag and Yaag, Inc., in a worse mess than Charlie Beech's.

Cook's pork butcher's in Mill Street came next. Mr. Cook knew as much about Germany at the time, I think, as I did. Later investigation proved that he came from strictly Yorkshire stock and was a devoted student of Mr. Kipling—dashing off a bit of patriotic verse himself once in a while. But he had a pork butcher's shop, and as pork and Germany were identical terms, we left his shop in a shambles and himself stretched across the counter groaning. I began to get sick from all the free sausage I'd been eating.

When all the pork butchers (the more obvious Huns) had been satisfactorily dealt with, attention was turned to the private houses. It worked something like this. The mob would pause panting for a moment and someone would address Joan of Arc: "You know that dirty auld man that lives in such and such a street. I think he's one of them!"

"I know he is!" someone who didn't like this particular person would agree. Then off at a gallop.

A rather pathetic case I recall was that of an aged couple who lived quietly in a house in Kent Street, just opposite St. Michael's Church. Of German extraction, they had lived so long in Liverpool they looked like natives. Moreover, they had taken out naturalization papers and were drawing their support from the Parish. At the moment our Joan converged on the front window with her trusty shillalah, they were in the parlor singing Lutheran hymns. In went the front window as Mrs. Seymour—our Joan—screamed: "You'll sink the bloody 'Lusy', will you? Then take that! And that! And that!" We left this old house practically wrecked, but no one hit the old couple.

Our next conquest was Annie Monnigan's little shack. Annie was just as Irish as Sarah Doran, German Bob Acte's wife, but she didn't contribute as generously to St. Vincent's and this made a big difference. Several reasons why Annie didn't contribute so much to the church as Sarah was that she had no sailors' boarding house, had six small children to feed, and her husband was interned. But she was quite as good a Catholic as Sarah. Years ago, she had married Charlie Thomas, fresh from a German four-masted barque. As the children came, Charlie quit the sea and matriculated, like all old sailors, to dock laboring—an occupation he was at when hauled off to the German detention camp on the Isle of Man. One of our crowd, with remarkable memory verified this—and the stampede was on. I shall never forget the hysteria of this last debacle, with the six young children screaming and Annie, like a good colleen, fighting back and asking no quarter. After doing a sound job here, we left loudly cheering our commander-in-chief, herself now sporting a black eye, given her by the fighting Annie.

Next—of all places—was my German uncle by marriage, Chris Hazeman's house in Chesterfield Street. Long afterward I was suspected of having suggested that the expedition go there, but it wasn't true. I don't know who started it; the only thing I do confess to was that when it *was suggested*, I seconded the motion. I remembered my beautiful Aunt Lizzie and a childish bitterness against the Hazemans grew rancorous within me. Now here was an opportunity to get even! But after we wrecked the little house that Auntie Lizzie loved so well (the Hazemans had fled when they heard we were on our way up there) I was glad she was not living then, otherwise she would have received the same fate as the other Irish girls whose husbands had become suspects.

And so far on into the night our gang, along with several others equally patriotic, went through the slummy section of the town wrecking everything we tackled. Up in the North End it was the same way; the foe for the brief moment had changed from England to Germany. Many mistakes were made. Most of the slummy women already mentioned early in this book took an active part in the campaign and not a few of them dispatched themselves with signal valor. If Germany had torpedoed the *Lusitania*, we certainly had torpedoed everything German in our immediate vicinity—certainly all the pork butchers' shops. The following day all was quiet, and the police, now mindful of their jobs, started taking an inventory. All damage was carefully checked and all the victims adequately reimbursed, the cost going on the tax rate as is the way with good British justice. Our commander-in-chief, the fiery little Irishwoman, was relieved from her chip-chopping activities and given six months in Walton for her valor, and only his adeptness at secreting himself behind chimney pots saved the Black Prince from going along with her. Several others got minor sentences.

There was some disguised blessings, too. Most of the

wrecked butcher shops were obsolete contraptions, but when the reconstruction architects came in, newer and gaudier edifices were erected. Little fighting Annie Monnigan had always detested the little shack in Frederick Street, so when the government offered to rebuild it according to the original plan, she threw up her hands in horror and suggested a cash settlement. Poor Charlie Beech and I were the worst sufferers. Charlie's son John dropped dead after racing with his father from the shop to his house in Aigbirth; and I got a pernicious bellyache on account of all the raw sausage I had eaten.

CHAPTER
THIRTY

SHORTLY after the *Lusitania* riots came the Liverpool Police strike. Perhaps the bobbies had just cause for their bitterness, for theirs were the only wages that hadn't skyrocketed with the war. I thought they were getting ample pay at the time, but like everyone else—not excluding the manufacturer, who almost always was the first to raise the cry of traitor to a striker—they wanted much more. It required a piece of legislation to raise the salaries of the bobbies and as none was forthcoming, they became very restless and finally, in direct opposition to the advice of their superiors who pointed out the severity with which such an unpatriotic act would be dealt, they struck.

Some people believe that the thing was engineered inside local government circles to obviate the paying of pensions to the older men, a great number of whom were about ready for retirement. But this I don't believe, for it isn't like British policy. Others had it that the plot was hatched in Berlin to give the local pork butchers a chance to get even with other tradesmen who had profited when the pork butchers were put out of business. But I don't believe this either. I personally blame the profiteering spirit, then all the go. When the bobbies saw men of the Murray stripe making three times their wages, no wonder they felt an injustice was being done them!

Like its inglorious predecessor, the strike resulted in wholesale destruction of property, much looting and the eventual repayment via the public taxes. It was upon us just as suddenly as the *Lusitania* riots and it was precisely to my liking, what with my new-found spirit of self-indulgence and my constant need of cash.

The bobbies were on strike! There were *no bobbies!* That could only mean one thing, and that thing happened. I was coming out of the Daulby Hall with Jackie Sanchez (having mooched the entrance fee from him) at the time when the fever first caught on. We went across the street to Skranvinsky's chip-and-fish shop and listened to speculations over this new and strange strike. As we stood in the crowd a couple of bucks walked in, ordered up some chips and fish and refused to pay for them, suggesting to the hysterical Mrs. Skranvinsky that she "get a bloody bobby!" Then they walked out, followed by others not yet paid up, who had taken the hint. Some leaned across the counter and grabbed handfuls of chips and fish and scallops and, without waiting to salt them, continued brazenly out into the street. Only Mrs. Skranvinsky's screams kept those on the outside at bay. *There were no bobbies!*

We were outside. On the corners here and there stood the bobbies, grimly passive and, to signify that fact, with no official labels on their arms. Excited groups of hooligans

232

eyed them wonderingly. A jewelry window just down London Road crashed in, and as the bobbies smiled wonder vanished from the hooligans. Another window crashed in. It was the *Lusitania* all over again, only much more intense, since now there was no restraining hand at all. Hands were out grasping through the jewelry store windows. Inside other stores whose windows were bashed in, respectable-looking men and women joined with slummies to gather up loot and flee homeward. Every store with anything worth stealing was broken into and the furnishings wrecked in the frenzy to get the best stuff available.

I did not have anything like good luck until Ben Hyde's pawnshop farther down London Road was reached. After the windows were bashed in, the place was ransacked; lockers pulled out; pledged articles tucked into aprons. I got hold of a couple of muffs that struck me, in my innocence, as very expensive things and once outside, fearing the riot would be short-lived, I skipped away from Jackie, tucked the two precious furs under my coat, and sped along the comparatively quiet streets for home.

Alice was sleeping on the sofa but my mother was up, as usual waiting for me to come in, and as I chucked the muffs down on the kitchen table triumphantly and told her how they had been gotten, she said determinedly: "Take them dirty, bloody, stolen things out of here!"

I thought her quite mad, after what I'd been through to get them. Besides, when again would such an opportunity present itself? I told her that they might be worth a lot of money; after which I brought up the sophistry that since everyone was stealing, it was no more than right I do it too. But after all this she said again quite firmly: "You'll take them bloody things out of here! I never thought I'd have a robber in the family. You're your daddy's son all right!"

Then I started feeling the muffs and got her to feel them. Poor woman, she'd never seen such quality, and they certainly impressed her. "They're worth something in pawn mammy!" I argued.

"Yes," she said feeling them again. "But they're stolen!"

Again she insisted that I take them back, and when I told her the impossibility of this and the dangers it entailed, she suggested taking them down the street to the dock and chucking them in. I wouldn't think of this, of course, and as I was quite a man then I had my way— my mother washing her hands of the whole affair, though wishing secretly she could find some way to keep the muffs and at the same time keep her conscience clear.

The following day, I took them up to a little fence I knew in Scotland Road and disposed of both of them, since the new police force (installed over night to the consternation of the neo-pensioner striking bobbies and to the remorse of the others) was doing a bit of detective work in recovering stolen goods and bringing the criminals to book.

But after disposing of the muffs, I passed the Palais de Luxe and succumbed to its lure. Once again I was in my own seat in the darkened gallery, and there, buried myself once more in the fantastic images of youthful dreams. . . . Then up and out into cold reality.

Ordinarily, with fourteen shillings in my pocket, out

of which I intended ten for my mother (to be borrowed back later by degrees), I should have been very happy. But walking homeward in the dusk that evening I was far from cheerful. Perhaps, I reasoned, it was the sense of guilt coming from the disposal of the muffs. But that explanation did not satisfy, and as I entered the darkened hallway of our home and proceeded along to our back kitchen, I *knew* by that peculiar intuition that never once has failed me, that something was wrong. As I opened the door, I prayed it was nothing started by my father, whom we were all content to forget.

Alice stood over the fire raking it into a blaze and mildly cursing the kettle for not staying steady on the coals. Her face was whiter than usual and, seeing me enter, she stopped fiddling with the kettle and stared at me. There was conflict in that stare, and instantly I thought of our mother and asked about her.

"She's down in Gordon's, Tim. I had to let her go down. You know what?"

"What?"

"Berny Roche. . . ."

"Is killed?"

"Yes. They just got word tonight. Mam's heart is broken. . . . Poor Berny! Just to think, he stood right there just before he went away. . . . You can't realize it, can you, Timmy?" Her little face was getting green; the big brown eyes catching some of the old terror they knew so well. "It seems like all your mates are going, don't it?"

Lepsey, Johnny Mangan, Joe Manassi, Harold May—and now Berny! What next and who next? That sickening sense of loss swept through me; the fourteen bob moistened in my hand. From the water of the Queen's Dock I could see my cousin and the others ready to dive from off the deck of the *Lagos* once again for the negro cook's sixpence. Now he was gone! No wonder Alice had consented to mother's drinking that evening.

CHAPTER
THIRTY-ONE

SHORTLY after the police strike it became necessary for Jackie and me to get to sea. In my own case this was easy enough, for my mother was as yet still blanketed under the sorrow of Berny's death. With Mrs. Sanchez it was different. This little woman knew the true story of the sea from the losses in her own boarding house, and when Jackie and I came into the place and told of both getting a ship, she screamed at him in Spanish and flashed her dark eyes viciously at me. Jackie had gotten on one of the Spanish Larrinaga boats, while I had shipped on something called the *Scarborough*. I had accompanied Jackie to his home, hopeful of congratulations; now I decided to get out quickly. . . .

The *Scarborough* lay over in the Eastham Locks, and the following day my mother, absenting herself from her charing duties, accompanied me across the river to see me off.

I was on the *Scarborough* three months. There is no need to describe the voyage in detail. It was the *Restitu-*

tion, Caledonia, Lowtyne all over again, with the same dirt, the same type crew and the same monotonous dragging through the ocean and back again.

Certain things, however, do recall themselves, particularly my lookout during the always hectic passage through the Danger Zone. In this convoy, as in the case of the *Lowtyne,* we had the front line. The sea was quite lovely as only the Irish Sea can be quite lovely, but the air was tense with expectancy. Around and around the twenty-odd ships circled the destroyers. On our right, as on the *Lowtyne,* was a China boat and on the left a Clan boat. The colors of a dilapidated Larrinaga boat showed beyond the Clan boat (I surmised at the moment that Jackie was on it, but I found later he was not).

Between two and four in the afternoon, I peered out over in the sea through the binoculars with the zest of the neophyte. Behind me on the bridge the second mate paced slowly and smiled at my enthusiasm; while down on the deck, the men went about their chores as though no danger threatened. Suddenly, over on the left bow a thin mysterious ripple speeded straight for us. Fascinated, I peered through my glasses at its tremendous speed. What was this ripple cutting the water at such tremendous speed? I had been told to look for periscopes; I knew nothing of torpedoes.

Then, suddenly, it dawned on me—this was a torpedo speeding our way that would probably strike us right under our port bow. My orders were if I spied a periscope to ring sharply and report to the mate on the bridge. But for this torpedo I knew I was too late. I held my breath watching the rippling wake dash toward us, toward our

bow, toward it, toward it, together they were coming—
it had passed! Straight across our bow, missing it by
inches and right on, right on—crash!—into the midships
of the China boat.

Instantly, the China boat lurched and heaved and a
huge gap showed in her port side. From her bridge then
came the eight short blasts warning the others in the
convoy that she had been torpedoed. Everyone on our
boat was galvanized into action. Zig-zag the course, came
the order from the officer to the sailor at the wheel; the
captain was called to the bridge.

Submarines! Crash! The ship behind the China boat
lurched and faltered and blew the warning whistles. The
red flags on the doomed ships were hoisted aloft. The
destroyers, guns bristling, were racing round and round
trying to locate the elusive and daring submarines. My
feet and hands were on the wire stay ready for the rapid
descent, for it might be us next.

Every second we awaited the inevitable crash as, with
the remainder of the convoy, we zig-zagged onward. We
were loaded to the scuppers with heavy iron rails and I
knew if the sudden crash we all expected occurred, we
would sink in a minute. My mind was made up—if it came
I was going to leap away down straight into the sea. On,
on we labored, as hard as the old engines could go, zig-
zagging all the time. In the distance three sinking ships
listed. Gradually the zig-zagging drew the ships apart,
and the destroyers could not be seen. The order of the
day then was to proceed alone, continuing with the zig-
zagging. The captain slid into the pilot house, consulted
his chart and rearranged his course—we were heading now

for South America alone! The firemen and trimmers came away from the engine room ladder and returned to their tasks. The air of anxiety lessened, even though at any moment that mysterious crash from the unseen foe might come.

The only things about South America that stick in my memory are the intense heat of the place, of the surprising number of Liverpool slummies on the beach there; much painting and soojy-moojying [scrubbing paint work]; the inevitable whorehouses and a return the same way and in the same monotonous manner as we went out.

As I anticipated, my father was at the Langdon Dock awaiting me, and I had great difficulty eluding him. I got away from him by giving him a shilling and telling him I had to stay aboard ship that afternoon as watchman and for him to go and get himself a pint and come back and rejoin me. After he had disappeared up the quay, I hoisted my sea-bag on my shoulder and made for the overhead railway.

It was the same old story and the same intensely affectionate greeting. My mother and Alice were both astounded at my improved physical condition, feeling my muscles and examining my chest. "Look 'ow big 'e is around the back, mam!" Alice would say, staring at me admiringly. "You wouldn't know 'im, would you? I hope now 'e'll stop goin' to sea."

Then after the size of my impending pay-off had been discussed (I fixed it so that two pounds would redound to myself), and after I had given a rather shameless account of eluding my father, over a cup of tea and a vast dish of bacon and eggs, my mother told me the more dramatic angles of the news. First, the government had tightened down on the rations. Next, news item: Ted Heaton's baths had been closed in Cornwallis Street and his wife had committed suicide. Seeing my surprise, they explained in detail. Did I remember that dirty water in the baths—the water that had sent me into a decline? Well, a boy had drowned in the pool and it was so dirty that they had to empty the entire pool in order to locate the body. Ted, the famed English Channel swimmer, had been dismissed in disgrace, after which he opened a pub at the bottom of Duke Street. Here, his wife, smarting under the disgrace, had taken poison.

And that was not all. No, their whitened faces and that strange, unfathomable look in my sister's eyes whenever something tragic was to be told, gave the game away. "Johnny Ford, your mate, was blown to bits in France— last week." Then, with her penchant for story-telling, my mother elaborated: "I was walking around Hardy Street and I saw Mrs. Ford and her sister Maggie. Johnny's mother was crying and I asked Maggie, 'What's to do with Annie?' She made a wink of her eye and said, 'Johnny's hurt'—then whispered, 'He's killed.' Maggie had got the wire before the War Office, from a woman in Bostock Street whose son was killed with Johnny and she didn't want Johnny's mother to know—right away. She'd told Johnny's mother that he was in a hospital, but the next day Mrs. Ford got the real wire from the War Office. . . ."

It was not quite the shock of Berny's death, for somehow I had expected news like this. Poor Johnny! Again the vision of the *Lagos* and the swimmers on its side in

A LIVERPOOL IRISH SLUMMY

the Queen's Dock came to me; again in my mind I counted them—only six left now: Jacko Oldham, Frankie Roza, Freddie Seegar, Jackie Sanchez, Mickey and myself.

CHAPTER
THIRTY-TWO

IN THE next two years I went steadily to sea, to various parts of the world, but few recollections remain of all these wanderings. But the loneliness of ship life did foster one great urge within me—the desire to write. The fact that I had no training for a literary career did not occur to me as an objection; I wanted to write and write I would.

It was with this writing urge upon me that I deserted in Philadelphia the British tramp on which I had shipped. I had touched the ports of San Francisco and Savannah and like all young men had decided that America was my land of opportunity.

All that I took with me when I deserted was my very English "American tailored" suit—and hope. But jobs were very plentiful then, for America had just declared war. Two days later I was a riveter at Hog Island helping to build the Emergency Fleet, at which task I stuck for about three months when ill-luck in a crap game, the lure of the sea and the first disillusions of writing sent me to New York in search of a ship.

This was my first visit to New York and, walking along West Street, with eighty cents in my pocket, the similarity to Liverpool made me a little homesick.

In the New York of late 1917, everything was hustle and bustle, steam engines, motor trucks, lorries with horses, merchandise going, going—my old Dock Road all over again. No beauty or symmetry of the Liverpool docks here, but more intense activity.

I must have gone aboard a dozen ships that afternoon without any success. American maritime arrangements and facilities for engaging and discharging seamen were in such a primitive state that it was difficult to tell when a ship was ready to hire its crew. Most of the ships I went on were American ships—new products of such places as the Hog Island shipyards, with new sailormen and new mates and new everything. Nearly all of them wanted sailormen (help, one youngish mate with downy cheeks told me), but they were not certain when they would start signing on. Maybe tomorrow, maybe next week—but come round again sometime. Where did they sign on? Why on the ship—where else could they sign on? I combed nearly all the docks clear down to the Cunard Line piers without success.

And then I saw something that made my heart beat faster. Ranged alongside the shed of the Cunard Line pier was the exact replica of that fine *Lusitania*, the sinking of which had precipitated our slummy riots and very likely had swept America into the War—the *Mauretania!* I retraced my steps quickly. I did not want to look too long at those four stately funnels, for in seeing them my mind reverted to Joe Manassi, Harold May and myself standing on the deck of the "Lusy" in Liverpool. So back down West Street I trudged to the Sailors' Home, where I knew I could check my suitcase for the night.

After checking my suitcase and purchasing a bed for the night I went up to the reading room and sat down, idly turning the pages of a geographic magazine, not reading, only looking at the colored pictures. Then suddenly the same impulse to write that had come to me aboard ship returned in even stronger form. Despite the disillusionment of my Philadelphia experience I knew I must somehow go on.

A hungry belly interfered with my second grim determination to settle down and write. I was sitting in the Reading Room the next day madly scribbling away when the impending pangs of hunger brought me to the realization that I was broke. There was also a place to sleep that night to be taken into consideration. It galled me to stop the abortive effort, but these stark economic facts had to be reckoned with. In my present predicament, a ship would have been the logical thing to seek. But it would be difficult to write in a ship's forecastle (your shipmates would think you quite mad); so the thing for me was a shore job—dishwashing or something like that. Dishwash of a day and write epics at night—that was it.

An hour later I found myself up on Canal Street in a strictly Kosher neighborhood of stores, restaurants, barber shops, etc.—a sort of miniature Scotland Road, with all its filth and turmoil and noise and polyglot tongues. In almost every restaurant window was the home-printed placard, "Counterman wanted—experienced." I wandered along—no good going in those places, for I knew precious little about American cuisine. On, on, I went, but always the sign mentioned "experience." My hunger forced me to take a chance, and I went into the next restaurant I passed.

An elderly Jew, very quizzical, faced me and behind him a stoutish Jewess and an elderly orthodox gentleman (obviously the man's father or father-in-law). Yes, the Manhattan Restaurant wanted a counterman (that much was obvious in the man's demeanor), but where had I counter-manned before? I hesitated, but hunger brought out the cautious lie: "I've never worked as a counterman in this country. But I've done pretty much the same thing on all the big English liners. Before that, I worked in most of the big London hotels. . . ."

The man's ears pricked up. "You are English, eh? Maybe you can cook, no?" He became very excited and consulted the others in Yiddish; gradually it developed into an argument among them. I could sense what was going on—in me they hoped to have a find. Perhaps I was a *chef* and if they only had a little patience with me (this was the owner's point of the argument, I took it) and signed me up to a long term contract, they would have the best *chef* in all Canal Street. A London restaurant chef! The argument ceased quite as suddenly as it started; again the owner cross-examined me. "Vot hotels in London you vorked at? The big ones, no?"

I had never been in London, so I was stumped. I gave the names of the bigger ones in Liverpool—the Adelphi, the Washington, the London & North-Western.

"You are on an English ship now—or maybe your ship it leave without you, no?"

I nodded and the deal was on. As I was taken back to
the kitchen, the smell of the food overcame me and I asked
right off for a meal—sensing the inevitable debacle that
was to come. "Sure, sure!" said the owner, expanding his
arms in gesture of his great generosity. Then to the big
Negro sweating over the pots—

"Here fix Mr.?" He looked at me inquiringly.

"Mr. O'Mara."

"Fix Mr. O'Mara something *nice* to eat . . . that's
me. . . ."

A big meal of a lot of stuff I'd never seen before was
placed in front of me and as I ate ravenously and the
family out in the dining-room again huddled in colloquy
over my prospects, the darky cursed the place roundly.
Sure, the counterman job was all right—he guessed;
that's why they could never hold one. So, too, was this
job he had, but he was jackin' up this week—yassuh!
What was I—Irish? There were Irish in Alabama where
he came from. Yes, I told him, there were Irish everywhere. Oh, no! he admonished—not in Canal Street!

After the plates had been placed in the sink, an apron
was gotten for me and I was put behind the counter. . . .
Half an hour later, I was walking nervously up Canal
Street with furious Yiddish curses ringing in my ears and
no apron on—a more violent eruption having taken place
than I had anticipated.

Round and round I walked, finally coming back to the
sailors' environs. I knew this from the narrow streets I
now traversed, so like Sparling Street in Liverpool. There
were Spanish signs and others in Italian and Greek and
almost every other continental language. In Christopher

Street it was, I think, that a Hungarian Restaurant had a sign in it: "Dish-washer wanted."

I needed some place to sleep that night and I felt, in view of my recent attempt, I could manage a dish-washer's job, so I went into this little murky hole-in-the-wall. It smacked strangely of that big kitchen dining-room of Mrs. Sanchez's boarding house at home. Swarthy men huddled at the tables talking in a foreign language. A nickel melodeon was playing. A big fellow rose from one of the tables and looked at me; I pointed to the sign in the window. He nodded and brought me back into the pantry and showed me a vast conglomeration of dirty dishes. A negro cook, not unlike the fellow in the Manhattan Restaurant, sulked over his pans in the corner.

How much did I want? How much did it pay? I countered. The man's seriousness and his determination to strike a hard bargain gave me the assurance I needed, and when he said "fifteen dollars" in fairly good English, I agreed and was hired immediately. The hours he told me were from eight in the morning until nine at night, with two hours off in the afternoon. I told him of my needing a room, hinting at an advance of salary when the day's work finished. He replied there was just one little room left upstairs, and I could use that. "It is small," he explained, "and it is not fixed up nice. But it will do you till you get another room." At that moment, a big, lumbering foreign woman came down the stairs, his wife.

I worked like a Trojan washing dishes that I thought never would stop coming through the little wooden receptacle from the outer smoky room—from six o'clock clear up till about nine, when the owner came in and told me I could quit. The restaurant's business had begun to quiet down now, and he intended taking charge of the dishes. A meal was served me by the Negro and two dollars pressed in my hand by the owner as he whispered smilingly:

"I pay you for all day Limey. Liverpool Irish—that's not *real* Irish, I know. Some Liverpool Irish all right—some no worth a good goddam! Down the street, a Liverpool Irishman named Kelley he runs a saloon—rat, bastard, sonofabitch! I'm Hungarian Jew, Budapest. Some Hungarian Jews good—some no goddam good. You all right. . . . How's all the Lime Juicers in Scotland Road, eh? I know Scotland Road. And the Legs of Man? And Lime Street? I been in Liverpool. How's the Sailors' Home? I know the Sailors' Home. I was ship's cook twenty years. . . . If you want to wash up, I show you."

He led the way upstairs to a stuffy front room looking straight out at the elevated railroad. "There's a bathroom there—you wash up." He went up one flight to the third back room and shrugged his shoulders. "It is not nice here, but it is better than pay fifty cents for one night. Tomorrow maybe down Christopher Street you can get a room —or you stay here if you want."

No it was not nice there, and it was my first definite proof that slums existed in God's Country too. Then the door of the front room opened and a wizened middle-aged fellow came out in his European drawers. He seemed genuinely pleased to meet me, fixing me with that peculiar stare so reminiscent of the *Restitution*'s old Spanish cook. "This is Mister Nikko," said the owner. "He been with me two years now. He's sailorman, too." Mr. Nikko kept eyeing me, cavorting around like a man about to go to bed with an attractive courtesan, and although I was not afraid of him I knew that we weren't going to get along. He seemed a second Don Alverez and I sensed I was in for some embarrassment. I insisted upon a key for my room, and this insistence seemed to puzzle Mr. Nikko. His eyes expanded in surprise—he had no key to his room and he had been there two years. Burglars? Poof! I made up my mind to look elsewhere for a room after that night.

CHAPTER
THIRTY-THREE

THE next day I cast about for a room away from this vicinity and was surprised to discover how very like Irish slummy Liverpool parts of this section were! Women with shawls there were, and men dressed not unlike the furtive and sooty artisans of our slums across the ocean. There were many Irish names—O'Hara, O'Reilly, Finnigan, etc. "Hell's Kitchen" lay a little farther west. It disgusted me, and it surprised me and it disillusioned me. I walked up to Fourteenth Street near Eighth Avenue, where I got a clean little room with a German family. From then on it was dish-washing and dancing at public "dance palaces" and trying to write. I remained only a week in the Hungarian restaurant; after that it was here, there, anywhere where dish-washers were needed.

I knew, of course, that mother and Alice would be worried to death when my ship got back without me, particularly now that three months had elapsed without hearing from me. One night I took the subway to South Ferry and repaired quickly to 25 South Street and its reading room, and did some genuinely imaginative writing. My mother has the letter to this day.

DARLING MOTHER:

Please don't worry about me as everything is all right. I have an excellent job in New York and I am going to stay here until I make enough money to bring you over with me. This is a lovely country and there is money everywhere and jobs everywhere. No, I'm not lonely: I'm in with another chap—in business for ourselves—and as soon as we get an office and get started right, I'll be able to send you some money. But don't worry about me. They make the moving pictures right here where I am and I see those actors and actresses you see at the St. James' pictures every day. I acted in a picture with Mr. Eugene O'Brien and you never can tell you might see me as a star in the St. James' sometime.

I can't send you any money right now, but buck up and it won't be long before I do send you some. This is God's Country and it won't be very long before I send you a few quid. I know both you and Alice would love it here. There is no such things as slums, and everybody is educated and talks well-off. I don't see why everybody in Liverpool doesn't come right over here and stay, for you can make more money here in one day than you can there in a year.

Unfortunately right now this friend of mine and I are just starting up a new office and it will be sometime before the money starts to come in. But it will come in, and when it does the first thing I am going to do is to send a few quid over to you. But whatever you do don't worry about me. I'm all right and I'm very happy.

At the present time I'm staying in a swell hotel up town but as I have a mail box in the Sailors' Home here it would be best for you to send your letters to me % 25 South Street, New York City. With lots of love and hoping you won't worry I am, your loving son,

TIM.

P. S. Tell my mates where I am if you see them—but don't let the government know! And give my best love to Alice. And dad, too, if you see him.

Then back to my little quiet room in 14th Street to lie in bed, listen to the rumble of the street cars, and to imagine some more.

From then on I made nightly excursions to 25 South Street, looking for a return letter. I got one about three weeks after I had sent mine. It was short and to the point and written by Alice in her impatient manner.

DEAR TIMMY. Mam is very sick and I think she is going to die. It's that old sickness she once had, and her heart's bad. Come home quick Timmy. . . . !

There was something else but that was as far as I read. I got that letter at seven o'clock that night. An hour later I was scouring the Cunard and White Star Piers for a job or a stowaway's crevice. I got the former on the *Megantic* —a trimmer's job, working my passage. The next day I was heading once again for Liverpool—only this time, instead of on deck, in the bowels of an inferno.

I always think of the short trip on the *Megantic* in terms of my first day trucking cotton at the docks, when I almost ruptured myself. Racing madly through the darkened bunkers with a "Jessie" full of coal, tipping it at the plates beside the ship's inferno and its perspiring firemen, and racing madly back for another load—this is the lot of the coal trimmer and if there be a more inhuman task I have never seen it. The "Deucer" (second engineer) yells for steam; the firemen yells for coal—the half-savage denizen of the Liverpool slums races for it. Coal-bunkers echo to the squeaking noise of the wheel barrows as these black-faced slummies race up and down the steel-decked passageway. Four on and four off—in droves they come up, go down. Any moment in the Danger Zone, a torpedo may blow death through these bunkers—and they laugh and joke at this. . . . Perhaps in my American suit I was the most bizarre figure in the *Megantic*'s bunkers. Certainly I was the least experienced and the most exhausted when—thank God!—the payless trip was over.

CHAPTER
THIRTY-FOUR

BUT fears regarding my mother's death were ill founded. It was always hazardous to guess about her health. Upon seeing her I knew perfectly well what had happened. She had suffered one of those complete collapses that had become so much a part of her later life and Alice had mistaken what looked like death for death itself. She must have recovered quickly, for when I got home she was puddling around in the same old manner with apparently nothing wrong.

I was glad to see that she was well and annoyed that I had incommoded myself in making the trip across the ocean and arriving penniless. In view of my splendid letter they were a bit surprised at my dilapidated appearance, but over the inevitable dish of bacon and eggs and tea for which by then I had a genuine nostalgia, I explained myself very satisfactorily. The business I had gone into with this hypothetical partner in America had tumbled due to his roguery, but that was nothing. America was simply full of businesses and partners and it would be no time before I got started up again, when and if I ever got back there.

Both of them were very excited. A "business" to them had to do with an office and a white collar and with "getting along in the world"—amenities never to visit the slums. What kind of business was it? I pressed my finger to my lips—I'd surprise them some day I intimated. Then gradually we fell into a discussion of America and like a good sailor I lied magnificently. I kept discreetly quiet about Christopher Street and the waterfront and its Dock-Road verisimilitude. But that gaudy atmosphere of Broadway and its dance halls and restaurants and perpetual electric lighting I gloated over. There were no such places as slums in America! Everybody dressed well and everybody had money. I described the truck-drivers smoking cigars and I elaborated upon that sight. Could she imagine a *docker* smoking a cigar? No, she smiled, she could not. Then I went on describing my adventure in the movies, how I had gotten a job (lie) playing in the films. *Inside* the films? asked Alice amazed. I looked at her reproachfully—why certainly! Did she know of an actor named Eugene O'Brien? Well, I had played right alongside of him. Then Alice's face fell. She was thinking that by calling me home she had ruined what very likely would have been a brilliant movie career. But here I comforted them both that, regardless of my present penurious state I would find a way very easily to start in right where I had finished—just leave it to me!

Then talk of Liverpool. It was pretty much the same as when I had left it almost four months ago, though certain vital things were happening. The first of these things had to do with the stolen muffs—my mother had atoned for my thievery and the money I had gotten from the fence had been returned. Returned—how returned and to whom? To the poor box in St Vincent's—that's where! With an occasional offering to St. Christopher to keep me safe too! But then a grave note was sounded by my mother. The American soldiers who had assumed command of the town were really having a bad effect upon the girls. Up in Knotty Ash, where they were encamped, barbed wire entanglements had had to be put around their quarters to keep the enthusiastic Liverpool flappers away from them. They had gone American soldier mad, listening to all the grandiloquent (and false she intimated) stories sprung by these great lovers.

Then Alice, for the first time, spoke of her own strange romance with the young soldier, Austin Jorgensen, whom she was later to marry when he returned from the war. It was peculiar to see her attitude toward love and the profound business of marriage. Not spontaneous nor from the heart—indeed it seemed only a patient acquiescence, to what Mother thought economically wisest for her. She would say to her mother, "It's much better to get an English boy that you know and can trust than to take chances with someone you can't trust."

To me this impending marriage seemed an even more ridiculously economic affair than my Auntie Janie's and had I been of superstitious make-up I might have blamed Janie's prayers for it. My mother, like all good mothers of the slums, was not concerned with the promptings of her child's heart (for young slummy women were never conceded to have anything approximating an expression of soul or heart), but only with her economic future. The highest thing that Alice could aspire to right then, was to get out of the clutches of the Board of Guardians atmosphere, of the Work House atmosphere, of this tenement shack atmosphere. Only by getting a young man not addicted to drink and a steady worker could she hope to realize anything like this, and in young Mr. Jorgensen my mother sensed just such a person. He was steady; he was sober, industrious—and he too needed a home. That their dispositions might conflict was not to be considered. The job was to marry them off—then hope for love! That, I think, was my mother's attitude toward this blossoming romance, and Alice, good little soldier that she was, and forever trusting the sincerity of her mother, was simply obeying orders.

Then there were some amusing anecdotes told about these very proud American soldiers. Courtships. One day during an altercation with her newly found American sweetheart, Annie Manassi—my dead pal's sister—in a flurry of indignation, threatened to leave him in the middle of Lime Street instead of continuing on into the pictures with him. "I'll go home!" she threatened, not meaning one word of it. "And," continued my mother, "what do you think the Yank said? He said, 'Wal, baby, I jest don't care whether you go and I jest don't care whether you stay!' And with that he turns around and picks up with another bloody omadhaun and takes her into the pictures and laves poor Annie standing there scratching herself!"

I asked about my father. He was completely neglecting his health, and if not for Alice he would have been infinitely worse off. She was attending to his wants as sedulously as though he had been the most exemplary father. The first thing she would do when she came home from work was go and clean his room, and fix him something to eat. He was doing an occasional day at the dock—just enough to ensure him room rent and ale money; the food he very foxily left to be provided by my sister. He was always talking about me, boasting of my prowess as a sailorman, much to the sardonic delight of his mates, who thought him a fool.

Then there was talk of my pals. No need of going up to the corner, my mother said, for there wasn't any corner any more—Aeroplane Joe having finally succeeded in breaking it up. Jackie Sanchez had come home from sea and had gone off to the country suffering with a bad leg, a tubercular outbreak which he was to carry with him all his life. I recalled those pains he used to tell me about in his ankle and my mother nodded understandingly. "Yes," she said, "and the doctor says there's no cure for it. He looked bad before he went away. I hope he doesn't go like the rest of your mates are going. He came down here to see you before he went away, about a month ago."

That was Jackie Sanchez. Freddie Seegar was still dancing at Daulby Hall and loafing as usual. Jacko, she'd heard, had gone to sea. Frankie Roza now an "improver" [one grade above an apprentice] engineer, was going with a very elegant English girl and getting to be quite a snob. Mickey she knew nothing about. She was on the point of reciting to me with that vividness of hers some more neighborhood deaths by torpedoes or shells in France, but I halted her quickly—the stuff was in the air, omnipresent, and she didn't have to elaborate upon it. I didn't want to hear of it.

With my brief sojourn in America I had caught a new glimpse of life—a different perspective—and I had no intention of losing it. I was going to get a ship by hook or by crook tomorrow, despite her pleadings that this time (now that I had lost my sea-bag and all the little religious things so dear to her heart) I should stay home and seek a safe job at the docks. I was still ineligible for both Army and Navy—so why must I risk my life again? But how, I argued in return, was I to get back into business with the office and white collar, or to get back into the moving pictures (and eventually to become a movie star) if I didn't first return to the land wherein all these things were possible? We ended that evening by my borrowing enough money to go to the Daulby Hall and dance.

Here I found the atmosphere very disappointing. The place was crowded with American soldiers, and the girls were interested only in them. I left there very early, disappointed particularly when Nancy, who had initiated me into the thrills of sex, deliberately snubbed me. Had anybody offered me a ship that night as I walked down London Road, past Ben Hyde's newer and more elegantly refurnished pawnshop, from which I had pillaged the two fur muffs, I would have taken it regardless of its destination. Anything to get out of Liverpool!

CHAPTER
THIRTY-FIVE

THE following day I set out looking for a ship that would take me back to New York. I was facing a peculiar problem in that I had no sailor's book, having lost it when I deserted in Philadelphia. Thus it was useless for me to go down to the Sailors' Home, because there I would leave myself open to arrest. The logical thing for me to do—indeed the only thing I could do—was to try to get what is known in Liverpool maritime parlance as a "jump." A "jump" meant filling the berth of an absentee sailor at the last moment; the question of pay being adjudicated when out at sea. Many sailormen have made their first trip this way. I would receive a new sailor's book at the end of the voyage and start under a new name, all debts and crimes recorded in the old sea book being automatically wiped out.

But as I wanted to get to New York as quickly as possible, instead of going around the docks and accepting a "jump" on some old cargo boat that might have brought me to heaven's knows where, I went down to the Landing Stage to obtain a last minute berth on one of the mail liners. The "jumps" on all Cunard and White Star liners took place here during the liners' brief stay in taking on mail and passengers. Here, the respective strengths of the "down below" and "on deck" forces would be computed by the junior engineers and mates, respectively. If there were any absentees (as there nearly always were) then the mate or the boatswain or the "deucer" or his "pusher" would trot down the gangplank and look through the inevitable group of baggageless nondescripts on the quay.

This particular morning, when I got there, the *Baltic* had just tied up and in about two hours she was due to sail to New York. On the night previous I had informed my mother of my intentions and so was fully prepared to accept a "jump" if and when it came. I think there were only two or three of us gathered around the gangway of the *Baltic*, all of whom were in the "down below" crowd, except myself. It wasn't long before the expected happened. The boatswain came down wanting to know were any of us "A. B.'s." I replied that I was. He motioned me to the gangway and turned to the others. No, they weren't A. B.'s. Then the boatswain followed me aboard ship and showed me into the vast forecastle; two hours later, in the once elegant American suit in which I had trimmed coal on the *Megantic* I was pulling and hauling on the *Baltic's* big Manila ropes as we sailed slowly down the river.

The following morning, along with a couple of firemen who had accepted the "jump," I was signed on and put on the starboard watch. We were making about fourteen or fifteen knots and traveling alone. Once clear of the

Bar Lightship, unlike the slow cargo boat convoys, this lean old greyhound leaped through the water on her own.

I was very happy. We would be in New York in eight days, I mused, and so I did not mind soojy-moojying and painting and "holy-stoning" the decks—this last a new experience for me. Four on and four off went the watches and always our watch consisted of pushing those big back-breaking holy-stones—night as well as day—over those long white wooden decks. This would be the routine all week except Sunday, and the chant among this group of shadowy figures as they pushed and pulled always was:

"Six days shalt thou work
As thou are able
And on the seventh, holy-stone the deck
And wash the cable!"

That was the routine of the sailor's life on a passenger boat—pretty much the landman's duties. For the steering of the ship there were the elegant quartermasters, and for the few genuine sea-going activities (such as sewing of canvas, splicing of wire, cable or rope) there were the special friends of the boatswain. But for the "mob" the charing duties sufficed.

All with the exception of one thing. The war was on and even we "charwomen" sailors, being Britishers, were initiated into its mysteries. On the second day out, six of the more husky of us, divided into two watches, were apportioned as "auxiliaries" to the regular royal-navy men who composed the "gun's crew." The *Baltic*, like all the other mail liners, had a six inch gun back aft on the poop manned by two regular navy gunners working in watches and forever on the alert for that ominous periscope as we zig-zagged our way through the Danger Zone. The shells were all piled near the gun and our duties as auxiliaries were to load it at the order of the regular navy men.

But we were green men and it necessitated showing us how to work the gun. As I remember it, the ritual went something like this: You hoisted a shell to your shoulder; next placed it in the crutch of your arm; then when the breech was opened you chucked it in. Then the gunner fired. We got two days of such practice firing at barrels thrown from the poop. On the third day we got some real action.

We were about in the middle of the Danger Zone at the time, with the wind blowing rather hard and churning the sea into a mass of rising white-caps. Suddenly, there was much activity on the bridge, and we turned a complete arc in our wake. Instantly everybody on the poop was galvanized into action. The gunner thought he saw the dreaded periscope, first sighted from the bridge, and we three auxiliaries were commanded to the shells. I was number two on the gun's crew, with number one a lanky and very excitable Yorkshireman. As the gun kept booming and we kept feeding it, his excitement increased and on the fifth shell up, instead of throwing his shell into number one position (on his shoulder) he brought it up from the deck a little hurriedly and it slipped over and landed on my right foot. It weighed somewhere around one hundred and twelve pounds, and had the tip and not the blunt end of it struck my foot first, it would have blown the poop sky high

In the excitement I didn't realize the damage that had been done to my foot. The shell was picked up by the lanky Yorkshire boy placed in the breech and the firing continued. Everything and everybody was in a state of frenzy. On the passenger decks the rails were lined with frightened spectators. The gun boomed out. The *Baltic* zig-zagged and zig-zagged and if there were any submarines near to us at the time they certainly might have been sunk by that incessant shelling from our poop.

When the shells would land, water would shoot up like geysers from whales. It was intensely exciting, and I think what kept me going more than anything else was the peculiar exaltation of spirit that overwhelms all patriots when their valor is witnessed. But even patriotism must bow before the limitations of the body. The last conscious thing I remember on that poop was slipping the shell into the breech followed by a dazzling phosphorescence appearing in both eyes—then out. When I came to I was in the ship's hospital, with the ship's doctor and several assistants working over my foot.

They had given me something to revive me and I could see what was going on. The doctor was cutting my shoe away as quickly as he could from the flesh. The right foot in the region of the great toe had been crushed to a pulp and as the leather and the flesh were quickly torn apart and the gruesome wound showed itself I realized, from the doctor's talk, that this was a dangerous matter. It seemed that amputation either of the foot or the better part of the great toe was imperative at once. A local anaesthetic was put around the foot and I saw a knife-like instrument in the doctor's hands. As I watched, the right toe was cut off. The agony was so great it went beyond mere pain, and as the blood shot out from the foot I lapsed again into unconsciousness.

From then until the time that I was carried in a stretcher down the gangplank of the *Baltic* in New York and rushed to St. Vincent's Hospital, I recall very little of that stuffy little ship's hospital. Nightly it appeared they were waiting for what the ship's doctor had thought was inevitable—blood poisoning and death. With the right great toe off and the severance cauterized as crudely as only those familiar with ships' hospitals can visualize, I was in a state of semi-coma during the remaining five days passage to New York. The ship's doctor was genuinely amazed at my living and told me as much when the stretcher bearers took me in charge.

I was in St. Vincent's Hospital about three months— all through the summer of 1918. With my Irish name I became a great favorite in that Irish-American hospital. I had more candies and cakes on visitor's day than any other patient. I lost count of how many women wanted to adopt me.

When I had entered the hospital my mind already was made up: toe or no toe, when I got better I was going to skip from the hospital and stay in New York. I wrote home to this effect, discreetly minimizing the lost toe to a bruise. Then, when everything seemed to be going along nicely, an upset occurred.

I was hobbling along the ward one evening when I felt myself steadily growing warmer—then intensely hot, and finally sick and dizzy. I lay on the bed, my crutches falling to the floor, and the last thing I recall was a dull pain in my right leg.

The next thing I knew was the priest and sisters by my bedside, the latter praying and the former murmuring the Last Sacraments in Latin as he anointed me. It was only a fleeting conscious moment, but I saw that screens were around my bed and my right leg was raised high in the air, almost perpendicular, on some sort of cage contraption. The praying and the Latin murmurings continued and I realized that this was death. A Catholic boy, I knew only too well what the Last Sacraments meant!

There is not more to tell in this section. Contrary to expectations I was there alive in the morning, the cynosure of all eyes. Specialist after specialist came behind those screens to comment upon my case. I did not know what it was then, but later I was told that I had been stricken with a severe case of phlebitis and cellulitis. A clot of blood had moved up from the blunted foot and gotten into the blood stream; it was checked just above my right knee and dispersed there. My right leg fell away to a mere shadow—almost as thin as my arm—and it was at least two months before I could get out of bed. It would be many months, too, before I could stand on that leg, I was told to my deep chagrin.

CHAPTER
THIRTY-SIX

My LAMED condition, when I was discharged from the hospital in late September and turned over to the joint care of the White Star Line authorities and the British Consul, ended all ideas of staying in America. I was very much alarmed about my right leg. It was strangely withered, and although the doctors reassured me that gradually it would come back into its former strength, I was very skeptical. I used to gaze disgruntled at my right foot, now not nearly so big as the left one and looking very peculiar with only a stub of its great toe.

There was, however, one consolation. Since I was not in the Royal Navy, I had a clear suit against the White Star Line either for compensation or for "damages." Entertaining visions of thousands of pounds being awarded to me, I was taken aboard the *Baltic* the day she was sailing for Liverpool. It had all been nicely arranged with good British economy. I was placed once again in the sailor's forecastle, a member of the ship's crew in name only. The liner had been converted into a transport, and there were troops, troops everywhere—everywhere where

I had formerly seen passengers and cargo. The soldiers were a gay gang, singing and dancing all the time. I found none of the old crew. I searched out the ship's doctor, but a younger man showed up, explaining that the doctor familiar with my case was on a brief vacation on his farm in Surrey. The Navy gunners, whom I had known, were gone too.

The voyage itself was uneventful. Back in the Mersey we went straight to the Landing Stage to discharge the troops, many of whom were sick and ready for the hospital and not the front. The others were headed for the American training camp at Knotty Ash. I was among the first to get down the gangplank, and as I had no money with me I had to make the old trek this time on my game leg.

CHAPTER
THIRTY-SEVEN

LIVERPOOL was the same as I had left it, with the exception that perhaps now the American soldiers were in even more absolute command. The young women had gone for them hook, line and sinker. They were everywhere, and as they had a great deal more money to spend than any other soldiers and spent this with startling generosity, nothing was too good for them. These staid Liverpool girls had never been up against such stuff, not only in the slums, where anything went, but also in the more respectable homes, where everything did *not* go. It was not long before the inevitable evidences of coming maternity began to appear—then the suicides.

In our shack things had not changed. Alice's romance with the young soldier still in France was progressing (via letters and presents) very nicely. Mother was still slaving as charwoman down in the Chicago Building in Paradise Street, but this, I intimated, she must cease the moment a satisfactory settlement of my big damage suit had been made. We discussed this case for two nights and on the third it was decided to call my father—who as yet hadn't heard of my home-coming—into conference. It appeared that senility and a general bachelor neglect had tamed his boisterous demeanor a bit—so much so that even my mother, to whom his name still was veritable terror, concurred in calling him into the case. "If anyone can get you the limit in compo, your daddy's the one all right," she said.

But she wouldn't hear of his coming into our rooms; instead, Alice and I went down to his abominable room in the Dead House and saw him there. After pawing over me sentimentally he looked at my leg and decided that it offered a damage suit case for a barrister, very popular with the dockers on account of his ability to extract substantial sums for minor accidents. " 'E's the boy for us!" said my father. "We'll see 'im tomorrow. Now 'ow about the price of a pint for yer poor auld man. . . ?"

The following day, after throwing volunteer Kitty Daughtery through the door, my father and I went down to the barrister's resplendent offices. Here my father, after much handshaking (you'd think he'd known the eminent gentleman all his life) stated my case, elaborating on exactly how the accident had happened, how the White Star Line had shown culpable negligence and was liable to suit, and almost going so far as to show the barrister how to handle the case when and if it came to court. "It's worth a couple of thousand quid if it's worth a bloody penny, h'ain't it now, me lad?" he asked the eminent man.

There is no use elaborating on what happened after this. All through October I drew compensation money from the White Star Company, while the barrister allegedly worked on my case. As I supplied my father with his ale, he in return supplied me with the latest news of developments from the barrister's office. Once he had me believing that the settlement at "a couple of thousand quid" was imminent. Jackie Sanchez, himself a hopeless cripple now with a tubercular leg, used to accompany me on his crutches down to the lawyer's office. Freddie Seegar, the only other member of the gang seen occasionally around the corner, also used to muscle in, anticipating, of course, the vast amount of money I was very soon to come by. Jacko Oldham, Frankie Roza, and Mickey were still alive, but I seldom saw any of them. Jacko, I heard, was going to sea and Frankie, despite his dark color, was making great social strides, what with his status as an engineer and his skill with the concertina. Of the rest of the gang, the only survivor of those directly connected with the war was Henry Roche, still over in France.

Then one day my father came around for me in a desperate hurry. "Get your collar and tie on, and come with me. Our man wants to see us. . . ." He attempted to get inside the kitchen door, but my mother stopped him determinedly and, growling, he awaited me outside. My attitude toward him was very friendly; but my mind was made up that after I got the huge "lump sum" I was going to give him so much (not very much) and then dispense with his services and as quickly as possible forget him, for the sight of him always reminded me of so many unhappy occurrences.

What the eminent barrister had to tell us was startlingly brief—the company had offered to pay me compensation

until I was able to work again, but no settlement. My
father stared aghast. "What, no lump sum?" No lump
sum, intimated the great barrister, a sadistic twinkle in
his eye. My heart dropped—no lump sum! No "couple
of thousand quid!" No passenger voyage to New York!
I looked helplessly at my father; my father looked skeptically at the barrister; the barrister calmly filled his pipe.
We could sue, he suggested. What were the chances in
Court, I asked. Very good, he smiled. "Well, gawd blimey,
sue!" said my father.

Two months later the case came up in the Dale Street
Court. Our barrister sat there like a sphinx, my father
doing all the speaking and saying everything he shouldn't
have said and omitting everything that I should have told.
Lump sum, lump sum, lump sum—that phrase was in his
every sentence, recurring like a *liet motif*.

"Do you know anything else but 'lump sum'?" asked
one of the company's barristers.

"Do you know *anything*?" retorted my father with his
usual flash of wit.

I think we were about the best hated pair of claimants
ever to stand in public court and I have often thought
that the jury was indulging in a little human spite when
they awarded me thirty pounds to wipe the slate clean.
Out of this came my barrister's fee of, I think, six pounds,
one to my furious father, fifteen to my mother and the
remainder for myself. An American tailored suit came
next, out of my end of it, and this was followed by an
accordion and a general dissipation in ale to drown my
disappointment and chagrin and general disillusion.

The prize money went almost as swiftly as my leg

regained its strength. Now the old dilemma faced me again—I should either have to go to sea or seek employment ashore; in the latter case the dock was the most logical place. Freddie Seegar was my constant companion now instead of Jackie Sanchez at the dance halls—a very important department for me right then. Regular girlies' men we were, constantly in St. Martin's or the Daulby dance halls and there grew up between our diametrically opposed characters—we were the last of the gang, so to speak—a very close friendship.

Then a week later a bomb burst in the sky. The armistice was signed! The war was over! Over? Yes, over! There was to be no more fighting. No more fighting? No! I'll never forget November the eleventh. A few days preceding the actual signing there had been gossip and a few news items predicting just such an event. But none of us took it seriously. With the pouring in of the American troops we had been confident that Germany was in for a big licking and that at any moment we would see their famed Hindenburg Line crack and the Allied troops march on to Berlin. But we never thought it would end any other way—to think of that mad, long-drawn-out conflict ending at the behest of anything like common sense was a little too much to believe. At eleven o'clock on that eventful day, the city paused and waited and listened, and presently the air was rent with sirens blowing and steamers' whistles in the river blaring out madly —the armistice had been signed! The Germans were licked. The war was over! Over! Over! Over!

Up our way everybody went clean mad. The pubs, working on a reduced output all through the war, now opened up wide and with a plentiful stock. No more need to conserve barley and wheat and all that stuff—drink and be merry! Early in the evening every public house was taxed to capacity. Dockers coming home for their tea found their shacks empty and no tea—their wives drunk in some pub. There was some muffled cursing at this, but a restraining thought of a son lost and a mother's releasing of her pent-up grief would in most cases send the husband scurrying out to the same pub to join in the celebrating. "Do's" there were outside every other house —in Sparling Street, with its Negroes, Pitt Street, with its Chinks, and Frederick Street (Flukey Alley) with its Flukes. Once again, these polyglot patriots were victorious Britishers one and all!

A tremendous "do" broke out late at night outside the Dead House and as Georgie Bell, the town's best accordionist, had been commissioned for this one, Freddie and I both attended it. The Dead House tenants were out in all their glory—my father rolling around in his dirty dungarees, Auld Harris himself, quite tipsy for a change now and trying his best to work up a tune on his fiddle, and daughter Emma, now a big lanky girl, screeching the more popular American tunes under the uncertain but enthusiastic guidance of her mother, the latter's mustache bristling with glee.

Mrs. Tar was there gloating through her one eye and hanging on to her stupid, half-blind son who was observing Emma very morosely. Mrs. Golding, the picker of select middens, was going a hilarious jig with her weakminded son, John, and recently married Bob and Leah were gazing wistfully into each other's eyes. My mother

275

and lugubrious Auntie Janie were there, both of them, however, constantly under the critical eye of my sister hovering nearby. "Bid" Callaghan and Jimmy, her husband, were waltzing gayly around. Mrs. Mangan and Mrs. Manassi lurched wonderingly on the sidelines. *Their* war had ended when Johnny and Joe had been killed. Johnny Ford's mother was very hilarious and, seeing her dancing around, I thought of my old mate and a great sorrow came over me.

Later on the Black Prince came roaring down the street (without his knife this time) calling the Kaiser the most fearful names and immediately endearing himself to the hearts of all. Then, Freddie's mother put in an appearance and threatened to tear Freddie's American tailored suit off his back right there in the street (and she would have too!) if he didn't oblige with "It's a long way to Tipperary. . . ."

Freddie, much embarrassed, stepped forward and twisted his mouth into shape, and on the second encore had the stage stolen from him by the irresistible Emma Harris, whom no one could restrain from singing any song at any time or place. Then Georgie Bell's accordion started into—of all tunes!—Strauss' "The Blue Danube Waltz." Nobody knew the difference and we all whistled the tune with glee and danced to our hearts' content. After this, and after the ale had been passed around and around and the Kaiser had been lambasted anew and fights threatened among the women over comparative losses sustained in the war, another Strauss melody was played to the extreme happiness and ignorance of everyone. These were our accordionist's chief stock waltz tunes, come down to him from the days of the gay young German sailormen from the Hamburg clippers putting into Liverpool.

Many times during the spree I became afraid for my mother, who upon occasion would glance at my father, blood in her eyes. I knew what was the matter with her, poor woman, with her pent-up, long-restrained bitterness fanned now with the ale and whisky. Always deep down in her soul was that human desire to even things up with my father, to repay him for the terrible life he had given her and her "two little chicks." I had to watch her pretty closely all the time, for had she once gotten out of hand there's no telling what she might have done to him. The Joan of Arc who had been our fighting little leader in the *Lusitania* riots, was behaving more peaceably and had become quite friendly now with Annie Monnigan, Charlie Thomas's wife, whose home she had helped wreck during those vicious *Lusitania* riots. Everybody and anybody— it was the same old gang, but the younger men, now dead in France or floating somewhere at sea, were sadly missing.

As the "do" reached its height, I saw a strange figure pass on the sidelines—Father Ryan, our parish priest, now a very sick man. He took one look at the mob, sighed, and passed on up the street to his debt-ridden church.

On through the night the "do's" proceeded, all over the city, certainly all over the slummy sections of the city. Sleep was out of the question anywhere. Bitter fights took place. Madness broke out; minds suddenly released from the tension were unable to control themselves. And finally there was the inevitable tragic note. While all this celebrating was going on, indeed (although I never saw her) while his very mother danced outside the Dead House in anticipation of his eventual homecoming now that the war was over, stark tragedy had already pointed its finger at another one of my mates.

Henry Roche, the boyish Irish figure so comical in his Scottish kilts, was killed this very night his mother celebrated! We did not hear of it for a few days—not until the recent casualties of his regiment, the Liverpool Scottish, were checked. He was killed about seven hours after the Armistice had been signed. It all seemed puzzling to us, but Austin Jorgensen explained the situation when he came among us for a brief leave from France. There was quite a bit of fighting that went on after the Armistice had been signed, because of the slowness in telegraphing the news around the line. Many lives had been lost that way, especially among the Liverpool Scottish, which had been in a bitter engagement with the enemy all that day.

I shall never forget the look in Freddie Seegar's eyes the night he heard that Henry, like the others, was booked to stay in France. Despite his general disregard for danger, there was a lot of Irish superstition in him. In Mrs. Mallin's pub we checked scores—seven gone from thirteen. Thirteen! That was a bad number. He left me very uneasy that night.

CHAPTER
THIRTY-EIGHT

For a month following the armistice, the convivial business kept up—at least in the slummy section. The pubs were taxed to capacity day and night and those that had made so much money as munitions workers and dockers while safe at home now spent it freely. Also, the returning soldiers spent their thirty pounds "gratuity" very freely.

There followed also a terrible splurge of "war weddings"—"economic romances" the nature of which I have touched upon before. My sister, Alice, married the young soldier from down the street, marching to the altar of St. Vincent's and poignantly staring up at Father Ryan as he performed the last marriage ceremony of his career.

Leave her mam and go to housekeeping elsewhere? The suggestion was preposterous, and more wonderment came into her lovely brown eyes when she saw her mother encouraging Austin's shrewd proposal. So the ambitious youngster, who had put in four years in France for his King and country and who wanted so badly to get a steady job and a little house and have children and eventually aspire to a foreman's job and a collar and tie, must come and share our two rooms with us. This meant that he had little chance to woo Alice from all the latter memories that were her heritage. Moreover, Austin liked to work hard, but when the work was done he wanted his reward. That reward consisted in the traditional pint of ale and visting friends and relatives. But Alice hated ale fiercely and shrank from visiting friends and relatives (the priests were the only friends I knew her to have), wanting only to live quietly in a world of her own making.

The wedding "do" sounded the ominous note. Alice, the bride, would not drink and, as might have been expected, frowned upon my mother's getting drunk. She went completely into her shell when her husband started to roll around and sing and disport himself in the traditional manner of a young man at his wedding. But under Alice's dark and frightened frown, the guests (slummies all of them whom Alice detested) soon began to wiggle uncomfortably and to depart one by one. The "do" ended on a note of anti-climax, and Austin, poor boy, went to his wedding bed wondering and doubting but loving.

He loved Alice intensely, but he could not understand her strange aloofness. He had spent the better part of his thirty pounds gratuity (a bitter pill for Alice to swallow) in furnishing a "do" that would be remembered and it had ended in this sad fashion, with the guests leaving and everyone silent, and gloom cast over everything.

I myself was placed in the uncomfortable position of the defending brother-in-law. Austin naturally assumed that he would have me to contend with in any family strife—that, I think, being one of his main reasons for wanting to get Alice out of our shack. In this, however, he was quite wrong. I, more than anyone, knew just what he was up against, and to no other man I have ever known did my sympathies go out so genuinely.

Immediately after the period of spreeing, the economic reaper began to take a hand. Among the bourgeoisie there had been erotic after-the-war tragedies and all that sort of "civilized" stuff. But none of this in our slums—it was simply economics, economics in everything including love. Poverty, that was the fellow to be reckoned with, not so minor a thing as an unfaithful wife or husband. I have known cases where a job has brought an erring slummy wife from the bed of her paramour back to the husband obtaining it. And nothing done about it. "Jim went back to work and Biddie went back to Jim"—that was all. Biddie would be beaten many times and severely for her aberration, but as long as Jim provided bread and ale he could feel assured that Biddie would not leave him.

With the glamor of the after-the-war spirit now spent (as well as the war gratuities) all we felt now was the increasing difficulty in finding jobs and the growing number of jobless as against the jobs to be distributed. The mills were all working on reduced schedules; no longer did ships in port work dock-wollopers overtime; overseers and bosses became very cocky and the stock question to the worker: "Will you go to a wedding?" became an ironic pun. The fact that soldiers returned from France to follow their pre-war occupation as merchant sailormen and, since they were regular sailormen, were given the preference, interfered with my plans for getting out of the country as quickly as possible. Moreover, I was handicapped by the fact that my record, prior to my desertion in Philadelphia, was a dead issue now. I had a coal-trimmer's discharge from the *Megantic* and an A. B.'s from the *Baltic*, but both these were White Star Line ships and I had sued the company in open court. Pierhead "jumps" were not the fashion now, with sailors anxiously looking for ships. It decreased my bitterness no little to think that in the same ratio that my general health grew better, my chances of getting back to New York grew slimmer.

Then economic conditions got worse. From reduced outputs, the mills one by one closed down; ships brought in much but took out little—a strange thing for Liverpool. Now Freddie and I found it increasingly difficult to get even the occasional day down at the docks—the wherewithal for the dance and the pub. My mother's charing duties were restricted to half a week, and most of my food came via my brother-in-law, who seemed to fare better with work at the docks. My clothes got seedy.

Like all things that alter the destinies of men, the opportunity to return to America came into my life as unobtrusively and quietly and fantastically as almost everything else had come into it. I had made my usual round of the stands at the various docks early one morning, and as usual there was "nothing doing," and I sat down on one of the many iron pins on the quay and gazed out at the Mersey. Across the river lay Hoylake and the sanitarium and the sands on which but a few years ago I had romped so contented and happy; the sands on which on another wilder day, I had seen the life-boat crew swirl out to their graves

Then a hand rested on my shoulder. It was a young American whom Freddie and I had got to know from meeting him at the Daulby Hall. He was a rather likeable fellow, not so aloof as most of the Americans that frequented the Daulby, and we had gotten along very well together. I had introduced him to Nancy, my old friend who liked Americans so well, and he and Nancy both appreciated the favor. It had never occurred to me that he was a sailor; I could see now that he was—very likely from off the American freighter *Courageous*, whose winches now ground out in the Queen's Dock just behind me.

He wanted to know what I was doing there looking out on the river—contemplating jumping in? As the idea of stowing away was very much in my mind right then, I replied facetiously that I was contemplating secreting myself aboard his ship. Well, why not? She was leaving that night for New York. (From conversations with me at the Daulby Hall he knew I'd lived in and liked New York.) I looked at the man; then to the ship. Was he serious? His expression was a blank. Why not? Would he help me? The blank expression never changed. As much as he could. He was on deck and if he knew where I was going to stow myself, he could slip me a few sandwiches maybe of a night—if I promised not to give him away if I got caught. He was going up to the Main Stem, but he had a few minutes to spare and suppose we went up on the *Courageous* and looked around the ship?

The month was December and, as I knew more about ships than my friend, I immediately suggested the engine-room, where, I knew from my Philadelphia experience in building such ships as the *Courageous*, a man-hole opened into the midships hatch—a warm spot nearby the boiler. The man-hole was there, all right, about half-way down the winding steel ladder. I went down and slipped it open. My guess was right, for peering through the darkened tunnel I could see the dockers putting in the cargo in the midship hatch. That was my spot!

When I came up to the alleyway, and he observed my quiet determination, the blankness in his face had given way to mild apprehension—don't forget if I got caught, there must be no squawking on him! After I had convinced him on this, I took him to the galley and pointed to a lower locker wherein he could leave whatever stuff he had for me. Then he gave me his American address—in Baltimore, Maryland—in case I ever wanted to look him up. Not a sailor, he smiled a little nervously, but a landsman—a dance-hall guy, he intimated, like me. We shook hands and departed—he to Nancy's home; I to explore further the mysteries of my future cabin to America.

Down the steel steps I went and through the man-hole and explored about. Several of the dockers, putting aboard the cases of tomato soup, nodded, thinking that I, like them, was working in the gang. All this tomato soup would be at my mercy when everything was battened down. Moreover, the man-hole in the engine-room was not bolted down, simply swinging open and shut, thereby eliminating the fear that I might be permanently imprisoned —always a chance with a stowaway. Also I assumed it would be warm and cozy.

A LIVERPOOL IRISH SLUMMY

I was very pleased when I came up from explorations. Tonight I would leave for New York! Three weeks later (at the outside) I would be there. In another month, perhaps, I would have a comfortable wardrobe, a nice room, several poems or tales written (and the publisher's checks received), to say nothing of an occasional tango at St. Nicholas Rink. That night, a curious plan in mind, I pawned my American tailored suit (had Auld Harris known of my plans, he would never have taken it in, it was so impossible to resell) for five shillings and got into overalls.

Would Freddie Seegar, the last active member of the gang, go with me? My curious plan was to fetch him. Assuredly I should like to have him and his infectious humor with me in that dark hole. He had always joined me in my wails against England and the desire to get away from it in any manner that offered. He had never been to sea—would he be wary of making his debut this way? When he heard the nature of our plan the answer came immediately—sure he'd go! I was elated and did everything in my power to give him the impression that there really was no difficulty about the whole matter.

But Freddie, like all good Irishmen, is very sentimental and what invites at eight o'clock may not look quite so agreeable at ten. Into Mrs. Mallin's pub we went, where I said under cross-examination by everyone present, that my money had come through changing my costume, and adding to Freddie that the moment he saw the swell clothes in New York, his too would be thrown into the discard. He doubted this, however, for he was very fond

of those bastard coat pleats that some ingenious Englishman had conceived and tagged "American tailored."

In Mrs. Mallin's we drank pint after pint on my five
bob, with the fear always present that I might finally lose
Freddie. Eight, nine, ten o'clock—the *Courageous* would
be about ready to go to sea now—was he? Outside in the
dark cold street he hesitated, and I took him by the arm,
looking him squarely in the eye—was he flunking, shirk-
ing? What did I mean? he demanded. Precisely what I
said, I admonished, bitter at spending all that my suit had
brought in pawn and then losing him in the end. Freddie
would fight at the drop of the hat and he stopped, pushed
me away from him, and demanded a fuller explanation.
I gave it to him.

"There's my cousin Berny, Joe Manassi, Harold May,
Johnny Ford, Johnnie Mangan, and Henry Roche, all
went down like men and you—you're scared to stow
away."

Undoubtedly, we would have fought it out then and
there, but just at that moment our common boyhood
enemy, Aeroplane Joe, showed through the fog swinging
his baton and eyeing us severely.

"And there," muttered Freddie discreetly quiet, "is the
lousy bloody bum that caused the most of it."

I took him by the arm. "Come on! We don't want to
get locked up now!"

He shook me off and started toward the docks; then
hesitated at the corner, making some excuse about going
back to his shack to get something. But I kept after him
—he had his tobacco and pipe, what more did he want?
Come on! Now wait a minute, Timmy! Come on! What

was the matter with me—was I goin' loony? Come on down to the ship and then if he didn't want to go, he could at least stay on the quay and bid me good-by.

All right then! All the way down Bridgewater Street, I kept assuring him how carefully the whole thing had been arranged and how simple it would be to work it out. Then abreast of my shack, it occurred to me I hadn't told my mother of my plan. Immediately I wanted to stop and bid her good-by, but here I sensed danger—if I did that, he would demand to do likewise and that would mean only one thing. As we passed the doorway of our shack, a terribly guilty feeling came over me. My mother would worry so! But then, what about Freddie's mother? They could bear it!

Coming up the street in the fog was a familiar figure— my young ex-warrior brother-in-law returning after putting in half-a-night down at the Cork boats, sweating and no doubt wondering what mood Alice would be in. I called him aside—Freddie and I were stowing away on an American ship and his job was to break the news both to my mother and to Mrs. Seegar, but not before tomorrow. Everything was all right—did he understand that? There was no danger to anyone concerned—just await the letters that would follow.

He tried to remonstrate with me, suggesting that perhaps I was not doing the sensible thing (all the time glad that I was going, if only to lighten his own economic burden), but I hurried off, Freddie a reluctant but very grim companion.

Up the companionway—on the quiet ship—at the engine room doorway. Hesitation by Freddie—now wait a minute! I literally pushed him down the steel steps, down toward the man-hole. I opened it feverishly, trembling lest we be seen at this crucial stage. Down, down I pushed him, and rejoined him in the darkness a moment later, discreetly pushing the plate back into place. He stood there in the darkness, uncertain, brushing his elegant suit, and I took him by the arm and led him out into the wider hatch. It was all right, everything had been arranged; there were the boxes of tomato soup, and up in the galley just as soon as we get started would be the sandwiches and coffee and desert and candies and cigars. And pretty soon the electrician would install the lights. What was he scared about? Scared? He stared at me, galvanized into action. Better smile when I say that to him!

And smile I did, for I knew my Freddie very well. He was here with me to furnish the much needed comedy, a reluctant partner perhaps but never a cowardly one. When the *Courageous's* engines started turning over a few hours later, he had already fixed himself a comfortable bed on the tomato boxes and was filling his pipe, philosophizing on what the ladies would now do, what with him away and nobody quite so attentive as he to their wants.

CHAPTER
THIRTY-NINE

THIS stowing away was one of the most bitterly painful journeys I have ever known. Everything went wrong. I had guessed wrong, for instance, in assuming that the proximity of the hatch to the engine-room would mean warmth for us. I had not taken into consideration the distance of the snake-like tunnel separating the hatch proper, where we were to live, from the engine-room. This narrow passageway was extremely hot, gradually getting cooler as it tipped out into the broad dark areaway of the hatch, where the temperature (particularly as we neared America) was like that of an icebox.

Then my optimism as regards the menu soon received an expected shock. We could not live indefinitely on canned tomatoes, and our American friend left the sandwiches in the galley locker on only a few occasions. Sometimes, after making the precarious ascent into the galley, I would find the locker bare and sometimes there would be little else save a mess left by the rats—the remnants of which I would take quickly down to the hatch, where we would eat ravenously. Bringing water down in a can was always a problem for me, because we had not taken water into consideration and were now using the small tomato cans exclusively. As I got through the man-hole in haste, invariably these cans would tip over, and I would lose some, occasionally all, of the water.

One time, when making the midnight ascent, I very nearly got caught. The ocean at night always fascinated me, and this particular night, with the waves riding high and the sky clear and ice in the wind, I couldn't help from staring out across the mystery for a brief moment and filling my lungs with the fresh keen air—so great a change from the stuffiness of the closed, darkened hatch. Then I heard voices coming up the steel ladder of the engine-room! I ducked into the galley and in desperation squeezed myself into the locker where the food cache was hid. The voices entered the galley—members of the "down-below" gang, Americans betraying their true nationality by their accents.

As usual, like good sailormen, they were talking about women, one of them saying something about a "tart's" expecting him to marry her on the return trip—but he was married already, he laughed. So the joke was on her! The other fellow laughed—he'd pulled the same stunt some time previous. They believed anything you told them, these Limey tarts! The coffee cans clinked; they went out. Then two sailors came in, Americans, cursing the mate, the captain ("the square-headed sonofabitch!"), the ship, the weather, the coffee. They went out and, after waiting a bit, I took a chance, gathered up the sandwiches (crushed black from my standing on them) filled the tomato cans with water and made the swift, furtive descent once again. On account of my greater ship knowledge, I deemed it best for me to make all the trips.

There was another and more vital reason for my not allowing Freddie to make an occasional trip. Though I hadn't any doubts about his personal courage, he had never before faced anything like this. This dark hole with rats as big as one's feet scurrying over one, with our blood frozen stiff and hardly any food and nothing to do but wait there with the prospect of a month of it (I kept telling him it took only ten days for the *Courageous* to make the crossing, in an effort to bolster his courage)—all this, in many ways, meant worse than facing death for him.

His pipe tobacco ran out, and pretty soon the enchantment of the Irish folk tales learned from his mother lost their tang. He mislaid his keen sense of humor and it wasn't long before he looked upon me as the greatest curse ever to come into his life. At the end of the third night, with the beams creaking terribly and the lightened ship tossing about in the ocean, seasickness got him and I had a devil of a time preventing him from scurrying up through the man-hole and surrendering.

He pleaded with me. "For God's sake, Timmy, let me get up out of here!" He wouldn't say anything about my being down there, he swore; but I held him fast, for I knew that his surrender would lead to a general search, and I had no intention of getting caught now that we had gone so far. He must have suffered the agonies of hell down that stuffy hatch with his belly full of old tomato soup and my steadfastly refusing him a breath of fresh air. One night, about the second day after his seasickness lightened, I thought I would have to let him go up. The darkness and the rats and the lack of food and general fear had finally penetrated into that region of the mind of which Freddie knew nothing, and I suddenly found him wandering around in the darkness, cursing me and rambling on in a most incoherent fashion.

I sat him on the hatch and talked to him severely, explaining with lying fury that the ship would be in port any day now (as a matter of fact we weren't nearly halfway over then) and for him to buck up! Then I talked playfully about the tarts in Liverpool and the dances and the pubs and of other stuff reeking with nostalgia for him, and gradually he came back.

But he was cracking, and once again I gambled with everything. The next night I took him along with me, up through the man-hole into the companionway and the air. We stayed there, leaning over the rails in the darkness, for fully ten minutes, with him filling his lungs with fresh air and his eyes brightening and a more sane expression coming into them. There were no sandwiches there that night, and I had a hard job convincing him that we better go back to our hiding place. But it had been a profitable trip, for he was a different lad from then on. His collapse had been as much physical as mental, for one increased the effects of the other. What he had needed was some fresh air.

From then on, however, we were like two strangers—two men united only by a single grim purpose—to stick this thing through to the end. We slept on the steel deck, with the broken boxes on top of us for warmth, and we had tomato soup whenever we chose. Sometimes watching the huge rats was his only diversion. I would fall asleep shivering with the cold and when I would awake I would find him breaking open another can of tomato soup and drinking it with disgust. We would not speak to each other for days at a time and did so only when loneliness threatened to send him mad.

Freddie began to cough with alarming regularity. One night he complained of sweats and of difficulty in getting his breath, and I began to fear the dreaded pneumonia. I did not want that on my soul—keeping him down here to die—and I watched him and attended to his needs now with genuine fear that the game might soon be up. Over two weeks had passed now, and the only thing that was keeping him going was my daily promise that any moment would hear the creaking of the beams stop and the silencing of the engines—and New York! New York of the plentiful, of the *real* American suits (not the preposterous Liverpool imitation he now wore), of the dance, of everything he claimed to like best. But, alas, Freddie's mind already was made up. All he wanted, his silence implied, was to get back to Liverpool and *never* be coerced into a mad thing like this again!

I must confess, too, that as the two weeks lengthened into three and still the beams creaked and the engines pounded and the ship tossed, that I too had lost much of my adventurous spirit. I had no desire to reship back to Liverpool—indeed I was determined not to—but the physical and mental strain were telling on me. My old chest weakness had returned and I was now coughing and spitting very badly. And I was in that state of acute and chronic hunger where food no longer entices.

The added strain of playing professional comforter to my depressed mate, whose total activities now consisted of lying on his back fretting and praying, was becoming too much. With the passing of the third week, I joined him in grim silence. There had been nothing in the galley for a whole week, and assuming that our friend had decided it would be wiser not to put anything in the locker and as I myself was chary of taking a chance now that we were so close to a realization of our goal, I was reluctant to make the ascent. We were almost starved and about as close to freezing that any two young men can be and still live. Freddie was so weak he found it difficult to stand, while in my own case the leaping I had formerly done over the tunnel toward the man-hole was replaced now by a senile caution.

Then something happened that buoyed up the spirits of us both. In the intensity of our suffering, we had not noticed the change that had come over the movement of the ship. The rolling that had, unnoticed by us, gradually subsided, now had stopped altogether and we were moving along creakless and as smoothly as a ferry boat. The darkness had deceived us, giving us the impression of night. In reality we were steaming up into New York's North River, during a heavy snow storm. Then the engines ceased their rumbling; a metallic bell sounded in the engine-room and presently everything was silent.

I jumped erect and gripped him by the knees, for I knew what this meant. "We're here, Freddie!" I gasped. "We're in New York! America!"

It was too big a temptation for me, and before he could make a reply, I bade him stay down in the darkness, while

I made sure about my guess. Up through the darkened tunnel I crawled, moved the man-hole plate aside and shrank back when the sunlight smote me in the face. Night down below, but up here sunlight! During the last five days our calculations had apparently lagged behind a full twelve hours—at any rate, figuring it to be night, it now showed as midday. There was much activity down in the engine-room.

I looked up the steel ladder. It was madness to go up there now that we had come so far without getting caught. It must be New York for what else would we pause? Then I heard up forward that unmistakable rumble that convinced me—the "hook" being let go! The anchor speeding off the windlass plunging its head into the water! Yes, we were here, no mistaking that! I closed the man-hole quickly and returned to the darkness and my mate. Were we there? Yes, I said, we certainly were! We would probably dock any time now, and then—all those luxuries I had told him about and for which he no longer cared one jot.

Irish optimism zoomed in my mate as soon as he realized the ocean with its mid-winter terrors had been crossed and that now he could cast about for a swift White Star or Cunard boat to carry him back home. His humor and his clay pipe, gotten from Mrs. Mallin's pub gratis with his first pint, came out strongly. Bits of tobacco dirt was recovered from the corners of his pockets and the pipe of happiness, of satisfaction, of conquest, soon blazed forth. When the *Courageous* docked and the longshoremen and other artisans came aboard, our getaway would be made comparatively easy. I seized the pipe from him and took a few draughts from it; then he snatched it back and squared off with the old mimicry—once again we were playmates and very, very happy.

I began curtseying around the darkened hatch, illustrating the steps I would soon be doing in some swell American dance-hall. On he smoked, and the smoke filled the hatch, and presently there was over our heads much scurrying of feet, followed by the desperate scratching of canvas. Then, lo! one of the hatches covering us— the one directly over where we sat—was lifted as by some mysterious force and daylight and snow streamed down upon us. Not only daylight and snow, but the big Scandinavian jowls of the chief mate.

I scurried for the tunnel, followed quickly by Freddie. But it was too late. The mate had seen us, a point he told us in his very best American: "Oh, there you! I yust saw you! Come oop! Come oop! I shoot by yo!" A couple of gallant sailors jumped into the areaway and hauled us back quickly. I glared down at Freddie's pipe—the cause of our debacle! The big Scandinavian mate was grunting down the ladder, followed by the boatswain and some other sailors, most of them Scandinavians, oilskinned and seabooted and covered with snow.

The mate glared at us good naturedly. "Vot you doin' down here—stowaways, no? Ho, ho, Limey stowaways! You been in here since we left *Liverpool*?" I nodded and he stared at me as though doubting my word.

"By yo! By yo!" He smiled at the pipe still smoking on the deck. I smiled too; so did the sailors; everyone save Freddie. He knew what he had done, and the sense of guilt weighed very heavily on him.

As they took us up the ladder he looked pensively at me and said, "I'm sorry, Timmy. . . ." But it was too late. Presently, we were up on deck drinking in the splendor of a wintry New York harbor and from here quickly whisked to the Captain's cabin, there to receive an excoriating speech. Then we were turned over to the law.

We were taken to Ellis Island and after being kept there a short time brought before a board and released. The two causes of the release I think were my name and the fact that I was an experienced sailor; because of America's enthusiastic ventures into big-time merchant shipping business sailors were much in demand then. We were allowed to enter the country on the condition that we "reship foreign." A member of the examining board, a sentimental kindly Irishman, immediately upon hearing my name and the fact that we were without funds, gave me five dollars, with the parting suggestion that I say a prayer for his aged grandmother now very sick in a Brooklyn hospital. This five dollars I split with Freddie, but only with the understanding he do the praying.

We landed at South Ferry about an hour after our release, and I took him in charge, barging into a restaurant as pompously and confidently as a native. I wanted to impress him so thoroughly with the amenities of America that he would forego his hankering to return home. However, it didn't work that way. After bumming around with me for two days, he suddenly disappeared, leaving word with the clerk at the Sailors' Home that he would see me there that evening.

I met him before the appointment, however, on West Street striding very jubilantly toward South Street—the British Consul had gotten him a mess-boy's job on the *Cedric*, leaving tomorrow for Liverpool! For Liverpool and the Daulby Hall and Lime Street and the Wine-Lodge and the tarts and all the other things so dear to his heart. It did not surprise me. He tried to influence me, but I couldn't share his enthusiasm. Why stick around here in the snow and cold with no clothes and money when I could be back home? I didn't know; I did know that Freddie and I were different persons altogether and our ways must part. Before bidding him good-by I split with him the two dollars I had left.

Again the sense of loss, the feeling of abysmal loneliness! To Freddie, going back home was getting on, doing something he liked, progressing somewhere. He would forget me an hour after he had gone. But to me, he was an indelible memory, a symbol of things past, another good-by, another leaf fallen from our common tree. I watched him hurrying along through the snow in West Street, the three funny looking box-pleats of his very British American-tailored suit swinging in the wind. I never saw him again.

CHAPTER FORTY

DESTINY had already shaped my course. The next day I shipped as boatswain on an American coastwise ship, a Clyde liner I believe. Anyone could get a birth on an American ship those days, and your British or Scandinavian sailorman could simply name his own job. What I wanted was some money quickly, and any ship suited. We put into Baltimore—into the dry docks. One day, while painting the ship's mast, I recalled our American benefactor's Baltimore address, and that night I looked him up. He was driving a Yellow Taxicab—a far cry from what I had at first imagined. We became fast friends during my stay there, reminiscing over mutual hardships on the *Courageous*—and of course about Nancy who, it seemed, had ceased writing love letters to him. He took me around among a lot of landsmen. I met many girls and danced a great deal. When the Clyde liner left the Baltimore Dry Docks, it had a new boatswain. Save for periodic sea interludes I became now an American taxi driver.

The periodic sea interludes I have reference to occurred

several times in the form of taking quick ship to Liverpool to see my mother. I was forced to do several unethical tricks at times to accomplish this purpose—particularly when a burst of maritime chauvinism sweeping over the country made it mandatory that all American ships be manned by Americans, native or citizens. I had taken out my first papers but had three or four years to await full citizenship. This new law brought with it a vexing problem. Ships left regularly from Baltimore to Liverpool direct, but now they would have to be manned by *Americans*. My passport shows how this problem was solved, and to the United States Commissioner that I so unconscionably humbugged, I offer my deepest apologies. It was my mother or the law—there could be no other choice.

In this new guise as a one hundred per cent American, I would go to Liverpool, always with a feeling of foreboding that any moment an erstwhile shipmate would betray me. Sometimes embarrassment would arise leaving ship in Liverpool, for when the one hundred per cent American crew would be going ashore, they would wonder why I would slink off and not accompany them to the usual American sailors' haunts. I had to put up with continual denunciation of everything British, but now, arrived in Liverpool, I couldn't very well afford to accompany this enthusiasm into places that knew me so well.

One day the *Quaker City* (that I had shipped on as a dubious American) docked in the Queen's, and my father clambered aboard in one of the dock-laboring gangs. Good God! what poignancy in having to elude *him*! What extreme embarrassment in working around the deck when at any moment I might be given away by any of the dockers who knew me so well!

But somehow or other, though I often came under direct suspicion, these dilemmas were met. Alice and my mother, of course, were my confidants and whenever I would visit them it would always be under cover of darkness. It was on one of these swift visits that my mother showed me the Weekly *Post* clipping about the Working Boy's Home waif who had listened to the sophistries of the Empire Builders, and who, after several attempts to escape the prairie solitude and peonage, had hanged himself on Christmas Eve in a barn in far-off Canada. Wasn't *that* my mate, Mickey? There was no picture, but the waif was from Manchester, an orphan, and his early life was more or less vague. Lacking definite proofs, I was convinced it was Mickey. I could have found out definitely from the Working Boy's Home, but that would entail giving my identity away. At any rate, I felt in my heart it was he. Empire Builder! Well, that made eight. I was a peculiarly sad American that night.

I never went near the barracks nor the corner on these surreptitious visits. Mother told me all I wanted to know. The barracks were as static as ever—the only difference was that my *elegant* relatives had moved to New York. There wasn't any more corner in the sense that I once knew it. Jackie Sanchez was always asking about me and was now, with his tubercular leg, a hopeless cripple. Frankie Roza and Jacko Oldham were "getting along fine with their trades." Freddie Seegar? That fellow always was in trouble! He hadn't done anything since he came home from stowing away save "blow his bloody 'ead off about 'ow much he'd done to 'elp you!"

Sometimes the news was a little heartening. With the dole abject starvation was out of the question. One could work three days at the dock for thirty-six shillings and draw the three days dole at three shillings per day to boot, making a grand total of forty-five shillings for the week of three days actual work! If one worked four days at the dock, there would be no dole, so the trick was to see to it that only three days were worked. And if no work were forthcoming, there would be eighteen shillings anyway. This beneficence was amazing when my mother compared it with former years.

And there were new houses being built by the Corporation, with all the new American gadgets such as gas and electricity in them! Several of the slummy crowd, particularly those who had salted a little away during the War, were taking social chances and moving into them. Several, however, finding life unbearable without the oil lamp and the bedroom bucket, were moving back.

Tragic news came, as I had feared, from Alice. Her marriage had failed and the young man, sad in heart and disillusioned, had "joined up" again, asking bitterly to be sent away "as far as possible." The Empire stretches very far, so they sent him to Peshawar in India. A little while later their child was born, and just a few months afterward the father died of malaria in far-off Peshawar. "Of a broken heart," said his mother—and there is much, I daresay, can be said for that.

Many such trips I made, but the last lingers in my memory longer than any of the others. One night, after paying the initial hurried visit to our shack, I was walking along Lime Street going, I think, to the American Bar, there to mingle with the other one hundred per cent Americans, when, coming abreast of the Palais de Luxe, a great nostalgia swept over me. I did not go toward that long stairway—a power much stronger drew me up into my old beloved darkened gallery. The same old thing! Nothing changed, the darkness, the shadows, the shapes, my very thoughts and dreams of years gone by! Only one thing was missing—my sandwiches.

The picture was some sophisticated nonsense, but I did not look at it. I closed my eyes and listened, patiently awaiting the tunes I loved so well, that particular one that moved me so! One, two, three hours I stayed up there in the darkness, waiting patiently for it to be played, but it never came—nothing but puerile imitations of American jazz.

Then I had an idea. I went downstairs, bought an orchestra ticket and walked straight up the aisles to the orchestra pit. In the semi-darkness I motioned to the orchestra leader and pressed a half-crown in his hand. No—no he could not do that, but what favor was it I wished? Would he play a certain tune for me? What tune? I did not know the name, but I could whistle it for him, and I did. He recalled it immediately upon the first whistling. "Dream of Autumn," he said. Yes, he would play it. Not right now I said—not for about five minutes, until I got back to a certain seat, then he could play it as many times as he could stand it.

As I walked down the darkened aisle and up the big stairway, I felt quite certain the orchestra leader put me down as a mad Yankee. But what matter—into the old seat now and after a bit that refrain started up. It is not Brahms, nor Wagner, but neither Brahms nor Wagner could not stir my soul so profoundly as this bit of sentimental whimsy. My eyes closed; in that darkness I was once again the little slummy in the bare feet munching his sandwiches and dreaming his dreams! Once again the consumptive waif coughing and fretting and wondering what awaited him when he left his dream-world for grim reality. I am thinking of Joe and Harold and Berny and the two Johnnies and Henry and Mickey; of my mates still alive; of Aeroplane Joe, the bobby; of St. Peter's School and Mr. McGinnis; of all those strange slummies; of my poor benighted father; of Alice—of my mother.

CHAPTER
FORTY-ONE

So THE story ends. Most of my experiences during the dozen years I lived in Baltimore driving a taxicab have been written in two volumes, TAXI HEAVEN, already published, and a TAXI JOURNAL, to be published at some future date. Four years ago my mother, then seventy years old, along with my sister, Alice, came over to live with me in America, and as I write this I hear my mother jigging it to an Irish air played on the radio—a great little colleen if ever there was one! My sister very proudly showed me the two medals the king had awarded me.

My grandmother died eventually and was buried beside her gravely strange husband. The barracks still live on, with my lugubrious Auntie Janie now in sole command. My elegant cousins were the only ones to follow us to America and, of course, to prosper. The ale finally got to my father's bowels, causing, I am told, some sort of cancer. But before coming to America, Alice, with that remarkable devotion to her father that has so characterized her, saw to it that he was placed very comfortably in the Little Sisters of the Poor Home. Here he lived in all the tranquil quietness of a retired monk, getting his bit of baccy regularly and also his pint of ale, always asking about me—"that lad o' mine!" and passing to his reward a year or so ago.

My reason for settling into the prosaic business of taxi-driving was because I wanted a shore job, freed of bosses, in which I could do some reading—something I was very much in need of. My friend of the *Courageous* showed me the rudiments of driving. It was about the worst possible task I could have undertaken, but once started I thought it best to see it through.

One day on my cab I read in a newspaper an article on reading and what should and should not be read, the article ending with the suggestion that perhaps a beginning reader's best friend might be a sympathetic librarian. That night, from the parlor of the semi-bordello in which I roomed, I wrote to Mr. Wheeler, the librarian at the Pratt Free Library, in Baltimore, explaining that I was an ignorant taxi-driver who wanted to write literature, but who hadn't read anything. Poor man, I must have frightened him to death, for although his reply was very nice and very courteous, the negative hint was quite apparent. I must say, however, in due respect to this gentleman, that when my first novel was published, he did under pressure buy *one* copy, placing it back among the early unread Greek philosophers, and refusing (to safeguard the morals of the community, I suppose) to allow it to be taken out of the institution.

So a new problem posed itself to me—what best to read? How appalling those long tiers of books looked upon my first visit to the public library! Why want to write

when so many books had already been written? I slunk
into a silent aisle where no one could see my self-conscious-
ness—and plucked one from its moorings: Conrad's *Heart
of Darkness*. I did not belong to the library, so I took it
to the reading room and tackled it. I read the book through
almost at that sitting, and when I got up my heart was very
heavy for I think I *knew* Conrad better than any man that
ever lived. How I should like to have known him,
talked to him in the silence of a night at sea! Had his spirit
placed the book there for me? I do not know. I only know
that it was a very *singular* start. Then the other great
spirits came—how, I do not know. Perhaps it was tradi-
tion asserting itself, or intuition. I knew nothing of literature, yet somehow I could *sense* the chaff from the wheat.
Homer, Virgil, Aeschylus, Shakespeare, Dante, Shelley,
Keats, to name but a few, all followed my immortal pilot.
Those hours spent in reading on my cab are among the
happiest of my life; God knows they fully recompensed
me for the twittings I received from my colleagues!

PORTWAY JUNIOR REPRINTS

Armstrong, Martin	SAID THE CAT TO THE DOG
Atkinson, M.E.	AUGUST ADVENTURE
Atkinson, M.E.	GOING GANGSTER
Aymé, Marcel	THE WONDERFUL FARM
Bacon, Peggy	THE GOOD AMERICAN WITCH
Baker, Margaret J.	A CASTLE AND SIXPENCE
Edwards, Monica	OPERATION SEABIRD
Edwards, Monica	STRANGERS TO THE MARSH
Hoke, Helen	JOKES, JOKES, JOKES
Hoke, Helen	MORE JOKES, JOKES, JOKES
Hoke, Helen & Randolph Boris	PUNS, PUNS, PUNS
Hourihane, Ursula	CHRISTINA AND THE APPLE WOMAN
Lemming, Joseph	RIDDLES, RIDDLES, RIDDLES
Lyon, Elinor	RUN AWAY HOME
Nesbit, E.	FIVE OF US — AND MADELINE
Parker, Richard	THE SWORD OF GANELON
Manning-Sanders, Ruth	CHILDREN BY THE SEA
Manning-Sanders, Ruth	ELEPHANT
Manning-Sanders, Ruth	MYSTERY AT PENMARTH
Severn, David	BURGLARS AND BANDICOOTS
Severn, David	THE FUTURE TOOK US
Sperry, Armstrong	HULL-DOWN FOR ACTION
Streatfield, Noel	PARTY FROCK
Stuceley, Elizabeth	SPRINGFIELD HOME
Pullein-Thompson, Christine	STOLEN PONIES
Pullein-Thompson, Christine	RIDE BY NIGHT
Pullein-Thompson, Diana	THE SECRET DOG
Pullein-Thompson, Josephine	ONE DAY EVENT
Williams, Elma M.	ANIMALS UNDER MY FEET
Williams, Ursula Moray	THE SECRETS OF THE WOOD

PORTWAY REPRINTS

NON-FICTION

Armstrong, Martin	LADY HESTER STANHOPE
Arnothy, Christine	IT'S NOT SO EASY TO LIVE
Barke, James	THE GREEN HILLS FAR AWAY
Bentley, Phyllis	THE PENNINE WEAVER
Bishop, W.A.	WINGED WARFARE
Blain, William	HOME IS THE SAILOR
Buchan, John	THE CLEARING HOUSE
Cardus, Neville	DAYS IN THE SUN
Cobbett, William	COTTAGE ECONOMY
Day, J. Wentworth	GHOSTS AND WITCHES
Dunnett, Alastair M.	IT'S TOO LATE IN THE YEAR
	originally published as *QUEST BY CANOE GLASGOW TO SKYE*
Edmonds, Charles	A SUBALTERN'S WAR
Evans, A.J.	THE ESCAPING CLUB
Falk, Bernard	OLD Q's DAUGHTER
Fields, Gracie	SING AS WE GO
Gandy, Ida	A WILTSHIRE CHILDHOOD
Gibbons, Floyd	RED KNIGHT OF GERMANY
Gibbs, Philip	REALITIES OF WAR
Gough, General Sir Hubert	THE FIFTH ARMY
Hart, B.H. Liddell	THE OTHER SIDE OF THE HILL
„ „ „	A HISTORY OF THE WORLD WAR 1914-18
Jobson, Allan	SUFFOLK YESTERDAYS
Jones, Ira	KING OF AIR FIGHTERS
Jones, Jack	GIVE ME BACK MY HEART
Jones, Jack	UNFINISHED JOURNEY
Jones, Jack	ME AND MINE
Kennedy, John F.	WHY ENGLAND SLEPT
Kennedy Shaw, W.B.	LONG RANGE DESERT GROUP
Keyhoe, Donald	THE FLYING SAUCERS ARE REAL
Lawrence, W.J.	No. 5 BOMBER GROUP
Lethbridge, Mabel	FORTUNE GRASS

Lethbridge, Mabel	AGAINST THE TIDE
Lowe, George	BECAUSE IT IS THERE
Masefield, John	THE BATTLE OF THE SOMME
Neumann, Major Georg Paul	THE GERMAN AIR-FORCE IN THE GREAT WAR (translated by J.E. Gurdon)
Price, Harry	THE MOST HAUNTED HOUSE IN ENGLAND
Price, Harry	THE END OF BORLEY RECTORY
Raymond, Ernest	IN THE STEPS OF ST. FRANCIS
Stamper, Joseph	LESS THAN THE DUST
Stoker, Bram	FAMOUS IMPOSTERS
Stokes, Sewell	ISADORA DUNCAN
Tangye, Derek	TIME WAS MINE
Torre, Lillian de la	ELIZABETH IS MISSING
Vigilant	RICHTHOFEN – RED KNIGHT OF THE AIR
Vigilant	GERMAN WAR BIRDS
Villiers, Alan	SONS OF SINDBAD
Von Richthofen	THE RED AIR FIGHTER
Whipple, Dorothy	THE OTHER DAY

FICTION

Aldington, Richard	DEATH OF A HERO
Aldington, Richard	ALL MEN ARE ENEMIES
Anand, Mulk Raj	SEVEN SUMMERS
Anderson, Verily	SPAM TOMORROW
Anthony, Evelyn	IMPERIAL HIGHNESS
Anthony, Evelyn	VICTORIA
Arlen, Michael	MEN DISLIKE WOMEN
Arnim, Von	ELIZABETH AND HER GERMAN GARDEN
Ashton, Helen	DOCTOR SEROCOLD
Ashton, Helen	THE HALF-CROWN HOUSE
Ashton, Helen	LETTY LANDON
Ashton, Helen	FOOTMAN IN POWDER
Ashton, Helen	SWAN OF USK
Ashton, Helen	FAMILY CRUISE

Caldwell, Taylor	THE STRONG CITY
Caldwell, Taylor	THE BEAUTIFUL IS VANISHED
Caldwell, Taylor	EARTH IS THE LORD'S
Caldwell, Taylor	LET LOVE COME LAST
Callow, Philip	COMMON PEOPLE
Chandos, Dane	ABBIE
Chapman, Hester, W.	SHE SAW THEM GO BY
Chapman, Hester, W.	TO BE A KING
Collins, Wilkie	ARMADALE
Collins, Wilkie	POOR MISS FINCH
Collins, Wilkie	THE DEAD SECRET
Collins, Wilkie	THE HAUNTED HOTEL
Comyns, Barbara	OUR SPOONS CAME FROM WOOLWORTHS
Cookson, Catherine	FIFTEEN STREETS
Cookson, Catherine	MAGGIE ROWAN
Cookson, Catherine	ROONEY
Cooper, Lettice	THE NEW HOUSE
Cooper, Lettice	PRIVATE ENTERPRISE
Cooper, Lettice	WE HAVE COME TO A COUNTRY
Cordell, Alexander	THE HOSTS OF REBECCA
Cordell, Alexander	RACE OF THE TIGER
Corke, Helen	NEUTRAL GROUND
Craik, Mrs.	AGATHA'S HUSBAND
Crockett, S.R.	THE GREY MAN
Crockett, S.R.	THE BLACK DOUGLAS
Crockett, S.R.	THE RAIDERS
Cusack, Dymphna & James, F.	COME IN SPINNER
Dane, Clemence	THE FLOWER GIRLS
Dane, Clemence	THE MOON IS FEMININE
Darlington, W.A.	ALF'S BUTTON
Davenport, Marcia	EAST SIDE, WEST SIDE
Davies, Rhys	RINGS ON HER FINGERS
Davies, Rhys	THE TRIP TO LONDON
Davies, Rhys	HONEY AND BREAD
Davies, Rhys	THE RED HILLS
Davies, Rhys	THE BLACK VENUS
Davies, Rhys	JUBILEE BLUES

MacGill, Patrick	CHILDREN OF THE DEAD END
MacGill, Patrick	MOLESKIN JOE
MacGill, Patrick	THE RAT PIT
Mackenzie, Compton	POOR RELATIONS
Mackenzie, Compton	THE ALTAR STEPS
Mackenzie, Compton	THE PASSIONATE ELOPEMENT
Mackenzie, Compton	EXTRAORDINARY WOMEN
Macpherson, Ian	SHEPHERD'S CALENDAR
Macpherson, Ian	LAND OF OUR FATHERS
Macpherson, Ian	PRIDE OF THE VALLEY
Macpherson, Ian	HAPPY HAWKERS
Macpherson, Ian	WILD HARBOUR
Marton, Francesca	ATTIC AND AREA
Masefield, Muriel	SEVEN AGAINST EDINBURGH
Maturin, Henri	MELMOTH THE WANDERER (the set)
Meredith, George	DIANA OF THE CROSSWAYS
Morrison, Arthur	TALES OF MEAN STREETS
Morrison, N. Brysson	THE GOWK STORM
Mundy, Talbot	TROS OF SAMOTHRACE
Mundy, Talbot	O.M. – THE SECRET OF ARBOR VALLEY
Mundy, Talbot	PURPLE PIRATE
La Mure, Pierre	BEYOND DESIRE
Myers, Elizabeth	A WELL FULL OF LEAVES
Myers, L.H.	THE NEAR AND THE FAR (2 vols)
Neill, Robert	HANGMAN'S CLIFF
Nicolson, Harold	PUBLIC FACES (with introduction by Nigel Nicolson)
O'Brien, Kate	THE ANTE-ROOM
O'Brien, Kate	MARY LAVELLE
O'Brien, Kate	THE LAND OF SPICES
O'Brien, Kate	PRAY FOR THE WANDERER
O'Brien, Kate	WITHOUT MY CLOAK
O'Flaherty, Liam	THE ASSASSIN
D'Oyley, Elizabeth	LORD ROBERT'S WIFE
D'Oyley, Elizabeth	YOUNG JEMMY
D'Oyley, Elizabeth	THE ENGLISH MARCH
D'Oyley, Elizabeth	EVEN AS THE SUN

Raymond, Ernest	DAPHNE BRUNO
Raymond, Ernest	THE FULFILMENT OF DAPHNE BRUNO
Raymond, Ernest	THE FIVE SONS OF LE FABER
Raymond, Ernest	FOR THEM THAT TRESPASS
Renault, Mary	THE FRIENDLY YOUNG LADIES
Riley, William	JERRY AND BEN
Riley, William	LAYCOCK OF LONEDALE
Roberts, Kenneth	OLIVER WISWELL
Roche, Mazo de la	DELIGHT
Roche, Mazo de la	GROWTH OF A MAN
Saunders, Margaret Baillie	QUALITY FAIR
Seton, Anya	THE MISTLETOE AND SWORD
Shellabarger, Samuel	CAPTAIN FROM CASTILE
Sherriff, R.C.	THE HOPKINS MANUSCRIPT
Shiel, M.P.	PRINCE ZALESKI
Shiel, M.P.	HOW THE OLD WOMAN GOT HOME
Sienkiewicz, Henryk	THE DELUGE (2 vols)
Sienkiewicz, Henryk	WITH FIRE AND SWORD
Sinclair, Upton	WORLD'S END
Sinclair, Upton	BETWEEN TWO WORLDS
Sinclair, Upton	DRAGON'S TEETH
Sinclair, Upton	WIDE IS THE GATE
Sinclair, Upton	PRESIDENTIAL AGENT
Sinclair, Upton	DRAGON HARVEST
Sinclair, Upton	A WORLD TO WIN
Sinclair, Upton	PRESIDENTIAL MISSION
Sinclair, Upton	ONE CLEAR CALL
Sinclair, Upton	O SHEPHERDS SPEAK
Sinclair, Upton	THE RETURN OF LANNY BUDD
Smith, Betty	A TREE GROWS IN BROOKLYN
Soubiran, Andre	THE DOCTORS
Sutcliffe, Halliwell	WILLOWDENE WILL
Sutcliffe, Halliwell	PEDLAR'S QUEST
Sutcliffe, Halliwell	A MAN OF THE MOORS
Sutton, Graham	NORTH STAR
Sutton, Graham	THE ROWAN TREE
Sutton, Graham	FLEMING OF HONISTER

PORTWAY EDUCATIONAL REPRINTS

ACADEMIC REPRINTS

Abbott, W.C.	COLONEL THOMAS BLOOD
Andrews, Kevin	THE FLIGHT OF IKAROS
Balzac, Honoré de	THE CURE DE TOURS
Braithwaite, William J.	LLOYD GEORGE'S AMBULANCE WAGON
Broke-Smith, P.W.L.	THE HISTORY OF EARLY BRITISH MILITARY AERONAUTICS
Cameron, A.	CHEMISTRY IN RELATION TO FIRE RISK AND EXTINCTION
Crozier, F.P.	A BRASS HAT IN NO MAN'S LAND
Crozier, Brig.-General F.P.	THE MEN I KILLED
Dewey, John	INTEREST AND EFFORT IN EDUCATION
Fearnsides, W.G. & Bulman, O.M.B.	GEOLOGY IN THE SERVICE OF MAN
Ferrier, Susan	DESTINY (2 vols)

This is the last and best of the three books written by the Scots novelist.

Galt, John	THE PROVOST

This comprises a series of short Baconian style essays on everyday events in which the Provost was engaged during his magisterial life.

Gates, H.L.	THE AUCTION OF SOULS

The story of Aurora Mardiganian, the Christian girl who survived the Great Massacres of the Armenians.

Gilbert, Edmund W.	BRIGHTON OLD OCEAN'S BAUBLE
Glass, David V.	THE TOWN – AND A CHANGING CIVILISATION
Gronlund, Norman	SOCIOMETRY IN THE CLASSROOM
H.M.S.O.	REPORT ON THE CONSULTATIVE COMMITTEE ON INFANT AND NURSERY SCHOOLS
H.M.S.O.	THE GEOLOGY OF MANCHESTER AND THE SOUTH EAST LANCASHIRE COALFIELD
Harrison, G.B.	THE LIFE & DEATH OF ROBERT DEVEREUX, EARL OF ESSEX

Hartley, Dorothy (Ed.)	THOMAS TUSSER – HIS GOOD POINTS OF HUSBANDRY
Hawkins, Doris M.	ATLANTIC TORPEDO
Haydn, J.	HAYDN'S BOOK OF DIGNITIES
Howard, G.E.	EARLY ENGLISH DRUG JARS

Mr. Howard had a celebrated personal collection of Early English Drug Jars or Pharmacy Vases as they are sometimes called. This book is recognised as a standard work on this subject.

Hughes, A.M.D.	TENNYSON POEMS PUBLISHED IN 1842
Hunt, Henry	MEMOIRS OF HENRY HUNT (3 vols)

Henry Hunt (1773–1835) had a stormy political life: elected to Parliament in 1831, he had previously served 3 years in Ilchester Jail once sharing a cell with William Cobbett, where he wrote the 3 volumes of his memoirs.

Duncan-Jones, Austin	BUTLER'S MORAL PHILOSOPHY
Jordan, Denham	ANNALS OF A FISHING VILLAGE
Kenyon, Robert Lloyd	GOLD COINS OF ENGLAND
Lamb, Harold	GENGHIS KHAN
Lewis, Saunders	A SCHOOL OF WELSH AUGUSTANS
Lewis, R.A.	EDWIN CHADWICK AND THE PUBLIC HEALTH MOVEMENT

This is an overdue appraisal of Chadwick's importance and significance, whose work has been hidden behind the traditional anonymity of the high level civil servant.

Lindsay, Philip	ON SOME BONES IN WESTMINSTER ABBEY
Ling, Princess Der	IMPERIAL INCENSE

This is the reminiscences of the author's life as a lady-in-waiting to the Empress T'zu Hsi of China. It gives a fascinating insight into the life of the Chinese Court.

Lucas, A., O.B.E., F.I.C.	ANTIQUES – THEIR RESTORATION AND PRESERVATION